POLITICS, GEOGRAPHY AND BEHAVIOUR

POLITICS, GEOGRAPHY AND BEHAVIOUR

by Richard Muir
and Ronan Paddison

METHUEN
LONDON AND NEW YORK

First published in 1981 by
Methuen & Co. Ltd
11 New Fetter Lane, London EC4P 4EE
Published in the USA by
Methuen & Co.
in association with Methuen, Inc.
733 Third Avenue, New York, NY 10017
© 1981 Richard Muir and Ronan Paddison
Printed in Great Britain
at the University Press, Cambridge

British Library Cataloguing in Publication Data

Muir, Richard, 1943–
    Politics, geography and behaviour.
    1. Geography, Political
    I. Title   II. Paddison, Ronan
    320.1′2   JC319   80–42216
    ISBN 0–416–31330–2
    ISBN 0–416–31340–X Pbk

c✓

Contents

Preface

Political geography, more than other branches of the discipline, has had something of a chequered history. It has nevertheless remained a recognized part of the geographical curriculum – albeit at times rather tenuously. Currently there are signs of it moving to occupy (we would argue, rightly) a more prominent position within human geography. In part this changed state of affairs can be traced to a growing awareness among geographers of the importance of politics as the means by which societies are organized and the realization that political processes focus on conflicts in the distribution of resources and the resolution of conflicts. It is against this background that this book has been written.

Any textbook is fundamentally a teaching aid, and in writing this one we have had certain objectives. Primarily we have tried to produce an introductory text on the interaction of political factors and spatial behaviour. The emphasis of the book is behavioural. In the early chapters themes are discussed which form the mainstay of behavioural geography – decision-making and its antecedents, ideology, values and perception. Subsequently, our focus has been to examine how the political system behaves and its impact on the spatial framework within which it operates. Given that politics is a means by which conflicts are resolved and resources distributed, we have chosen to study the impact of political behaviour in a number of selected fields – the environment, the state, the allocation of public goods and the interrelationships between states. Covering such a wide field our intent has been to highlight major principles and to illustrate them with case-studies. To both teacher and student, however, we would urge that the notes on further reading form an essential part of the book and the references cited are disigned to act as the basis for seminar discussion.

A preface gives the author an opportunity not only to state the objectives of the text but also any necessary qualifications (at least those of which he is aware!). In common with a number of other political geographers we adopt a systems framework as the basis of our discussion. For the most part, however, this is used simply as an ordering device (it is doubtful whether the systems theory *sensu stricto*, is a theory). The reader, however, will look in vain for any analysis of homeostatic mechanisms, negative or positive feedback or other attributes commonly used to describe the operation of systems. Our emphasis is decidedly on the process element. This does not mean that the other main perspective of political geography – structure, or the organization and functioning of political territories – is ignored. We have not discussed, however, such topics as core areas, capital cities and the like which hitherto have been such an essential element of the political geographer's tool kit. Rather, our aim has been to discuss structure only insofar as it relates to and is influenced by political processes. This stress on processes and behaviour is deliberate in that it allows us to focus on the ways in which political factors may be incorporated within the wider field of behavioural geography.

R. Muir
R. Paddison
February 1980

Figures

Tables

1 The Political System and Space

Among human geographers there is much debate on the current state of their discipline within which there are a number of distinct methods of approach. Internal debate has characterized the subject for much of its historical development. Indeed, a case can be made that such argument both reflects a vigorously expanding discipline and is necessary for it. Within geographical circles, if the 1970s have been witness to greater discussion and doubt than heretofore, this is attributable to the recognition that neither quantification nor its handmaiden, positivism, is wholly able to meet the problems human geographers face. In spite of these problems, however, there is a broad consensus on what human geographers study, that is the structuring and interaction of spatially observable patterns.

If human geographers are divided among themselves this has been even truer for political geographers. What Whittlesey said of the subject in 1939 – that 'there is even yet neither a universally accepted approach to the subject nor a consensus as to its content'[1] – is probably still largely true more than forty years later. A glance at the content of a recent symposium on the curricula in political studies taught in British universities and polytechnics would amply demonstrate the variety of approaches.[2] Yet few, if any, academic disciplines are founded on conceptual frameworks which are universally accepted, and what we have argued as the value of internal debate can also apply here.

Nevertheless political geography, particularly in relation to its economic, urban and other human counterparts, has been at a disadvantage through its ill-definition. Unable to agree a common definition of their subject, political geographers have argued over such substantive issues as the appropriate unit for analysis (hence criticism of the overemphasis on the state) or whether questions of structure should be given precedence over those of process. Not unexpectedly, such discussion has frequently been less than helpful;

structure and process are different sides of the same coin. The outcome of the subject's ill-definition is that it is seen as lying somewhat loosely between geography and political science, and within it it is possible to trace movement towards more overtly geographical or political approaches.

Whatever the reasons underlying what Dikshit has termed 'the retreat from political geography'[3] – and these are too well-rehearsed to pursue again here – there have been signs of revival in the discipline. Several reasons may be adduced, including the contribution played by the systems theory model in providing the discipline with a workable general framework applicable to a variety of spatial scales.[4] Hindsight will probably suggest another factor as having been important, namely the growing awareness among human geographers of the importance of political factors as influencing their spatial analyses. To an extent this relationship has long been recognized, as in the law–landscape thread outlined by Whittlesey in his article 'The Impress of Effective Central Authority upon the Landscape'.[5] Human geography has advanced beyond the stage of merely describing spatial patterns to the more demanding questions of explanations, and more recently, to the question 'what ought the pattern to be?', a problem more fundamental to the nature and organization of societies, which necessarily include political factors. As politics is in essence an exercise in how societies are (should be) governed it is clear that for geography its importance is that political processes not only operate within spatially bounded units but in so doing also influence spatial distributions.

The political geographer's sister discipline, political science, has also been studied in a variety of ways. One of the basic conceptual differences, as in political geography, has been that between structure and process. The more traditional, and certainly earlier, school of thought within political science emphasized the role of institutions, particularly through the theory, organization and government of the state; as an alternative within the same general school the discipline was viewed in terms of the governance of a geographical territory and the range of functions for which governments are responsible. A later school adopted power as its central theme, examining its nature, locus and how it is utilized. More recently we can identify several approaches, each of which is concerned more with process and whose common ground is an understanding of political science as concerning the production and allocation of values within society. Politics, therefore, is a process by which rewards are distributed and conflicts resolved, and how it functions brings to the fore such issues as decisions and decision-making or, to another school, policies and policy-making. These more recent foci constitute what Young[6] terms a 'broad view' of the subject in contrast to its more narrow conception as the study of political institutions.

In this book our aim is to demonstrate how political factors and processes influence and interact with spatial behaviour. Where the behavioural approach in human geography has sought to unravel explanations of spatial behaviour the more influential studies (with the exception of voting analyses) have been in fields other than political geography. A study of political processes in their spatial setting will also help to re-focus the political factor within the corpus of human geography.

By necessity our approach has had to be selective. At the risk of contradicting ourselves with a point made previously, the book emphasizes process over structure although, because of the obvious importance of the latter in providing the fora within which political activities take place, the issue of (territorial) political structures is not ignored. In other respects the study focuses on certain 'key' aspects of process, notably decision-making and its antecedents, and the interaction of politics and the environment. In the remainder of this introductory chapter we shall outline the systems model which provides the broad conceptual framework for the study and the nature of the behavioural approach in human geography.

The Political System

Systems theory has been an influential methodological device within political geography. Although systems concepts have been applied elsewhere in human geography, political geographers have relied equally on the systems ideas developed by political scientists, notably David Easton,[7] and by the sociologist Talcott Parsons.[8]

A system is fundamentally a set of relationships. Most definitions of a system embody the idea of a number of components which interact with one another with a certain degree of order and regularity. An example of a simple physical system which is frequently used for illustrative purposes is a hot water system, comprising a number of components or elements (tanks, taps, pipes, etc.) which interact. The links interrelating the elements take the form of flows of various sorts, enabling the system to maintain its organization. These will allow it to adjust to changes in its environment, so that (for example) the drawing off of water results automatically in the filling of the tank while through the use of a thermostat (which is able to receive and interpret feedback) the water is kept at a constant temperature, i.e. the system is capable of self-regulation in order to attain some goal.

In Easton's analysis political activities are linked in behavioural terms to the environment within which they take place (Fig. 1.1).

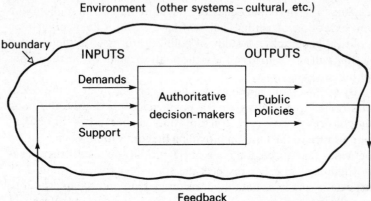

Fig. 1.1. A simplified model of the political system.

Thus, political activities constitute 'a system of behaviour embedded in an environment to the influences of which the political system itself is exposed and in turn reacts'.[9] The political system acts as a self-regulating mechanism divisible into four sub-systems: (1) the set of inputs, (2) the methods by which the inputs are received and translated into (3), outputs which through (4), the feedback sub-system can be relayed so as to modify new inputs or outputs. The political system will survive as long as it is able to balance the sets of inputs and outputs within the structure, the inputs being either in the form of demands made on the political system or those supports it receives, particularly through the ballot box.

A political system, however, is not only a means of converting those demands which arise more or less continuously from the environment (e.g. for improved services of different types) into outputs, or binding decisions. It is also a vehicle which is capable itself of being purposive and goal-directed. One fundamental goal will be its own survival which it will strive to meet by regulating its own behaviour or altering its internal organization.

This question of survival or persistence of the system was discussed by Parsons[10] in his functional analysis of society. In order to survive any social system needs to meet four imperatives: (1) pattern maintenance, (2) adaptation, (3) goal attainment, and (4) integration. We can illustrate what Parsons meant by using the state as an example of such a system. Once established the state will quickly develop its own institutions, laws and bureaucratic machinery necessary to preserve its main characteristics. Those institutions of the state which are responsible for making political decisions – national legislatures, bureaucracies – will need to adapt themselves to their environment. The responses of the system to the various demands generated by the environment vary but ignoring them will court the possibility of losing essential support. The notion of goal-attainment and goal-seeking behaviour is important to all kinds of organization. For the state it is not enough that its goal be survival; it must have some other goal(s) which motivate society, providing it with a *raison d'être*. These goals might be the establishment of an egalitarian society, the conquest of some coveted province of a neighbouring state or any other objective which has been broadly accepted by both political leaders and the citizenry. The interaction of these three activities will create stresses within the state so that only when integrated will it be able to meet the needs of the other characteristics. Integrated states, however the term integration is defined (see Chapter 6), will be able to function more effectively in meeting the needs for their own survival.

The value of the systems model is that it can be applied to political units operating at a variety of spatial scales. (Its use is not restricted to areal political organizations, though it is these with which political geographers are often concerned.) In this way each level of government operates as an open system adapting to its environment, purposively seeking stipulated goals.

Political Processes and Behaviour

The behavioural approach offers a different way of looking at geographical problems. The behaviouralist's main interest is unravelling the sequence of events underlying some decision which has resulted in a spatially observable pattern. It is a mode of approach which accentuates the question of process, which in political geography can be defined as 'that succession of events, actions, or operations which man uses to establish, maintain or change a political system'.

The central tenet of the behavioural approach is that what determines spatial patterns is man's appreciation of his environment and his behaviour within it. Rather than reactions to the real world, man's actions are responses to a 'smaller' world, one which he perceives, his perception being an amalgam of his values and attitudes, his inherited culture traits. Their effect is to channel his attention to certain features of the environment so that given the same physical environment the responses of two individuals (or two social groups) can well vary. Opportunities (e.g. economic resources) recognized by the one may go unrecognized by the other, depending on the way in which their different cultures – the core of traditional ideas and values which contribute to the conditioning of actions – channel their perceptions.

Within geography much of the pioneering work of cognitive behaviouralism was by Kirk in his articles of 1951 and 1963[11]. Kirk modelled what he termed the behavioural environment as distinct from its phenomenal counterpart (Fig. 1.2). The latter constitutes

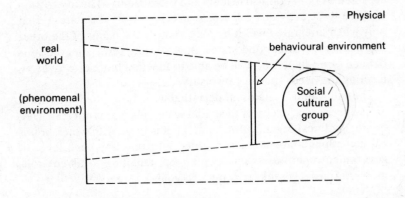

Fig. 1.2. The behavioural environment.

Source: Adapted from W. Kirk, 'Problems of Geography', *Geography* (1963), **48**, 366.

the real world, including the totality of human and natural systems. The behavioural environment is the environment as perceived, the formation of which is influenced by the individual's social background.

Geography has in fact been concerned with certain aspects of human behaviour for much longer than there has been a separately recognizable behavioural approach to the discipline. In the French school of geography, through the writings of Vidal de la Blache and others, the agreement that cultural factors influenced man's interpretation of his environment was central to their analysis. More recent behavioural studies, however, have differed from these earlier studies by examining in greater detail the factors underlying spatial decision-making, particularly in economic geography where there was widespread dissatisfaction with the model of economic man as one perfectly able to optimize his spatial arrangements. In a review of work prior to 1973 Bourne[12] identified three major types of study: (1) analyses of the spatial outcomes of individual and group behaviour patterns, (2) the decision and decision-making processes, and (3) the preconditions of these decisions, particularly how people view their environment.

As we could expect from earlier comments, behavioural studies have not been applied with equal incidence to the subdisciplines within human geography. In a review of behavioural work up to 1970 (now itself somewhat dated) Golledge, Brown and Williamson,[13] though dividing their analysis under similar headings to those used by Bourne, showed that most studies, other than those of a primarily methodological focus, were in the economic and urban fields. Major fields of interest have concerned locational decision-making, the factors underlying the diffusion of innovations, perception studies particularly of urban structure and of the use of services (shopping, recreation) within urbanized areas. Within political geography voting studies have provided the only developed area using the behavioural approach, though there are studies dealing with other topics in the political field.

As such this is only a partial reflection of the potential of behavioural studies within political geography. Politics has been defined as primarily a process by which rewards are distributed within society and how conflicts are resolved: viewed geographically our interest is in how these processes interact with the spatially organized environment in which they take place and their effects in turn on this environment. Viewed thus several key areas, within the range of studies explored by behavioural geographers, can be identified. These are decision-making, its antecedents and effects on the environment. These form the focus of the early chapters of this work together with an analysis of voting behaviour and the influence of elections as supports of the political system. In the last three chapters we look at political behaviour from a somewhat different emphasis, that of the political system and particularly of areally defined governments. These questions of behaviour focus upon the problems of how to integrate the political territory, of conflict-resolution, of how the system allocates goods and services spatially and how political units interact with one another.

Discussion Points and Further Reading

Systems theory provides a broad framework within which to examine the interactions between politics and geography and a convenient starting point for discussions. Geographical differences, as measured by variations in the environment in which the political system operate, function as inputs which in turn are modified by the outputs of the political system. Political geographers have used Easton's systems model widely, though in different ways. Bergman's analysis (1975) provides a comprehensive study of the field in systems terms, while a landmark article is that by Cohen and Rosenthal (1971). The wider implications of systems theory as applied to political relationships, including a critique of the theory's shortcomings, is touched upon in Young (1968) and Morgan and Kirkpatrick, (1972).

No attempt has been made here to trace the history of the subject or alternative methodologies. Kasperson and Minghi (1969) provide an excellent review of the heritage of political geography, while more recent discussions of the current state of the discipline are contained within Minghi (1980), Muir (1976), and Dikshit (1976). An important alternative methodology placing political geography firmly within the welfare field of human geography is presented in Cox (1979).

Bergman, E., *Modern Political Geography*, Brown, Dubuque, 1975.

Cohen, S. B., and Rosenthal, L. D., 'A Geographical Model for Political Systems Analysis', *Geographical Review* (1971), **61**, 5–31.

Cox, K. R., *Location and Public Problems*, Basil Blackwell, Oxford, 1979.

Dikshit, R. D., 'The Retreat from Political Geography', *Area* (1977), **9**, (4), 234–9.

Kasperson, R. E., and Minghi, J. V., *The Structure of Political Geography*, University of London Press, 1969, esp. pt I.

Minghi, J. V., 'Recent Developments and Future Trends in Political Geography Research in North America', paper presented at I.B.G. Conference, Lancaster 1980. Forthcoming in Burnett, A., and Taylor, P. J. (eds.), *Politics and Geography, Anglo-American Perspectives*, Wiley, London, (1980).

Morgan, D. R., and Kirkpatrick, S. A., *Urban Political Analysis*, Free Press, New York, 1972, pp. 1–27.

Muir, R. E., 'Political Geography: Dead Duck or Phoenix?', *Area* (1976), **8**(3) 195–200.

Young, O. R., *Systems of Political Science*, Prentice-Hall, Englewood Cliffs, 1968.

Notes

1. D. Whittlesey, *The Earth and the State: A Study of Political Geography*, Holt, New York, 1939, p. iii.
2. A. Jenkins and D. McEvoy, *Teaching Political Geography*, Oxford Polytechnic Discussion Papers in Geography, no. 7, 1977.
3. R. D. Dikshit, 'The Retreat from Political Geography', *Area* (1977), **9** (4), 234–9.
4. A full statement of the systems approach to political geography is to be found in W. A. D. Jackson and M. S. Samuels, (eds.), *Politics and Geographic Relationships*, Prentice-Hall, Englewood Cliffs, 2nd edn, 1971, pp. 1–40.
5. D. Whittlesey, 'The Impress of Effective Central Authority upon the Landscape', *Annals of the Association of American Geographers* (1935), **25**, 85–97.
6. O. R. Young, *Systems of Political Science*, Prentice-Hall, Englewood Cliffs, 1968.
7. D. Easton, *A Systems Analysis of Political Life*, Wiley, New York, 1965.
8. T. Parsons, *The Social System*, Free Press, New York, 1950.
9. Easton, *Systems Analysis*, p. 18.
10. Parsons, *The Social System*.
11. W. Kirk, 'Historical Geography and the Concept of Behavioural Environment', *Indian Geographical Society, Silver Jubilee Edition* (1951), pp. 152–60; W. Kirk, 'Problems of Geography', *Geography* (1963), **48**, 357–71.
12. L. S. Bourne, 'Through the Looking Glass: Comments on Behavioural Approaches in Geography', in J. Rees and P. Newby (eds.), *Behavioural Perspectives in Geography*, Middlesex Polytechnic Monographs in Geography, no. 1, 1973, 94–106.
13. R. G. Golledge, L. A. Brown and F. Williamson, 'Behavioural Approaches in Geography: An Overview', *The Australian Geographer* (1972), **12**, (1), 59–79.

2 Values, Attitudes and Images

In the previous chapter we noted some broad interrelationships which exist between political processes and space. Politics; it was seen, could be broadly defined as the authoritative allocation of goods and services which is effected through a series of adjustments so as to achieve harmonious interrelationships among individuals and groups within a political community. Such allocations are synonymous with the outputs of the political system and concern the making of decisions as to the distribution and redistribution of resources within society.

The systems model provides the conceptual framework within which we can analyse how the political process operates. When considered as a system it is possible to demonstrate how governments are able to adapt to changes in the external environment and also modify it, because of the existence of a two-way flow of information linking inputs and outputs. The outputs of the system are made up of the set of decisions formulated by governments and expressed through its laws and policies.

Within this rather formal description of the political system it is the decision-making stage of the process which is of central importance to the political geographer. It is through decisions made by the political machine that the environment in which it operates is altered. Regardless of the significance of the decision in altering the environment – whether, that is, it results in some relatively minor landscape change or in some major international initiative linking countries in a formal trading agreement – we need to trace the course of the decision back to the likely forces influencing it.

The purpose of this chapter is to discuss the main components underpinning the decision-making process. These will be discussed under several headings, namely culture, values, ideology, attitudes and images. Each concept follows logically within the model to be discussed in the next section. While their relationship within the decision-making process is clear enough it is perhaps relevant to stress that particularly when discussing such factors as differences of political culture and ideology we are dealing with broad issues which permeate the polity and influence its mode of operation. Their spatial impact, however, may not be immediately obvious and their influence tends to be indirect through the decision-making process. This is not to underestimate their importance, and it will be possible to illustrate the kinds of spatial outcomes resulting from differences of political culture. The interrelationships between political attitudes and space also need to be closely scrutinized, and the growth of national orientation is used as a vehicle to explore the two sets of factors. In the final section we shall take up discussion of images in political geography and their influences on decision-making.

A Framework For Decision-Making

Any decision can be traced backwards to two principle groups of 'influence variables', i.e. those relating to the environment and those relating to a set of predispositions which determine the decision-maker's orientation. Under environment is included the political, social and economic setting within which the individual is located, while his set of predispositions refers to those values and attitudes which are of importance to him. Fig 2.1 shows how the two

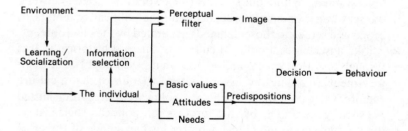

Fig. 2.1. A simple model of decision-making by the individual.

Source: Adapted from L. W. Milbrath, *Political Participation*, Rand McNally, Chicago, 1976 p. 26.

groups of variables interrelate to decision-making by the individual. Within the area to the left of the diagram the various components are interconnected by information flows which the individual receives, structures and selects prior to making a choice. The flows relate, on the one hand, to the set of beliefs, attitudes and needs of the individual and, on the other, to the understanding of the environment in which he is located and which he interprets through his store of past and current experience. These two factors – the set of predispositions and his image of the world – form the basis of how the individual makes a decision.

It is in looking at the set of predispositions influencing the individual that it is possible to trace how political factors enter the process. Political scientists have devised the notion of political culture to denote those values, attitudes and beliefs which can be viewed as a basic determinant of action. Although the term is variously defined the definition provided by Almond and Powell highlights the interconnections between values, attitudes and political objects:

> Political culture is the pattern of individual attitudes and orientations towards politics among the members of a political culture system. Such individual orientations involve several components including (a) cognitive orientations, knowledge, accurate or otherwise, of political objects and beliefs; (b) effective orientations, feelings of attachment, involvement, rejection and the like, about political objects; and (c) evaluative orientations, judgements and opinions about political objects which usually involve applying value standards towards political objects.[1]

A political culture acts, therefore, as a conditioning factor on our behaviour in that it incorporates not only the aspects of the environment which appear important to us but also our attitudes towards them. Within our systems framework it is located between the set of environmental influences and the political system itself, acting as a screen to those demands generated by the environment.

Like any culture a political culture is amassed historically. It is through historical accumulation and what psychologists call 'reinforcement' (learning through repeated experience) that a culture acquires value patterns and beliefs. A political cutlure is transmitted between generations by the process of political socialization through which the individual acquires his knowledge of the environment and the set of predispositions which determine his orientation to the political system. This learning and acquisition of political skills is effected through several agencies which act as information disseminators, notably the family, peers, schooling and the media.

Our model in Fig. 2.1 outlines the factors underlying the process of decision-making by the individual. Yet many decisions in political life are not taken by the individual, but rather by representatives on his behalf. These include representatives within national legislatures, or local governments or local community groups. As an alternative to the individual's decision-making schema, Fig. 2.2 illustrates the process distinguishing between decision-makers and the citizen. The model re-emphasizes the influence of the environment and the set of predispositions, while illustrating how these interact sequentially.

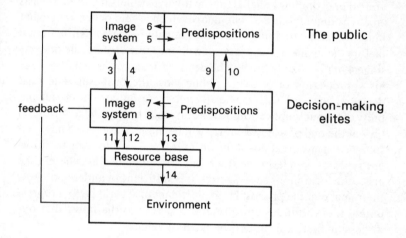

Fig. 2.2. An alternative formulation of the decision-making sequence.

In Fig. 2.2 the process begins with some change in the environment which is perceived separately by the two types of actor and incorporated into their image systems. These images refer to the interpretation of the environment, and though this might differ between the citizen and the decision-maker, as stages 3 and 4 demonstrate, the image systems of the two groups do mutually influence one another. Subsequently in stages 5, 6, 7 and 8 there is interaction between the values and attitudes of the individual and the decision-makers and their image systems. The actual decision (13) is taken following an evaluation by the decision-maker of their image, predispositions and the constraints placed by the resource base. The effect of the decision is to alter the environment whereupon the cycle recommences.

At this juncture a simple example might help to illustrate the operation of the model. As issues posing an apparent threat to one or more groups within a community frequently pose a problem demanding political resolution they will furnish us with a suitable example. Suppose some large factory (though not a noxious industry) employing substantial numbers wishes to establish itself in a small town, a situation which is common enough. The situation will be differently viewed by the town's citizens and probably also by its local government representatives and administrators. Thus to some the proposal may be seen as an opportunity providing employment and other economic benefits for the town; to others it may be seen as an environmental threat. The image which is held depends on what kinds of values are important. If these values stress environmental factors the image of the proposal will probably be a hostile one. As stage 4 in Fig. 2.2 illustrates, the decision-maker must acknowledge his appreciation of how the public view the proposal. The final decision, however, will also be affected by resource factors – availability of labour, implications for the financial base of the town and so on – at the end of which a choice will be made. Though we have not followed in any great detail the different images belonging to different types of people in the town (e.g. the unemployed, the middle class, the local shopkeepers, etc.), it is sufficient to understand how their image of the proposal is an amalgam of several factors representing their attitudes and preferences. It is to the latter that our discussion first turns under the label of values.

Values

Within recent years geographers have become increasingly aware of the concept of values and of the need to incorporate some understanding of these as part of their discipline.[2] Values may be defined as 'things or relationships which people would like to have or to enjoy'.[3] Attempts, therefore, to understand political decision-making, given that their output is the distribution of rewards, without recognizing the existence of values is clearly a fallacious exercise. Yet in many studies the values underlying the process being analysed are left unarticulated, frequently because they are considered so fundamental that their position is assumed, as for example where these refer to such broad issues as equality, democracy and the like. Greater emphasis has in fact been placed on the analysis of attitudes or opinions which are generated by values.

The range of possible values which underwrite a given society can conveniently be subdivided on the basis of the scale over which they apply. Table 2.1 lists some of the values which would be commonly subscribed to in America, grouped under reference to self, group, society, nation and mankind. The individual will subscribe to a whole set of values, his own needs and wants being expressed through a series of value preferences which both complement and sometimes conflict with those belonging to the larger scale. Because especially individual values can conflict with those of the group, such as the local community, some collective means is necessary to resolve problems.

As far as the individual is concerned his needs and wants are in large measure the determinants of his values. His needs will include those items which are essential to survival. His wants, though less

Table 2.1. **Some Common American Values.**

I Self-oriented values
1. personal material welfare, e.g. physical/mental well-being/economic security
2. self-respect – the right to be treated as a person and as a 'full' member of the community
3. personal liberty – freedom/privacy/property rights
4. self-fulfilment (the pursuit of happiness)

II Group-oriented values
1. respectability, e.g. conformism
2. civic virtues/involvement, good citizenship
3. friendship/loyalty
4. generosity

III Society-oriented values
1. social welfare
2. equality, e.g. civil rights, fairness
3. justice
4. liberty
5. law and order
6. equal opportunities

IV Nation-oriented values
1. patriotism
2. democracy and 'the American way'
3. service for country

V Mankind-oriented values
1. human welfare – peace, material progress
2. humanitarianism
3. internationalism

Source: Selected values from 'A tentative register of American values', Appendix 2, from N. Rescher, 'What is Value Change? A Framework for Evidence', in K. Baier and N. Rescher (eds.), *Values and the Future*, Free Press, New York, 1971, pp. 68–109.

essential to survival, neverthless help to determine the level of satisfaction the individual gains from the life experience. Psychologists have suggested various typologies of human needs and wants among which Maslow's hierarchical classification has been influential.[4] Maslow listed five main categories of needs and wants which are considered hierarchical in that the attainment of one level leads the individual to strive to the 'higher' needs: (1) physical (food, water, sex); (2) safety (an orderly and predictable environment); (3) love and belongingness in relationships; (4) self-esteem, the establishment of prestige and status, and (5) self-actualization by which the individual achieves his full potential.

The available evidence tends to support Maslow's basic ideas. In a comparative study using survey data from ten West European countries, Inglehart has shown that as individuals become more affluent and therefore secure their value preferences alter from the mundane to more abstract concerns.[5] In each of the countries (but particularly in West Germany) memories of the Great Depression and the Second World War influence the older generation while, in contrast, the younger generation is accustomed to greater affluence and has a less materialistic orientation. This also means, however, that the latter lays greater store on questions of power and gaining respect within the community. We can also seek explanations within this framework for the greater concern for the environment among the 'haves' than the 'have-nots', a trend which is frequently true for sovereign states themselves as much as it is within them.

The values listed in Table 2.1 relevant to larger scales, society and the nation, clearly underpin these individual values, besides providing the ground rules for much political behaviour. In the liberal democracy it is the subscription to values such as popular sovereignty, political equality and majoritarianism which are essential for its survival. Although democracy can be defined in a number of ways one essential component is its recognition of the public or common good; a democratic government functions for the benefit of society at large rather than for particular sectors or élites within it. Yet determining what is the public good, as indeed who decides on such questions, remain constant problems particularly since what appears appropriate at one level (in time and/or space) often conflicts with what appears so at another. Thus, the partitioning of Cyprus, based on the *de facto* division following the Turkish military invasion, may help reduce interethnic conflict in the short term (though even this is questionable given the sensitivity of the issue of partition) while being at variance with the longer-term common good of the island as a political and economic entity.

In the modern democracy the state is too populous, and matters of government frequently too technical and complex, to allow for direct democracy as it was espoused by the classical political theorists. The task of identifying the common good is decided less by the citizen than it is in effect by his elected representatives. In the representative liberal democracy, therefore, the emergence of political élites is an accepted and reasoned development, yet one with important consequences for the decision-making process. It is axiomatic to the liberal democracy that its citizens, as voters, are able periodically to renew or replace their representative and by so doing affirm the regime's acceptance of the concept of political equality.

Voting is of importance to the question of values in another way, in that it provides the means for deciding between a set of preferences. Any decision will normally contain some value-judgements and because these will vary among people it is through voting and the establishment of the most favoured alternative that the conflict will be resolved. On this basis the decision-rules by which we decide voting outcomes are of crucial importance. One commonly recognized method is the acceptance of the majority choice – majoritarianism – as an indicator of the common good, though this can put at risk the rights of the minority group. It was this fear of the 'tyranny of the majority' which led the Founding Fathers of the American constitution to incorporate a number of constitutional checks, not least of which was to be the federal structure itself. In other countries majoritarian decision procedures are modified to ensure that political allocations do not necessarily discriminate against minority groups (see Chapter 6).

Values and Ideology

The role of ideology in relation to values is central. By a political ideology is meant 'a belief system which explains and justifies a preferred political order for society, either existing or proposed, and offers a strategy for its attainment'.[6] Frequently an ideology has become bound up with a self-oriented set of ideas promoting the advantages of a particular group, justifying and maintaining its own position, as Marx argued, at the expense of others.

Several functions are served by political ideologies. As a belief system it provides a cognitive structure, 'a map and compass', with which the individual is able to orient himself politically. Ideologies channel human perceptions selectively and provide a normative set of rules by which the basic framework of the political community should be structured. A second function of ideology is its provision of prescriptive formulae for individual and collective action, e.g. it provides the means for explaining and justifying, or disclaiming, how societies distribute resources. Furthermore, political ideologies, by articulating a core of common wants and the methods by which these can be gained, give a basic framework within which conflict can be resolved. Thus a commonly expressed goal for greater economic equality might be met through various redistributive policies. Finally, by providing the outline and rationale for the political community, ideologies supply the individual with political motivation and channel collective action within purposive lines.

One way of appreciating the interaction between ideology and values and the differences between rival ideologies is to look at the different political parties within a country. In terms of their political ideologies parties can be classified according to their location on the 'left–right spectrum'. Figure 2.3 illustrates the spectrum within a West European context, extending from the radical left through liberalism to the reactionary right. Bersch and others[7] have shown how the parties vary in relation to those values which an earlier political scientist, Harold Lasswell, had emphasized, i.e. power, well-being, respect and enlightenment. Parties to the right of centre will tend to give less emphasis to (for example) issues providing for economic redistribution and well-being than parties of the left while proportionately more to the idea of individual freedom (Table 2.2).

Table 2.2. **Attitudes of political parties towards the redistribution of basic values.**

Party	Value			
	Power	Well-being	Respect	Enlighten-ment
Radical Left	R	R	R	R
Communist	A	R	R	R
Democratic Socialist	N	R	R	R
Liberal	S	R	N	R
Christian Democrat	S	A	A	A
Conservative	S	S	S	S
Reactionary Right	R	S	S	N

Note: R – redistributive tendency   S – status quo
A – ambivalence   N – neutral
Source: G. K. Bersch *et al.*, *Comparing Political Systems*, Wiley, New York, 1978,
p. 87.

	Radical Left	Communism	Democratic Socialism	Liberalism	Christian Democracy	Conservatism	Reactionary Right
Britain	—	—	Labour Party	Liberal	—	Conservative	National Front
West Germany	—	German Communist Party	SPD	FDP	CDU	CSU	NDP
Italy	Proletarian Democracy	Italian Communist Party	Italian Socialist Party	Republican Party	Christian Democrats	Liberal Party	Italian Social Movement
Ireland			Labour		Fianna Fail	Fine Gael	
Netherlands		Communist	Labour	Radical People's Party	Catholic People's Party	Calvinist	

Fig. 2.3. Political parties and the Left–Right spectrum in Western Europe.

Note: Not all parties in each country are listed.
Source: Adapted from G. Smith, *Politics in Western Europe*, Heinemann, London, 1972.

This model assumes that political parties provide the means by which value preferences, expressed through ideologies, can be transmitted collectively. Political parties do exist for this reason though there are many other reasons, such as providing the means for mobilizing and channelling political support. Nevertheless the extent to which parties differ ideologically varies between countries. American parties, in this respect, contrast with the typical West European pattern in that the two major parties (Democrat and Republican) are separated by a smaller ideological distance than are parties of the left and right in Europe, presumably reflecting the greater agreement in America on the basic goals of society.

Not all party systems or individual parties are so easily categorized on the basis of their location within the left–right spectrum. In the Irish Republic the distinction between the two major parties, Fianna Fail and Fine Gael, is partly an historical one in that their origins are traceable to their position regarding the legitimacy of the 1922 treaty partitioning Ireland. Furthermore, there are a number of other parties whose ideologies are not easily classified as left, centrist or right such as the nationalist parties of Scotland and Wales. Their nationalist objectives tend to override their other ideological goals, though even in these cases it has become apparent that demanding local autonomy by itself is an insufficient ideological platform from which to attract electoral support.

Some political scientists have suggested that in the Western democracies ideological differences are narrowing. S. M. Lipset has suggested the basic reasons that underlie the process:

> Greater economic productivity is associated with a more equitable distribution of consumption goods and education – factors contributing to a reduction of intra-societal tensions. As the wealth of a nation increases the status gap inherent in poor countries is reduced. As differences in style of life are reduced so are the tensions of stratification. And increased education enhances the propensity of different groups to 'tolerate' each other.[8]

Although there is some evidence from a wide variety of countries to suggest that party-based ideological differences have diminished it would be more accurate to describe the development as the decline rather than the end of ideology.[9] Thus in Britain, beginning with the post-war Labour Government initiatives, successive Conservative governments have endorsed regional aid programmes, though they have (as in 1979) reduced the amounts of aid and the areas over which it is offered, reflecting their own ideological preferences against state intervention. Elsewhere, many other cases of policies with spatial impacts could be cited which stem from ideological differences between political parties.

Political Culture, Values and Policies

Much of our discussion of the themes of political culture and values has been in very general terms. It might, therefore, help discussion to illustrate some kinds of geographical differences which stem from these factors. Taking the very broad definition of political culture – basically as the set of attitudes and opinions individuals have towards politics within a political system – its influence is clearly pervasive. Somewhat paradoxically, however, there have been few attempts by geographers to examine the implications of differences in political culture.

One of the most far-reaching discussions of this question has been by a regional political scientist in an analysis of political cultures in the United States.[10] D. J. Elazar's thesis is that within the United States three main political cultures can be recognized geographically whose origins can be broadly traced to different migration streams. The three consist of: moralistic – in which the emphasis is on the society rather than the individual and the role of governments is to provide for the common good; individualistic – in which private concern is the primary motivating factor so that community control of resources is limited; traditionalistic – in which politics is considered the preserve of a political elite, and the social and political order is essentially a conservative one.

Figure 2.4 shows the broad geographical distribution of Elazar's cultural types. Although Elazar ignored state boundaries for the purposes of his analysis certain regional differences and patterns are strongly evident. Thus in the north-eastern states a moralistic culture was the result of Puritan and Yankee influences. Subsequently New England settlers migrated to north-western states, and the moralistic culture was also established in that region. What is important, however, for our discussion is that these culture types can be related to differences in public policy.[11] Thus in moralistic states there was a strong commitment to mass education and to the idea of popular rule (indicated by the time at which the secret ballot and female suffrage were introduced). By contrast, traditionalistic states, notably in the south, were relatively late in adopting female suffrage.

As geographers have become aware through their discussions of

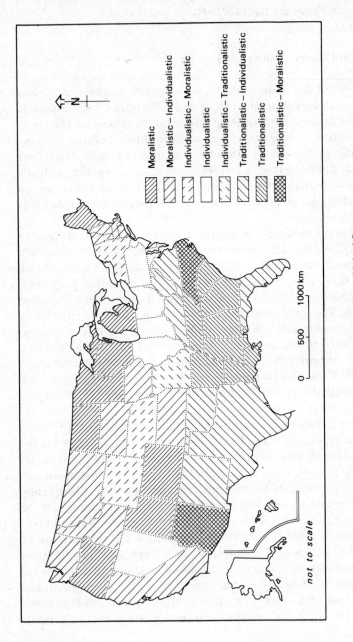

Fig. 2.4. Political cultures in the United States.

Source: D. J. Elazar, *American Federalism. A View from the States*, Crowell, New York, 1972.

value-judgements it is well known that value preferences vary among individuals as they do among groups within society. J. S. Furnivall, who introduced the term 'plural society', in his study *Netherlands India* showed how each ethnic group had its own set of values which for the most part were incompatible with those of other groups.[12] Other social divisions may serve further to segment society into a number of 'value subcultures' based on characteristics such as age, social class and the like.

The study by Williams and Adrians[13] of value preferences among a system of local governments (in the US) demonstrates their impact on public policy-making. Williams and Adrians were concerned primarily with how local governments defined their community role, an issue which would reveal their broad preferences for particular objectives. Their local governments fell into four main types:

(1) Those acting on the belief that expansion is to be positively related to community prosperity. Policies such as preferential zoning and taxing arrangements were designed to promote active economic growth and characterized these jurisdictions.

(2) Local governments whose preferences were directed to securing a high quality of life for their residents. A high-amenity environment and the provision of good services were advocated above growth which was effectively discouraged. In order to meet these high standards of service provision specific policy fields were selected for upgrading, e.g. parks and libraries, on the basis of local preference.

(3) Local governments whose main objective was the maintenance of traditional services (meaning only basic support services). Local governments of this type were evidently oriented to individualistic rather than collectivistic ends, their goal being to reduce local taxes to a minimum.

(4) Those local governments which placed the greatest priority on ensuring that resident, industry and commerce interest groups were given access to the policy-making process.

While Williams and Adrians were able to show how policies, based on value preferences, varied between the four types of local government bodies, it is clear that such preferences are not the sole determinants of policy-making. Indeed, in another study of intrametropolitan governments in the United States, Williams and others demonstrated that needs and resources were further important factors governing policy choices.[14] This is not to detract from the importance political geographers ought to attach to the question of values, for they are significant both for individuals and for governments in furnishing the motivational stimuli which, by moulding attitudes to various policy options, lead in turn to the selection of specific choices.

Attitudes

An analysis of attitudes follows logically from the study of values. For the most part our attitudes towards (political) objects are dictated by our value preferences. Attitudes can be defined as 'those feelings, favourable, unfavourable or neutral, which are held in relation to specific political objects'. Their specificity provides one way in which they differ from values. Another is the way in which, while the values of a society in many cases command general support, attitudes towards political events provide a more continuous source of conflict. Thus by definition democratic societies subscribe to the idea of one man one vote, though attitudes towards reapportionment, the type of electoral system to be used and the like, all of which affect the equality of the vote (Chapter 4), reveal a far greater diversity of opinion.

Attitudes are categorizable on the basis of several criteria, notably their intensity, dimensionality and stability.[15] Emotive issues tend to produce extreme opinions, particularly where interests are perceived as being directly in threat. The related issues of bussing and school desegregation following the Supreme Court decision in the United States provides a case in point in that the attitudes of black and white populations, especially in some cities, are so entrenched that confrontation, rather than compromise, has resulted. Environmental issues (e.g. the second Tokyo airport and some developments in British national parks) have also generated intensely felt attitudes. Secondly, attitudes are usually multidimensional. Thus opinion may favour regional aid programmes while also, and in apparent contradiction, support the cutting of public expenditure. Both attitudes are in effect compatible in so far as they measure different 'dimensions' or problems, the one being an assessment of a broadly social objective, the other an economic one referring to national policies at large. Finally, attitudes may be more or less stable dependent upon their intensity, changes within the environment which influence an alteration in our attitudes, and individual personality factors.

The measurement of political attitudes is not easily achieved,· though methods such as the semantic differential (in which the respondent locates his attitude between bipolar pairs of adjectives, good/bad, etc.) do afford quantitative assessment. Davis and Sinnott[16] have examined attitudes in the Irish Republic to the Northern Ireland crisis. Because of the complexity of the issue they based their analysis on multiple indicators, each group of indicators relating to a dimension of the attitude. Factor analysis was used to unravel the clusters of attitude items – these included such items as their attitude to partition, to whether they supported IRA (terrorist) activities and their feelings towards Northern Ireland Protestants. In Table 2.3 are listed the statements used to assess attitudes towards partition in each of which the response could vary between the following opposites:

PRO	1	2	3	4	5	6	7	ANTI
	strong	moderate	slight	neutral	slight	moderate	strong	

Overall attitudes to the question of partition were then assessed by looking at the combined responses to the set of statements.

Table 2.3. **Attitude Statements to Partition of Ireland.**

1. Reunification is essential for any solution to the problem in Northern Ireland.
2. This is an island and it cannot be permanently partitioned.
3. The presence of British troops in Northern Ireland amounts to foreign occupation of part of Ireland.
4. There will never be peace in Northern Ireland until partition is ended.
5. The sooner we get the idea that the North belongs to us out of our heads the better.
6. The major cause of the problem in Northern Ireland is British interference in Irish affairs.

Source: E. E. Davis and R. Sinnott, *Attitudes in the Republic of Ireland*, p. 95.

Political Socialization, Attitude Formation and Spatial Awareness

Given that the individual's view of the political world surrounding him will closely reflect his set of values and, more specifically, attitudes then a key question must relate to the acquisition of these. Broadly speaking such values and attitudes are acquired gradually as a continuing process related to our development. There are stages within the life-span, particularly during childhood and adolescence, when the acquisition process is probably more intense. While schooling marks a formative stage in the learning process it does not mark the end of it; in subsequent periods of life being a member of a trade union, an employers association or an informal group will provide other prolific sources of information which will continue to influence how the outside world is viewed.

The term political socialization is employed to denote the processes by which values and attitudes and the political culture of a society are inculcated.[17] Effectively it is a learning process by which the individual acquires those skills and beliefs necessary to orient him to the political community of which he is part. We will examine here as a case study how the individual acquires information orienting him to the nation and national territory as a vehicle to illustrate the process of political socialization.

Nationalism and the nation provide one of the major objects of political organization and support. The term 'nation' commonly refers to groups of people united by common cultural traits, occupying a definite territory and frequently organized as a separate state. Trent defines nationalism as a 'conglomerate of human attitudes and behaviour with high priority on the defence and assertion of the values, interests and the institutions of a particular people'.[18] Both nation and nationalism are defined by cultural, ethnic and historical factors on the one hand, and by psychological characteristics on the other. In gaining awareness of the nation the individual must acquire its cultural and political habits (predispositions) and be able to relate these meaningfully to a spatially bounded community.

Political Socialization

One way of studying the development of national orientation in the individual is to examine his awareness of political space at various stages in the life-span. In the first place the analysis would emphasize the designative aspect of the process, the knowledge of the world as a partitioned set of territories. A second stage would be evaluative in which the individual is able to make preferences between countries.

Psychologists, in studying the evolution of spatial (territorial) perception, have analyzed its development within children and adolescents. Broadly, as children become older their cognitive awareness of political space increases while their political attitudes alter from being expressed in affective terms, in simple like/dislike terms, to being more evaluative in nature.

Several theories of the child's growing awareness of political space have been developed by psychologists, the common

denominator among them being the idea that cognition is a cumula- ·
tive and developmental process. Piaget's 'centre–periphery progression'[19] of cognitive awareness has been one of the more influential models, which specifically uses the political area to test ideas of
changing spatial orientation. (His major ideas were propounded in
1918 though the work quoted here was with Weil in 1951.) Piaget's
ideas of the development of the child's idea of homeland and
nationality were based on survey evidence from Genevese children.
Taking the three age groups, 7/8, 8/9 and 10/11 years onwards
Piaget outlined a progression from where the child is unable to
rationalize properly about his local area (Geneva) in relation to the
state (Switzerland) or to other states to the position where he is able
to rationally locate himself and recognize the coequal existence of
other states. The overall sequence is one from egocentricity to ·
reciprocity (that of being able to understand others) though 'in
practice the sequence is checkered, with development periodically
giving way to regression as a result of some strain or conflict or
pressure in the child's environment'[20] (e.g. where a return to
egocentrism is manifested as ethnocentric behaviour).

Subsequent research evidence has added support, if sometimes of
a qualified nature, to Piaget's thesis that the child's political world
extends outwards as a progression through city and region to country, finally embracing other states. Evidently class and ethnic differ- ·
ences account for differences in spatial orientation. One study
amongst Pittsburgh children using Piaget's research techniques
showed that the centre–periphery progression followed the same
pattern as for Genevese children but that it was most developed (at
the same age) amongst middle-class whites and least among lower-
class black children who were less oriented to the national than the
more local level.

Parallel to the centre–periphery progression is a growing understanding of how and why countries differ. The child learns of the
social and political characteristics which distinguish his own country
and national group; sometimes this takes place through civics
courses which aim to socialize him to the political system of which
he is a member. Equally, the child learns of other countries, his ·
attitudes towards which develop from affective opinions (preferences) to evaluative judgements in which the child is able to
appreciate basic differences between states and begins to understand other points of view. Learning about other countries is also
important because it helps to foster the child's own sense of national
identity. Lambert and Klineberg[21] in their international survey of

children (at 6, 10 and 14 years of age) demonstrated that it was by comparing the cultures of alien countries that national identities were forged. Further, the children began to group countries into 'international blocs', sometimes revealing their preferences, based on such factors as spatial proximity, cultural similarities, Western versus Oriental and African countries and the like.

Agents of Political Socialization

Much of the foregoing survey evidence shows that the child's spatial orientation (view and attitudes) towards the political world develops from a localistic/egocentric frame of reference to a more cosmopolitan and reciprocal one. The accumulation of information about the political world helps to explain the child's more effective spatial reasoning not only in being able to locate himself properly but also in being able to categorize other countries.

The inculcation of this spatial orientation as part of the child's (and adult's) political culture is moulded by information flows stemming from a number of agents of political socialization. These include the family, schooling, mass media, and governments. While varying in importance, as also in their incidence at various stages in the life cycle, their role is the dissemination of ideas and values which the individual should acquire in order that he can subscribe to the norms and values of society in which he lives.

At this point a caveat should be entered as to the role and effects of such agents, particularly those which operate on a mass basis. Channels of mass communication as a means of moulding the values and attitudes within individuals and groups (which are spatially segregated from the communicator) are popularly considered as powerful agents of (political) socialization. Illustrative of this is the frequently close scrutiny, if not direct control, by national governments of the mass media, while in countries with a history of regime overthrow the centralization of broadcasting within the national capital is of obvious significance. However, analysts of mass communications have been less anxious to suggest that the relationship between the communicator and his audience either produces a definite response, or that, given there is a response, it is 'produced' directly. Studies of the effects of mass media on such subjects as violence and social problems have underpinned the importance of the media in influencing attitudes and sometimes behaviour patterns, though evidently individual personality factors play a part in this. If the question of effects is in doubt so is the relationship between the communicator and his audience. An early media model suggested that the relationship was direct, a process described graphically as akin to a hypodermic needle 'pecking and plunging at a passive audience'.[22] An alternative and in many cases more realistic model,[23] besides maintaining a direct link, introduces the role of an intermediary, perhaps a member of a (political) elite, through which information is channelled and processed en route to a wider audience.

Duchacek[24] has used the term 'territorial socialization' to mean the process by which individuals acquire identities with their political area (state, region, etc.). Several agents, notably governments, the educational process and mass media, can be taken to illustrate their influence upon the development of territorial socialization.

A continuing role (and an essential one) of a national government is the establishment among its citizens of allegiances to itself. The absence of such loyalties will undermine its legitimacy and, consequently, its basis of support. Loyalty to the state is sought and attained by the 'production' of symbolic goods by governments which act as information stimulants linking the individual to the state. Gottman[25] used the word iconography to denote the set of symbols allied to a particular area. These might include the national capital, national flag, etc. – symbols which stimulate positive attitudes and which form part of the national legacy, demanding respect, for successive generations. Symbols provide potent agents linking the individual with the national territory and the idea of friendly or hostile nations, even amongst the very young. In a study[26] of kindergarten children in New York State the US flag was the most preferred and that of the USSR the least. Similarly to the child figureheads, the queen or a president, act as strong referrant symbols.

Schooling provides a major source of influence on values and attitudes. School systems are normally organized on a national basis, so that they afford a vehicle for establishing standardized interpretations of past and current political events. The structure of the school itself, with its emphasis on authoritarian, hierarchically organized relationships, contributes to influence the child's acquiescence in authority. More important, in many countries formal political education courses are taught as part of the curriculum though their influence on political awareness is less than might be expected. Nevertheless, as a recent report[27] in Britain proposing the introduction of political literacy courses shows, the syllabus would ideally include the teaching of those values and attitudes and political processes typical to a plural democracy. It should also be remembered that within the educational process the teacher acts as an influential intermediary. Thus it may be of importance to find that only a minority of primary school teachers in America appear willing to introduce, within the curriculum, material that is critical of the nation and its political machinery.[28]

Parts of the educational curriculum have had a more pronounced influence in communicating the idea and virtues of the child's own nation and of alien countries and political cultures. The teaching of history in particular is typically biased, to a greater or lesser extent, to a national perspective. Certainly countries of the 'Free World' are not immune to such educational bias. Duchacek quotes the example of the burning of Washington by the British which all the junior high school textbooks mentioned without in a single case indicating that it had been similar action by American forces in the Canadian city of York which had led to British retaliation.[29] The problem of biased (national) perspective has been recognized as particularly acute in Europe with its history of violent conflict between states, so it is interesting to note that, under the aegis of the EEC, there are attempts to rewrite the history texts used by member countries.

The treatment of alien political ideologies by the educational system also exemplifies how the study of foreign ideas is used to bolster the values of the child's own country. School essays entitled 'Better Dead than Red' carry their own thinly disguised message. Communism in American schools is typically drawn as an evil, conspiratorial ideology dominated by the Soviet Union. Ziegler and Peak[30] illustrate the bias, citing the case of four student projects accompanying one text which included 'Write a short paper on agreements with other nations broken by the Soviet Union and (2) draw a chart contrasting the way of life in a democracy and in a totalitarian government'.

Mass media furnish an ongoing source of information. In most countries – the United States is an exception – the media, broadcasting and the press, are organized nationally and in authoritarian regimes tend to be closely controlled. Control of mass media, however, is not restricted to authoritarian regimes; French radio and television is closely scrutinized by the government influencing, for example, the treatment of European questions.

In spatial terms the special influence of the educational system and governments has been to emphasize, to the point of bias, the national territory. The media reinforces this spatial bias as it relates to the communication of political events. Localism, as Cole and Whysall[31] demonstrated in a content analysis of the world areas mentioned on the BBC and in *Pravda* (see Fig. 2.5), was the major characteristic. Subsequent analyses of *Time* and *The Rolling Stone* magazines have reaffirmed the parochial bias. Nevertheless, through television in particular, the individual is able to learn of 'far places' visually though value-influenced by news communicators. As several programmes on British television on social problems, such as homelessness and the plight of the teenage migrant in London, have demonstrated, graphic portrayal can trigger 'instant' debate and even policy-making in the national legislature.

The significance of the agents of territorial and political socialization is primarily in their nature as disseminators of information which the individual receives and incorporates into his political make-up or rejects. Orientation to the nation and the national territory has been examined as a case study to demonstrate the nature of the process. Not all the agents of political socialization have been discussed – clearly the family, peers and membership of organizations such as the Boy Scouts, with its accentuated loyalties to queen, country and good citizenship, generate further value cues. Nor, perhaps more critically, has it been possible to 'measure' the importance of such agents, particularly as individual personality factors enter the equation as 'noise'.

A final qualification must also be raised where this behavioural interpretation, through processes of political socialization, conflicts with the ethologist's interpretation of nationalism. Hence to ethologists instinct is a driving force leading man to organize and defend a defined territory; possession of a political territory satisfies such basic human needs as security and identity.

While such ideas attract some support and can point to a certain amount of empirical evidence[32] to bolster their argument it is clear that as a mode of explanation they conflict with the processes outlined in this section. Attitudes and values are based on man's ability to reason with the physical and human world that surrounds him. And it is precisely because man, as opposed to animals, is able to rationalize events on a collective basis, with coalitions, for example, that drawing a one-to-one correspondence between animal and human behaviour tends to oversimplify. However, as a caveat to much of our current understanding of behavioural processes it is by no means clear that there are direct links between attitudes and values and overt behaviour. Psychologists have been hard pressed

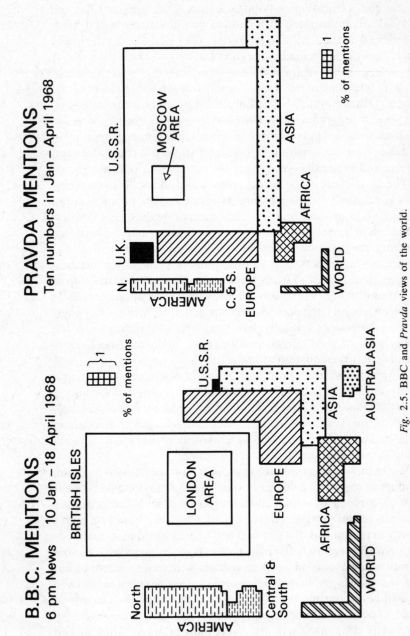

Fig. 2.5. BBC and *Pravda* views of the world.

Adapted from J. P. Cole and S. Whysall, 'Places in the News', *Bulletin of Quantitative Data for Geographers* (1968), **7**, University of Nottingham.

to show that this is the case; Wicker[33] in a review of 46 attitude versus action type studies found only a weak link joining the two.

Images of the Political World

Earlier in this chapter it was suggested that it is through our 'image systems' that much of our decision-making is based. Images represent a subjective interpretation of reality and are formed by an amalgam of the interaction between attitudes and values and our understanding of events in the real world. Perception has been used as a term to cover the processes by which man understands his environment while the image is the end-state of such processes. Downs' model of environmental perception places the various components in perspective:

> The real world is taken as the starting point and it is represented as a source of information. The information content enters the individual through a system of perceptual receptors and the precise meaning of the information is determined by an interaction between the individual's value system (predispositions) and their image of the real world. The meaning of the information is then incorporated into the image . . .[34]

A change in the image may demand readjustment, which is achieved through an appropriate decision.

In this model it is the image of reality that determines decision-making behaviour. As a student of international politics has argued, 'Once a statesman has formed an image of an issue, this image acts as an organizing device for further information and is a filter through which this information must pass. Images, not detailed information, govern political behaviour.'[35] Besides their function in providing the basis for decision-making, images also act as the agents by which individuals can sort and classify information about the real world.

The role of image formation as it impinges on the political process has been clearly discussed by Brecher in his analysis of Israeli foreign policy-making.[36] He distinguishes between an operational and a psychological environment. The operational environment includes external variables (political conditions outside Israel) and internal variables (military, political, economic and social characteristics of the state). Information concerning the operational environment is channelled through the 'attitudinal prism', the psychological environment, where it is modified by the predispositions of the decision-making elite to become their images of the internal and external environment. Unlike other spatially-related images governing the relationships between sovereign states – Dulles' interpretation of the domino theory in south-east Asia, for example – Brecher concluded that Israel's image of a largely hostile and rigid world was close to reality. Nevertheless he was able to argue that not until the Israeli image of the Arab, as only understanding force, altered would any peace initiatives be likely to succeed, a prognosis which the signing of the Sinai Agreement of 1978 has supported.

Image-formation

Images, it has been argued, are formed by the interaction of attitudes, values and the comprehension the individual has of the world. An alternative way of looking at images, stressing their mode of formation, is the result of the interaction of a large number of communicated signals from the environment and the individual's response to these. The signals relate to events in the real world which are received more or less continuously through a number of communication channels, e.g. media, face-to-face communication. Once an image has taken form then fresh signals can augment it, give it greater salience or leave it unchanged.

How the individual defines his environment is closely linked to the 'openness' of his images. An open image is flexible and can adjust to new information, while a closed image will likely suffer from being anachronistic. Evidently the continuous stream of information must be processed by the image, even if this is only the rejection of such signals. The extent to which new information is incorporated depends on the openness of the image. Traumatic events can force openness and a realignment of images and in turn of policy-making behaviour. The race riots in American cities in the late 1960s forced a new image of the urban black problem, particularly among Federal administrators, leading to new urban policies. On the other hand, the American débâcle at Pearl Harbour illustrates that the signals demanding a readjustment of images must in themselves be clear. Many examples could be cited of governments that have failed to heed warnings from the environment because their images were more closed than otherwise and because the clarity of the signals was insufficient.

Because of the complexity and uncertainties in the world it is apparent that as decision-makers our images are 'relatively closed'.

This degree of closure affords security. Hence the extent to which new information is incorporated ensures that only such events that can be readily assimilated are usually accepted. In the well-researched theory of cognitive dissonance psychologists have shown that when a belief or value is contradicted by a new message (a 'dissonant cognition') generally the belief will be retained and the message rejected or its 'adaptation' secured to fit the facts as they are seen. Only reluctantly will the individual alter his beliefs or images on the basis of new information.

The existence of stereotype images of foreign nations was studied in an early work by Buchanan and Cantril, *How Nations See Each Other*.[37] Based on questionnaires they carried out a cross-national survey to expose the attitudes held towards various foreign nationals. What their study showed clearly was that people's views were frequently stereotyped and therefore oversimplified. Thus to the British the Russians were described as hardworking, domineering, cruel, backward and brave, the adjectives most frequently chosen in order of importance. Interestingly Buchanan and Cantril showed that the American image of the Russians was radically different from their own self-perception, an observation which White subsequently refined and termed the mirror-image phenomenon. That is, both Russia and America see themselves as peace-loving nations and the other party as aggressors. American bases in 'rimland states' and the theory of containment is seen by one as an act of defence and by the other as one of aggression. Clearly such images can be, and are, used as the reference devices by which further information can be categorized and also selected.

Images of foreign nations will generally be formed through the influence of secondary sources of information. Books, newspapers, television and other sources of communication provide the main channels from which our images are derived. It has already been shown how spatial biases frequently characterize how information is imparted. More generally the ideological differences between mass media serve as a wider influence of image formation.

Research into urban imagery[38] has shown that the images people have of cities are given greater salience where they are reinforced by activity patterns and actual usage. Such active interaction with the image-subject is less possible in many of the issues covered in the political geographer's field. Americans did not, nor could they, 'know' North Vietnam. Likewise the middle-class householder anxious to reroute a new road through a nearby local authority housing estate does not necessarily 'know' what the view from the estate is –

at best he can have an image of this which may bear scant likeness to reality.

The Chinese image of the world order (see Fig. 2.6) provides one of the better known examples of spatial imagery.[39] Based partly on the historic position of China, which as the dominant East Asian power was surrounded by a number of tributary states, and partly on an ideological commitment to world revolution since the communist assumption of power, the world is divided into a number of zones which define an 'ideal' pattern. Countries adjacent to China are the most immediately important from the viewpoint of national defence and in a number of cases were lost by the 'unequal treaties' of the nineteenth century. Communist China has committed itself to regaining some of these territories: thus the first zone includes China, Taiwan, the Soviet Maritime province and Sakhalin. Military conflicts between Communist China and Soviet forces on the one hand and Nationalist forces on the other support the behaviourist's thesis of image-based action. Yet the example as it applies to Taiwan can also be used as a word of caution to the ready acceptance of direct links connecting image and behaviour, in that the advantages of world recognition and the greater perceived threat of the Soviet Union have reduced the image's salience as it affects Nationalist China. Images may underlie behaviour though other constraints also fashion decisions and actions in the political world.

Discussion Points and Further Reading

Though fundamental to understanding why particular decisions are made, geographers have all too infrequently studied the question of values and value-systems. Put simply, it is values and value-systems which determine which courses of action are likely to be taken by the decision-maker. Besides the sources cited earlier an influential and stimulating article on the impact of values as an input (through the ballot box) to the political system is provided in Wilson and Banfield (1964). The question of regional political cultures generates complex methodological issues, in terms of the criteria by which they can be recognized, their spatial delimitation and possible effects on the political system. Savage (1973) presents a detailed time-series analysis of cultural regions in the United States, helpfully enumerating the variables used as the basis for regionalization.

Spatial images and attitudes in political geography are discussed in the case studies by Kristof (1968), Saarinen (1973) and Sprout and Sprout (1965).

Kristof, L. K. D., 'The Russian Image of Russia. An Applied Study in Geographical Methodology', in Fisher, C. A. (ed.), *Essays in Political Geography*, Methuen, London, 1968, pp. 345–87.

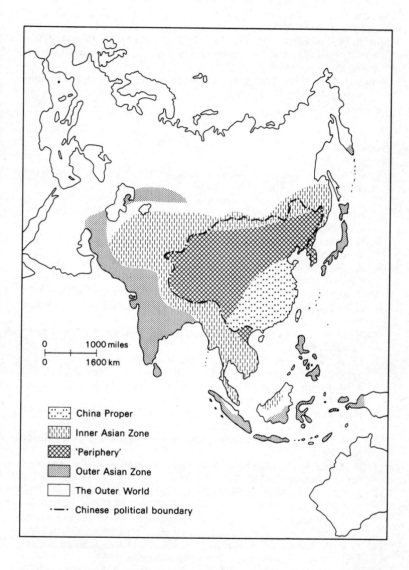

Fig. 2.6. China: The traditional world order. Reproduced from N. Ginsburg, 'On the Chinese Perception of World Order', in Tang Tson (ed.), *China's Policies in Asia and America's Alternatives*, University of Chicago Press, vol. 2, 1968, by permission of the author and the University of Chicago Press.

Saarinen, T. F., 'Student Views of the World', in Downs, R. M., and Stea, D. (eds.), *Image and Environment*, Aldine, Chicago, 1973, pp. 148–61.
Savage, R. L., 'Patterns of Multilinear Evolution in the American States', *Publius*, (1973), **3**(1), 75–108.
Sprout, H., and Sprout, M., *The Ecological Perspective on Human Affairs with Special Reference to International Politics*, Princeton University Press, Princeton, 1965.
Wilson, J. Q., and Banfield, E. C., 'Public-regardingness as a value premise in voting behaviour', *American Political Science Review* (1964), **58**, 876–7.

Notes

1. G. A. Almond and G. B. Powell, *Comparative Politcs: A Developmental Approach*, Little Brown, Boston, 1966, p. 50.
2. Sr A. Buttimer, *Values in Geography*, Commission on College Geography, Resource Paper No. 24. Association of American Geographers, Washington, 1974.
3. K. Deutsch, *Politics and Government. How People Decide their Fate*, Wiley, New York, 1975.
4. A. H. Maslow, 'A Theory of Human Motivation', *Psychological Review* (1963), **50**, 370–96.
5. R. Inglehart, 'The Nature of Value Change in Postindustrial Society' in L. N. Lindberg, *Politics and the Future of Industrial Society*, McKay, New York, 1976 pp. 57–99.
6. R. M. Christenson, *et al.*, *Ideologies and Modern Politics*, Nelson, London, 1971, p. 5.
7. G. K. Bersch, R. P. Clark and D. M. Ward, *Comparing Political Systems: Power and Policy in Three Worlds*, Wiley, New York, 1978.
8. S. M. Lipset, *Political Man: The Social Bases of Politics*, Doubleday Anchor, New York, repr. 1963, pp. 442–3.
9. R. D. Putnam, *The Beliefs of Politicians: Ideology, Conflict and Democracy in Britain and Italy*, Yale University Press, New Haven, 1973.
10. D. J. Elazar, *American Federalism: A View from the States*, Crowell, New York, 1972.
11. R. L. Savage, 'Patterns of Multilinear Evolution in the American States', *Publius* (1978), **3** (1), 75–108.
12. J. S. Furnivall, *Netherlands India*, Cambridge University Press, Cambridge, 1939.
13. O. P. Williams and C. R. Adrians, *Four Cities: A Study in Comparative Policy Making*, University of Pennsylvania Press, Philadelphia, 1963.
14. O. P. Williams *et al.*, *Suburban Differences and Metropolitan Policies*, University of Pennsylvania Press, Philadelphia, 1965.
15. D. T. Reynolds, *Politics and the Common Man*, Dobey Press, Illinois, 1974, pp. 7ff.
16. E. E. Davis and R. Sinnott, *Attitudes in the Republic of Ireland relevant to the Northern Ireland Problem*: vol. 1, *Descriptive Analysis and Some Comparisons with Attitudes in Northern Ireland and Great Britain*, Economic and Social Research Institute, Dublin, 1979.

17. See M. Rush and P. Althoff, *An Introduction to Political Sociology*, Nelson, London, 1971.
18. J. Trent, 'The politics of Nationalist Movements – a Reconsideration', *Canadian Review of Studies in Nationalism* (1974), **3**, 157.
19. T. Piaget and A. Weil, 'The Development in Children of the Idea of Homeland and of Relations with Other Countries', *International Social Science Bulletin* (1957), **3**, 561–78.
20. B. Stacey, *Political Socialization in Western Society*, Edward Arnold, London, 1978.
21. W. E. Lambert and O. Klineberg, *Children's Views of Foreign Peoples*, Appleton, New York, 1967.
22. E. M. Rogers and F. F. Shoemaker, *Communication of Innovations*, Free Press, London, 1971, p. 203.
23. P. Lazarsfield, *et al.*, *The People's Choice: How the Voter Makes Up His Mind in a Presidential Campaign*, Owell, Sloan and Pearce, New York, 1944.
24. I. D. Duchacek, *Comparative Federalism*, Holt, Rinehart and Winston, New York, 1970.
25. J. Gottman, *Le Politique des Etats et Leur Géographie*, Colin, Paris, 1952.
26. E. D. Lawson, 'Development of Patriotism in Children – a Second Look', *Journal of General Psychology* (1978), **55**, 279–86.
27. B. Crick and A. Porter (eds.), *Political Education and Political Literacy*, Longman, London, 1978.
28. Quoted in Stacey, *Political Socialization*, p. 14.
29. Duchacek, *Comparative Federalism*.
30. H. Ziegler and W. Peak, 'The Political Functions of the Educational System', *Sociology of Education* (1975), **43**, 115–43 (quotation, p. 133).
31. J. P. Cole and S. Whysall, 'Places in the News: A Study of Geographical Information', *Bulletin of Quantitative Data for Geographers* (1968), no. 7. University of Nottingham.
32. For a reasoned discussion see R. Pettman, *Human Behaviour and World Politics*, Macmillan, London, 1975, pp. 176–99.
33. A. W. Wicker, 'Attitude versus Actions: The Relationship of Verbal and Overt Behavioural Responses to Attitude Objects', *Journal of Social Issues* (1969), **25**.
34. R. M. Downs, 'Geographic Space Perception: Past Approaches and Future Prospects', *Progress in Geography* (1970), **2**, 65–108 (quotation, p. 84).
35. J. Frankel, *National Interest*, Pall Mall, London, 1970.
36. M. Brecher, *The Foreign Policy System of Israel: Setting, Image and Process*, Yale University Press, New Haven, 1972.
37. H. Cantril, W. Buchanan *et al.*, *How Nations See Each Other: A Study in Public Opinion*, University of Illinois Press, Urbana, 1953.
38. D. C. Pocock and R. Hudson, *Images of the Urban Environment*, Macmillan, London, 1979.
39. N. Ginsburg, 'On the Chinese Perception of a World Order', in Tang Tson (ed.), *China's Policies in Asia and America's Alternatives* (2 vols.), University of Chicago Press, Chicago, 1968, vol. 2, pp. 73–91.

3 Decision-Making

Why Study Decisions?

Political geography concerns interactions between products and processes that are political and products and processes that are geographical. Study within the discipline involves two broad categories of question: 'How has geography affected politics?' and 'How has politics affected geography?' The general conception of this relationship may be clarified by using some kind of Eastonian model embodying a political decision-making system receiving inputs from an environment, of which a portion is a geographical environment, and transforming these inputs via policy-making processes into outputs, some of which effect modifications of the geographical environment. It follows that answers may be elucidated by substituting the original questions with the reconstructed questions 'How have the inputs from the geographical environment influenced behaviour within the political system?' and 'How has the behaviour of the political system affected the geographical environment?' Accepting, as we must, that the transformation processes are the products of political decision-making activities, the centrality of decisional analysis to political geography is established.

While there is no currently recognizable movement to circumscribe the field of political geographical inquiry, the portion of the discipline's literature which is explicitly concerned with decisional analysis is minuscule. Even so, in so far as we can sniff the breezes of change, there seems to be an acceptance, amongst the younger practitioners at least, that attention should be directed towards the more analytical investigation of relevant political processes, in which case studies of decision-making must constitute a vital component in the overall development of the subject.

Although the decision-making question has been sidestepped, a considerable amount of political geographical research can be done, and has been done, in relevant fields which do not require decisional analysis. Normative modelling, for example the design of optimal administrative areas, is practical without reference to real world decision-making. In the area of dynamic analysis, interactance rather than decisional approaches may be more appropriate to a proper understanding of a situation, for example when aspects of behaviour other than decision-making and policy formation occupy the centre of the stage. Such studies would include, for instance, the useful applications of interactance hypotheses to the analysis of trading or communication patterns. For the purposes of a wide range of inquiries, decisions can be regarded as facts rather than subjects for research in their own right; for example it is possible to conduct a variety of geographical investigations into the political partitioning of the maritime environment, regarding claims to spheres of control as facts rather than as products of decision processes. However, in most cases where decision-making has been discussed by political geographers, the approach adopted has been descriptive rather than analytical; stages in the decisional process may be identified and the reader may be informed as to *what* decisions were taken and when they were taken, but the question of *how* is completely bypassed.

But if what is required are accurate and comprehensive answers to many of the questions about 'How does politics affect geography?' then sidestepping, either by beginning analysis with the policy which is the end product of the policy-making process or by treating decision-making in terms of historical description, will prove inadequate. The great advantage of a decisional approach to empirical problems in political geography is that it provides an organized framework for understanding how political processes occur, in detail, and with a minimum of abstraction. Like the systems approach, into which it is frequently integrated, the decisional approach will inevitably emphasize the dynamic relationship between the actors, the policy and the environment, and therefore it constitutes a highly suitable vehicle for geographical inquiry.

This is not to say that the adoption of the approach will automatically vouchsafe answers to all questions about the politics–space relationship. In practical terms there may be insuperable difficulties encountered in the collection and interpretation of information necessary to the understanding of the processes concerned. There may also be difficulties of a more philosophical nature, and it could be argued that if geographers concern themselves with questions of decision and policy formation, they will be as novices in an unfamiliar land, obliged to grapple with procedures identical to those developed by political science initiates. The only truthful reply is 'Yes, they will'.

Academic opposition to the study by geographers of decision and policy formation can be refuted partly by the use of analogies drawn from other branches of geography, and partly by the consideration of the interdisciplinary dependency of the social sciences, of which human geography is one. First, bearing in mind the longer history of process–emphasis in the physical branch of geography, we might ask ourselves whether, confronted with an unfamiliar landform, a geomorphologist would be content to measure it, map it, and catalogue its structural components. No, he would not fully comprehend the landform until he had identified and investigated the processes that had formed it, even if the techniques required were those of the chemist, physicist or mathematician. Secondly, decisional analysis is neither the product nor the property of any one disciplinary heartland but has developed from the exchange of ideas between the fields of psychology, economics, political science, management studies, cybernetics, public administration, and several others. Within the social sciences, human geography functions as a perspective rather than as a core and the development of human geography advances hand in hand with the general development of the social sciences through the refinement of the spatial perspective upon the subject matters of related disciplines.

In terms of problems of analysis, the decisional studies likely to engage the geographer (with the possible exception of those concerning small aggregates of voters) will be of the more difficult kind. In the political branch particularly, the relevant decisions are usually those taken by organizations or collective decision-making units rather than by individuals, while for the processes concerned to be political there must be an element of conflict involved, and since it takes two to start a fight, political geographical investigation is likely to be concerned with interplay between at least two decision-making collectives with conflicting goal structures.

Some Basic Concepts

In general terms, the geographical involvement with decisional behaviour can be criticized first because of the widespread failure to explore decision-making by way of an organized and analytical framework, leading to descriptive writing and arbitrary selection of

items for mention, and secondly because of the disproportionate
emphasis upon locational decisions. The scant nature of the political
geographical contribution has been noted, though Brunn included a
section on decision-making in his text on geography and politics in
the USA. The significant point is made that:

> Many of the public institutions and facilities that dot the map of a city,
> state or nation are in that particular place because of political and
> geographical considerations. While there is a demand for such services,
> the decision of where to locate that institution or facility may not be
> reflective solely of economic or social considerations . . . Political power
> or clout in the form of an influential citizenry, lobby, politician or organ-
> ization may have been involved subtly or openly in the eventual decision
> regarding location.[1]

Interesting discussion follows on the role of political activity in
influencing the spatial allocation of 'desirable' installations like
state capitals and military academies which are expected to produce
positive externalities, and prisons or nuclear testing or dumping
sites which could produce negative externalities, but the two weaknesses identified above are apparent. It must be emphasized that
there are decisions other than locational ones that are interesting
from a political geographical standpoint; notably those that indi-
rectly affect spatial structure, including the designation of land for
conservation or development uses, the subsidizing of certain
strategic industries, the policy on ethnic minorities amongst a host
of other examples. Furthermore, it is self-evident that the detailed
analysis of decision-making requires the use of appropriate analytical frameworks, concepts and theories if good research is to be
distinguished from good journalism.

Patients often relate the efficacy of a tonic to the difficulty
encountered in swallowing it. A decisional approach will often
permit a clarity and precision of analysis which is denied to other
approaches, but it cannot be adopted lightly or employed without
due attention to a host of intertwined variables. The beginning of an
understanding of this complexity and an appreciation of some basic
decision concepts can be attained through the step-by-step demoli-
tion of a normative model of the decision-making process.

The following is a digest of several of the more widely accepted
verbal formulations of the process. On encountering a problem (I),
the decision-maker defines a goal (II) which is an image of a desired
future state, and proceeds to evaluate strategies for attaining the
goal. He identifies the range of possible alternative actions (III),
evaluates the effects of the implementation of each alternative (IV),

estimates the probability of each effect occurring (V), and ranks the effects and the probabilities, leading to a generalized view of each alternative (VI). He then ranks each alternative in order of value or preference (VII), and his decision involves the choice of the most preferable alternative (VIII). Represented diagramatically, the process appears as in Fig. 3.1.

The normative model (see Fig. 3.1) shows what would happen if the decision-maker had total information and was absolutely rational, and the model would have many weaknesses if presented as a model of real world decision-making. We may start with the 'problem', and begin by noting that in the real world a problem may

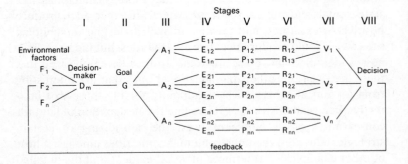

Fig. 3.1. A normative model of the decision-making process.

exist without being recognized. The appearance of a problem does not produce an automatic response from the appropriate decision-maker; for a long time there has been a problem concerning the inequality of width of territorial waters claimed by the various maritime states, though it has only been recognized as being a major global problem during the last two decades. A problem may only become a problem when a level of social or technological advance determines it to be such; twenty years ago there was no problem about the extraction of minerals from the bed of the High Seas. Different problems are open to different interpretations; what one politician might perceive as an immigrant problem, another might identify as an immigrant opportunity – the presence of a pool of labour prepared to accept the low-paid menial labour rejected by the indigenous workforce. Moreover, as Lindblom shows, policy-

makers are not always faced with a *given* problem, they may have to
identify and formulate their problem; thus when rioting broke out
in several US cities in 1967, President Johnson did not immediately begin to define a problem-solving goal, he appointed a commission to discover what the problem was.[2]

When it is misinterpreted in a descriptive sense rather than in the
normative sense, most of the objections to the model concern the
characterization of the decision-maker who appears as a mechanism
for converting perfect information into rational decisions. Most
decisions of interest to political geographers are the products of
collective rather than individual decisional behaviour, but we find
nothing in the model which identifies the decision-maker as a
member of a particular society, culture or class, or as an individual
with a particular personality or value system. The information
concerning environmental conditions is shown as travelling directly
to the decision-maker without being selectively screened off or
distorted by his own distinctive perceptual apparatus. Perception
concepts will be familiar to most readers; for the remainder, the
following quotation from Simon must suffice:

> The perceived world is fantastically different from the 'real world'. The
> differences involve both omissions and distortions, and arise in both
> perception and inference . . . The decision-maker's model of the world
> encompasses only a minute fraction of all the relevant characteristics of
> the real environment, and his inferences extract only a minute fraction of
> all the information that is present even in his model.[3]

As well as being prey to the weaknesses of his own perceptual
apparatus, the decision-maker operates within a context which will
colour, condition and constrain his decisional behaviour; he is an
element of several interlocking systems, a member of a society, a
culture, a class, an organization and a situation. The nature of a
particular society, that is to say whether it conforms most closely to
a ruling class, ruling elite or pluralistic model, will greatly determine
the form, membership and goals of the decision-making activities
existing within it. For example, in the Soviet Union, where important decisions are the prerogative of a ruling elite, they are formulated within a context of a kind known as 'conflict interdependence'
the decision-makers being primarily motivated to safeguard and
develop their own particular vested interests, and the decisions
produced are likely to reflect compromise influenced by given
power distributions rather than the pursuit of the most rational goal
implicit in the normative model.[4]

Returning from the context to the individual, it has been said that 'behaviour is a function of the environment or situation in which an individual is located and of the psychological predispositions which that individual brings to the situation'.[5] There are several political science and political–sociological approaches to personality and to the attitudes, beliefs, opinions and values held by individuals, while there have even been attempts by psychologists to provide psychoanalytical explanations for the policy-making behaviour of certain US presidents. While bearing in mind the importance of context, the researcher may only find it practicable to identify what the decision-maker wants rather than the psychological motivation for wanting it. Obviously, the decision-maker cannot be 'taken as read'; given similar information, goals or tasks and environmental or situational contexts, different individuals will produce significantly different decisions as a result of differences in their personality, cultural and value systems.

An added dimension of complexity is encountered when the decisions under scrutiny are the products of group rather than individual decision-making, and the researcher is confronted with interplay between different personality types, and probably contrasting value systems, motivations, levels of participant dedication, intelligence and information, and with behaviour that reflects the varying locations of individuals on the dominant–submissive spectrum, all of which may find expression in the decisions produced, or at least in the way that decisions were reached. Group structure is a variable to be considered; it may be an independent variable imposed upon the group as is likely in decision-making within a formal organization, or a dependent variable emerging as the result of interaction within the group, as is likely in the case of a group engaged in community protest politics. Each group is likely to develop its own communication network (see Fig. 3.2) and this will influence the decision process; research suggests that given a central position in such a network an individual who does not normally display the psychological attributes of a leader may begin to display leader behaviour.[6]

The normative model endows the decision-maker with the capacities to identify the alternative strategies, their effects, the probability of each effect occurring, to rank the effects and probabilities, and so to acquire a general view of each alternative, making possible the ranking of alternatives and the selection of the one which is most desirable. In reality, the decision-maker will have neither total information nor the ability to evaluate the information that he does have with total rationality. Rather than striving for the optimal decision, he is likely to satisfice: 'In most psychological theories the motive to act stems from *drives* and action terminates when the drive is satisfied'.[7] Satisficing becomes acceptable when costs are considered; in searching for relevant information, the decision-maker will incur costs, expressed in terms of time, energy and resources expended by the information search. 'Costs are not willingly borne unless there are benefits from the decision. The benefits are frequently referred to in terms of *utility*. Costs are borne until the actor or group sees that further participation is worthless.'[8]

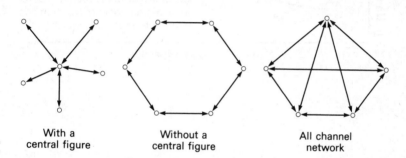

| With a central figure | Without a central figure | All channel network |

Fig. 3.2. Some communication networks.

In so far as he can assess costs, the decision-maker is likely to terminate his information search at some point before the marginal costs exceed the marginal utility, and consequently there is some economic rationale attached to making a decision upon a basis of imperfect information (see Fig. 3.3).

At least the decision represented in the normative model would seem to be clearcut and unambiguous. But unless appropriate techniques are employed, the detection of a decision may depend upon that decision being implemented. A model of the decision process has been developed by Levin (see Fig. 3.4) which allows for the detection of a decision which is independent of its implementation. He writes:

A decision is a deliberate act that generates commitment on the part of the decision-maker towards an envisaged course of action of some specificity and is moreover an act that is made in the light of – and is

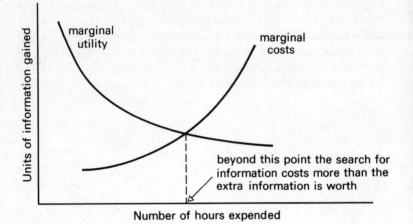

Fig. 3.3. Costs and the information search.

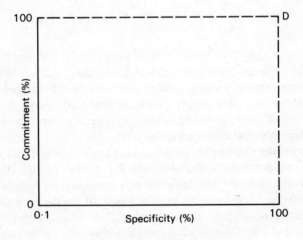

Fig. 3.4. The 'Levin model' of a decision.

consistent with some at least of the elements of – an action schema, the components of which are classifiable under the headings of action, outcome, and action/outcome realtionships.[9]

In essence, Levin says that as the decision process proceeds, the decision-makers become increasingly specic in the indentification of a desired outcome, and increasingly committed to a specific course of action. The decision is made at the points of maximum commitment and maximum specificity.

Political Geographical Applications

We have already stated that interest in decision-making transcends many disciplinary frontiers, and have suggested that the theories and concepts developed by political scientists are the most relevant to political geography. However, the political geographer must be selective in his appropriation and modification of such material, for 'it should be explicit at the outset that "decision-making theory", like most terms in political science, lacks a commonly accepted meaning. Some equate it with the elitist-pluralist debate over assessing the distribution of power. Others equate it with mathematical game theory . . . '.[10] To the extent that it is possible to generalize, the political geographer's attention will focus upon the politics – landscape relationship, and his *prime* concern will not be with the study of decision-making as a means of discovering 'who rules?', while game theory, as associated with the familiar pay-off matrices and a highly formal and quantitative nature, is likely to prove too abstract and limited for the elucidation of his empirical problems. In the preliminary developmental stages at least, political geographical investigation is likely to focus upon specific real world processes and the testing and subsequent modification and development of spatially oriented models of the decision process.

Decisional analysis can be attempted at all political levels, but generally speaking the higher the level the more likely is the researcher to encounter the main logistical weakness of the approach, the persistence of 'blank spaces' or information gaps which result from security, secrecy or privacy. At the national governmental level in the UK, for example, parliamentary debates are meticulously reported but the researcher does not have access to the crucial processes of lobbying, private conversations between participants, the counselling of ministers by civil servants, committee meetings or cabinet meetings. Particularly with the normal organization of policy-making and voting upon rigid party lines, the public portion of the decision process, the debate upon the floor of the House of Commons, becomes largely ritualistic, a necessary constitutional preliminary to the sanctioning of policy that was formulated in detail before it reached the chamber.

Thoroughgoing research cannot be based upon the tantalizing snippets of information that periodically seep through the filter of secrecy as reminders that policy formation is a highly political process. Neither can one rely upon the veracity or disinterestedness of those who leak:

> Callaghan barged in [on a Cabinet discussion about new docks for Bristol in the summer of 1968] as Home Secretary and also as Member for Cardiff, saying we couldn't have a port at Bristol because Newport and Cardiff wouldn't like it. So Callaghan, Cledwyn Hughes and George Thomas [two other Ministers who had Welsh constituencies] provided the weight to defeat the Bristol scheme. This is politics at its worst. I don't think any of them were thinking in terms of Government policy or politics but merely in terms of Welsh regional self-interest.[11]

While admitting that 'decision-making by governmental bodies in Britain is notoriously difficult for an outsider to study because of the inaccessibility of material, especially where central government is concerned',[12] a geographically rare and highly interesting attempt to study decision-making within an organized decisional framework has been produced by Levin (a specialist in social administration). He studied the planning processes concerned with the establishment of new towns and expanded towns in the UK, taking the Central Lancashire new towns and the Swindon expansion scheme as case studies. Some of the concepts employed have been outlined above, and they include commitment, specificity, the action schema, information and interest, the decision, the planning process, administrative, technical and political processes, and the planning framework. Particular emphasis was placed upon the ways in which the planning or decision-making process involved the decision-makers in incurring commitment to selected strategies, with the growth of commitment serving to endow a project with momentum. The administrative process is concerned with the various set procedures which surround planning, the technical process with the activities of planners in tackling particular planning problems, and the political process, with the activities by which consent for a particular development is obtained, or opposition overridden. The planning process is viewed from different perspectives by members of the administrative, technical and political groups, all of which have a stake in the planning process. This process was studied first within the context of the planning framework which consists of the prescribed procedures; secondly with the patterns of contractual connection, professional affiiliation and communication linkages associated with the organizational context, and thirdly with the distribution of interest, power and obligation within the world of planning. These three sets of elements, though not wholly independent of one another, bear particularly upon the administrative, technical and political processes respectively.

Due recognition was given to psychological factors, both in the identification of the different perceptions that participants from the administrative, technical and political groupings have of the planning process, and in the study of the formation of commitment. By acquiring rising levels of commitment to particular strategies, decision-makers increasingly stake their self-esteem, reputations and valued relationships upon the pursuit of a selected course of action, the abandonment of which will involve them in a loss of credibility and 'face', and this may lead to a reluctance to consider information and interests that are at variance with the developing policy.

Levin's involvement in the study of planning policy-making led to a recognition of the enormous influence of personal interest and commitment on planning decisions, and to the view that, particularly in the case of the Central Lancashire new towns, the development of strong levels of commitment to particular courses of action at an early stage in the planning process produced undesirable levels of inflexibility and an unreadiness to consider alternative options objectively as fresh information became available.

Working at the international level (rather than the national and intranational level with which this text is primarily concerned), Wise, one of the few political geographers to have become deeply involved in the decision-making field, has investigated a policy-making situation of extreme complexity involving multiple actors. His research has concerned policy-making processes concerning the development of the EEC Common Fisheries Policy between 1958 and 1972. The political process involved was of a diffuse and complex nature, with numerous governments, governmental agencies, EEC agencies and economic vested interests having an influence upon policy, while the 'rational' solution could be identified differently according to the criteria adopted. For example a solution which was rational in terms of conservation needs might not be rational in terms of its acceptability to the national participants who were motivated by national concerns to maintain particular shares and sizes of catch.

Wise points out that

> the political process producing the spatial distribution of fishing rights within the EEC did not conform to any synoptic or pure rationality model. Instead 'disjointed incrementalism' was much in evidence as those involved bargained, threatened and persuaded their way towards mutually 'satisfactory' compromises on a variety of issues in the whole 'package deal' underpinning the CFP.

Although the Commission was able to outline policy-making goals, formulated from the Common Agricultural Policy (which can be listed as follows: 1, to develop a rational and optimum production of fish; 2, to ensure a fair standard of living for fishermen; 3, to stabilize fish markets and ensure supplies; and 4, to ensure reasonable prices to the customer), Wise demonstrates that such a goal structure did not provide a basis for rational decision-making.

> One cannot act rationally in the pursuit of goals about which one is not clear ... Many decision-makers with conflicting values in different national and EEC institutions were active, thus making purely rational action in the pursuit of common 'European' objectives impossible ... there was no attempt to rank (the goals) in any order of priority or think rigorously about possible conflicts amongst these multiple goals.

His conclusion that the decisional and policy-making processes researched conformed to a disjointed incremental and satisficing model rather than to any normative system, is obviously correct, but in a sense the decisions reached were optimal. If politics is the art of the possible, then the only rational decision is one which can be accepted by the influential actors whose support for a decision or policy is crucial. Thus a decision which embodies a satisficing compromise may be the only decision which is acceptable to the different interests participating in decision-making, and is therefore the rational decision. Such a process is represented in Fig. 3.5 suggesting that each actor has a most desired outcome which is surrounded by an area of general satisfaction or toleration within which, according to circumstances, he may be prepared to satisfice. The satisficing decision is made within the small area of overlap of the satisficing spheres of each influential actor. Though no attempt is made here to represent scales or axes, it could be said that the decision which is near optimal in terms of political practicality might be far removed from a truly rational decision. Remaining with the fishery policy example, a politically acceptable compromise might well be totally inadequate in terms of conserving the fish resource upon which the fishing industries of the various actors depend. Thus we have another instance of the conflict between political expediency guided by perceptions of the short-term national interest and the radical innovation which constitutes a part of the long-term national and global interest.

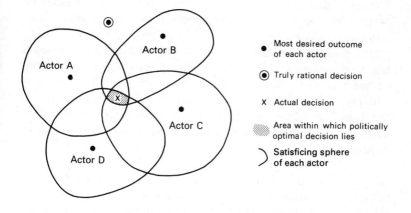

Fig. 3.5. Satisficing spheres of decision.

Probably the greatest potential for comprehensive and detailed decisional studies is to be found at the local (substantial) level, and the recent development of community protest politics, producing associated demands for 'open government', has greatly reduced the ability of officialdom to defend 'blank spaces'. Decision-making approaches are applicable to research into the allocative behaviour of a variety of organizations which operate at the local level, but it can be argued that the richest vein of intensely political-geographical material is associated with conflict situations where the allocative behaviour of one decision-making unit has imposed, or seeks to impose, externalities upon other units and the ensuing decisional processes either result in the coordination of the interests of the conflicting units or the legitimization of the activity which has created the externalities. The externality effects may concern an intangible, such as noise, but almost invariably they are associated with interventions in the physical environment, such as motorway or airport construction, urban redevelopment or the building or activities of polluting enterprises; consequently the associated conflict and decisional processes have a strongly geographical dimension.

Towards a Decision-Making Model

The remainder of this section concerns suggestions for a model or framework for political geographical decisional analysis. The framework will be developed in relation to a scenario involving actors, goals and processes, and it would be possible to employ a real world example. However, in attempting to do justice to the unique aspects of such an example, the prime intention of model-building might become unnecessarily complicated. Therefore a situation has been created which has much in common with a number of real world examples, and is loosely based upon one case in particular.

Actors and goals   The actors concerned are a town council with plans for central redevelopment, a development company, an interest group composed of residents in the proposed redevelopment area, and a college which owns much of the property in the area concerned. The council supports redevelopment but lacks the financial resources to do so; the development company has the financial resources, but needs the sanction of the council as the planning authority in order to proceed; the local residents seek to preserve the *status quo*, and the college is motivated to safeguard its investment and has a general concern to preserve the character of the local environment. The development of this conflict situation can be analysed in terms of goals, action schema, power relationships and outcomes.

According to Parsons, 'a goal is an image of a future state, which may or may not be brought about'.[13] To develop a perception of a goal, an actor must be aware of a problem or opportunity, its relationship to himself, and the outcome of that relationship which appears most desirable from his point of view. Each of the actors in our scenario has developed a goal structure; the goal of the council is to undertake redevelopment using the development company as its agent and source of investment, while at the same time not compromising its responsibility as a planning authority or alienating too much public support; the goal of the property company is to undertake redevelopment in such a way as to maximize profitability while recognizing the sensitivity of the council upon which it depends for contract and sanction; the primary goal of the interest group is to resist all redevelopment and preserve the residential environment in all its essentials, and this failing, the secondary goal is to minimize disruption and channel it along least unfavourable lines; the goal of the college is to protect its assets and condition the form that redevelopment takes.

Viewed in economic terms, through goal-seeking behaviour, each actor is attempting to maximize utility: the council is seeking to maximize utility for the urban community as a whole by pursuing what is perceived as an improvement in the urban environment; the development company is seeking to maximize its utility as a profit-making concern by engaging in a profitable enterprise, while the interest group and college are seeking to preserve the utility that they already enjoy. But the nature of the situation is such that the utility-maximizing activities of the council and development company may impose negative externalities upon the members of the interest group and the college through compulsory purchase and the transformation of the built environment. To the extent that the development company is dependent upon the council, the council upon the company and also upon an electorate which includes the interest group and its sympathizers, and the interest group and college upon the council in its capacity as arbiter rather than innovator, all the actors have an interest in coordination, and the decision process will partly involve an exploration of the limits of coordination. Furthermore, since none of the actors can predict the eventual outcome with certainty, the process involves the discovery by the actors of constraints upon their actions which will require modifications of their goal structures through time.

Ideas about goals and perception and goal-seeking behaviour can be integrated in the concept of an 'action schema', 'an active and self-consistent organization of old and new information'.[14] A decision-maker's action schema focuses upon what is perceived as the need and scope for action and it will contain 'elements which – in the context of his personal set of "values" – contribute perceived "desirable outcomes"'. It will also contain elements which reflect the resources seen as being available to him, and constitute perceived 'scope for action'.[15] Levin classifies the components of an action schema under three headings: 'action', including all perceived

courses of action, those called for by specific outcomes, and all
perceived constraints on actors; 'outcome', which includes desired
outcomes or goals and perceived constraints on outcomes, and
'action/outcome relationships', the implicit relationships between
specific actions and expected outcomes, and assumptions about the
influence of independent variables such as economic conditions or
autonomous actors upon outcomes. The decision-making process
comprises the behaviour of the actors concerned which is in each
case determined by the dictates of an evolving action schema.

Decision processes, behaviour and power   As in a war situation, the
conflict process develops through the exchange of strategies, with
action by one actor provoking reaction by others. In our scenario,
the council initiates the conflict by announcing a policy which
attracts the attention of the development company. The development company reacts to the initiative by evaluating the potential
profitability of this opportunity in relation to the profitability of
alternative opportunities and decides to produce a development
plan. The interest group reacts to both these initiatives by evaluating different strategies for resistance and decides to mobilize public
opinion against the proposal and to lobby council members. The
college reacts by evaluating the proposal, decides there is a threat to
the quality of the college environment and uncertainty as to the
level of compensation for its assets, and adopts a strategy of using its
influence upon council members as an employer, land owner and
leading institution of the town. A number of stages may be discernible in the developing conflict situation, one decisional stage terminating with the adoption by one of the actors of a particular
strategy; the adopted strategy then constitutes the starting point of
the next stage which involves reaction by the opposing actors.
   The successful analysis of conflict situations and decision-making
will not be possible without an evaluation of the nature and distribution of power. Writers associated with the pluralist approach to
politics have described the intricacies of power relationships and
permitted a more comprehensive understanding of power than
would otherwise be possible. Dahl has identified some of the
characteristics of a political system as 'the *magnitude* of the power of
the Cs' (controlling units) with respect to the Rs, (responsive units)
how this power is *distributed* in the system, and the *scope* and
domain of control that different individuals or actors have, exercise,
or are subject to'.[16] In his investigation of politics in New Haven,
Dahl considered that decision-making involved the processes of

initiation, modification and veto, this broader approach to power making possible the inclusion of groups and individuals whose contribution to the decision-making process might have been overlooked by adherents of the elitist approach.[17] While recognizing that political scientists normally distinguish between power and influence it is convenient here to consider different kinds of power being distributed unequally between our actors. These kinds of power are reflected in abilities to initiate, veto and influence.

The council has the power to initiate developments and, through its exercise of planning regulations, the power to veto them too. But because of its shortage of funds, its ability to initiate is in this case constrained and its power to initiate is dependent upon the forging of an alliance with a development company. The development company has the funds to initiate, but its ability to initiate could be negated by the council's power of veto over developments that are considered unsatisfactory from a planning viewpoint, though the company's monopoly of investment gives it the ability to influence the nature of the initiative (in a different scenario, the company might have been an initiator through the speculative purchase of property with an independent view to redevelop, but its power to initiate would still be similarly constrained). The college and the interest group have neither the powers to initiate nor to veto development, and their strategies revolve around making the most effective uses of their capacities to influence outcomes. Conceivably though, the situation could be affected dramatically by the fact that despite its possession of the powers to initiate and veto, the council is not a sovereign actor; the college and interest group could wield sovereign powers by proxy if they could provoke the intervention of the sovereign actor (the government) and influence the decision of that actor (by presenting evidence at a public inquiry). The main power relationships which can be identified are displayed in Fig. 3.6.

An Analytical Framework

The analytical framework which is set out below can be adopted for research into a number of decision-making processes of interest to the political geographer. Like the decision-maker of the theoreticians, the researcher should begin by conducting an information search. This could include a structural functional analysis of the institutions involved and an identification of the various items of

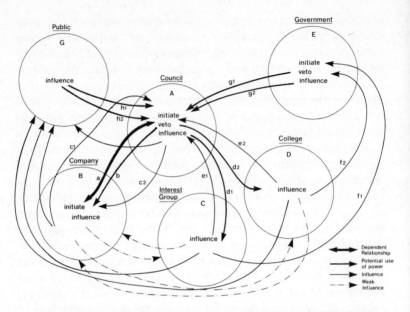

Fig. 3.6. Power relationships between actors in a hypothetical situation.

Notes:

Line a shows that A is unable to initiate without the support of B and *vice versa*. B does not completely control A's ability to initiate as another developer could be found, but the relationship would be similar given a different B.

Line b shows A's potential to veto B's initiative.

Line c_1 shows that B will seek to influence A's initiative, e.g. A may be requested to exercize its right of compulsory purchase over C and D. Line c_2 shows that A as a planning authority will influence B's initiative.

Lines d_1 and d_2 show that A could override the influences of C and D by exercising its legitimate right to initiate development even in the face of opposition.

Lines e_1 and e_2 show that C and D are attempting to influence A to abandon the development initiative and operate its power of veto on the initiatives of B.

Lines f_1 and f_2 denote the use of influence by C and D in an attempt to invoke the attentions of sovereign (potential) actor E.

Lines g_1 and g_2 denote E's potential ability to veto, or influence the form of A's initiative (and hence the initiative of B).

Lines h_1 and h_2 denote the potential of public opinion to influence A, either to proceed with its initiative or operate its veto. Where the situation is an election issue, G might theoretically operate a power of veto, i.e. by replacing an initiating council by a vetoing council.

existing legislation which may constrain and direct the formation of decisions. The preliminary analysis should lead to the discovery of every actor exerting a significant influence upon the process and it should produce relevant information concerning the historical development of the situation and the geographical characteristics of the environment concerned.

In the second stage of analysis a more thorough investigation of the actors and their motivations is necessary. This will involve the identification of the initial goal structures adopted by each actor, and in many cases these will be found to be conveniently encapsulated in the form of a map or plan; in the case of our example, the goals of the development company are partly embodied in the development plan and those of the protestors in a map of the undeveloped environment. Up to this point the actors have largely been treated as individuals, whereas in reality each actor that we have been concerned with is a collective decision-making system composed of several or many individual decision-makers. A thoroughgoing analysis should examine decisional behaviour *between* and *within* the collectives, and the adoption of a strategy by one unit, not only provides the starting point for a phase of conflict or bargaining between units, but also represents the culmination of a phase of decision-making within the unit concerned. Referring to our example, it might emerge that the interest group really consists of a core of middle-class activists whose claims to represent the interests of the working-class population of the area concerned are spurious, while the council's behaviour might be found to be affected by penetrative linkages with other systems; for example, Liberal councillors may be influenced by Liberal party policies concerning 'open government' and 'grass-roots participation' in local politics, consequently the Liberal group might seek to delay an initiative until satisfied that public opinion had been adequately sensed. The complexities of behaviour resulting from individual councillors' attachments to party, place, class and group – in so far as this is practicable – should be identified and assessed.

The preceding structural functional analysis should have revealed the spheres of legal competence and responsibility as prescribed, but it will not explain how the wielders of power will employ their power resources and the next analytical stage should investigate the power relationships between the units. Power can be explored in terms of its magnitude, how much power each actor controls; its distribution, the way that it is distributed between the actors; its scope, the activities over which the different kinds of power are effective, and its domain, the degree to which the power of a controlling unit in one relationship extends to other power relationships. Actors may choose not to mobilize their power resources to their full extent; in our example, the council while having the power to proceed with an unmodified initiative might at some stage choose to coordinate and seek a compromise with the protestors. The accuracy of the analysis will depend in part upon the realism of the characterization of the empirical power relationships.

The researcher is now in a position to analyse the dynamic processes of interplay between the actors and their strategies and the resultant revisions of goal structures and action schema, culminating in the ultimate decision. This stage involves the investigation of the formulation and implementation of strategies of action developed within the context of action schemas and in relation to defined goal structures. Attention should be paid to the ways in which the adoption of a decision by one actor affects the formation of decisions by other actors. None of the actors concerned will have total knowledge of the outcome and consideration should be given to the processes by which unperceived constraints upon their goal structures are discovered and incorporated into revised action schema developed in relation to revised goal structures.

Reference has already been made to Levin's model of the decision-making process as representing a progress towards a state of 100 per cent specificity and 100 per cent commitment. His diagrammatical representation of the Roskill Commission's progress towards the decision to recommend Cublington as the site for the third London airport is represented in Fig. 3.7 where stage 3, for example, represents medium commitment to recommending one of nine sites on the first reduced medium list of possible sites; stage 7, full commitment to recommending one of four sites on a detailed short list, and stage 8, full commitment to a specific site, Cublington.

Levin chose to focus his attention upon decisional behaviour *within* one actor, the Roskill Commission, a non-sovereign actor, and of course pressure from other non-sovereign actors on the sovereign actor led to the dismissal of the Commission's proposals. The idea may be developed and modified in such a way as to allow the methodical analysis of decision-making in a situation involving multiple decision-making units and could reveal the effect of decisions made by one actor on the formation of decisions by others. It is possible to retain the valuable concepts of commitment and specificity and represent the parallel decision-making processes of different actors upon one diagram. The model is modified to assume

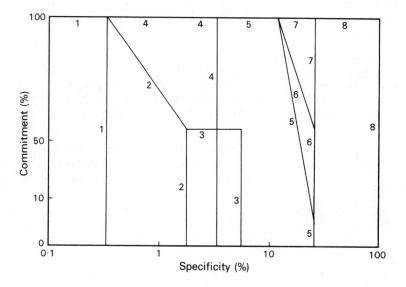

Fig. 3.7. Levin's model of decision-making by the Roskill Commission.

a three-dimensional form, with time forming the third axis, and the revised model below represents the following scenario:

t_1 The council announces medium commitment to a general principle of central redevelopment.

t_2 The announcement attracts the attention of the development company which has medium commitment to a general plan of development. It has also led the college authorities to discover their general feelings of opposition to redevelopment, though specific policies remain to be formulated. The interest group is in the process of formation. The council's support for redevelopment in principle has hardened.

t_3 Following consultation between the councillors and the company, a mutually agreed development plan is approved by the council. The interest group and the college are each united around specific strategies of opposition.

t_4 Following the delivery of a petition to the council, the organization of a public demonstration by the interest group and the lobbying of individual councillors by the college authorities, the council remains committed to development in principle, but is anxious to coordinate and prepared to consider alternative plans. The company is discouraged by the council's lack of resolve, considers withdrawal and evaluates substantial modifications of its plan. The interest group and the college remain committed to opposition, but the nature of their strategies will depend upon the council's next move.

t_5 The council and the company announce their decision to proceed with a modified plan.

t_6 The interest group and the college each decide to appeal for a public inquiry into the situation.

t_7 The minister decides to reject the appeal.

t_8 The council and the company begin to implement the plan. The college authorities decide to accept defeat. The interest group members are divided upon whether to continue their opposition, and if so, what strategies to adopt.

When represented according to the principles of the original Levin model, the council's progress in decision-making would appear as in Fig. 3.8. When plotted in the revised manner, the

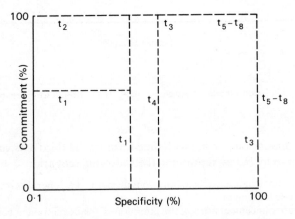

Fig. 3.8. Decision-making by a hypothetical council.

parallel decision-making processes of the different actors can be represented on one diagram (Fig. 3.9), which reveals changing levels of specificity and commitment, and suggests responses by actors to the decisions of other actors, but which does not describe specific goals, only levels of agreement about goals which may change as the process develops.

The final stage in political geographical analysis becomes possible when an agreed decision is implemented and concerns an investigation of the effects on the geographical environment of this implementation, the effects largely being measured by the degree of difference between the environment as it was before, and as it comes to be after the implementation of the decision. The only

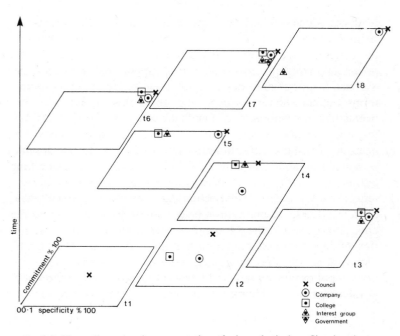

Fig. 3.9. Three-dimensional representation of a hypothetical conflict situation.

decisions which have direct political geographical significance are those which produce an intervention in the real world system (as opposed to the institutional system). The real world system comprises the tangible geographical phenomena (buildings, communications, landscape and so on), and all those activities engaged in by the population at large, and in a sense the political geographical significance of a particular decision can be measured by the extent of the transformation of the real world system that is engendered by the implementation of that decision. The political, social or economic significance of a decision will not directly determine the geographical significance, for example a government decision to abandon legislation concerning Green Belts would have much more geographical significance than one to double the old-age pension.

Interest in decision-making processes should not terminate with the adoption of the crucial decision which permits a specified intervention into the real world system; further decisions concerning the detail of the intervention may remain to be taken, while imperfections resulting from an inadequacy of information or a misinterpretation of information during the decisional process may produce feedback which will initiate a new generation of decisional activity. In many cases this will be found to result from a faulty perception of the geographical, rather than the political environment. Political processes, involving the mobilization of support, bargaining and the exercise of power may make an intervention possible in political terms, but coordination with the dictates of the geographical environment is not guaranteed. Feedback analysis should be undertaken in any cases where a further phase of decisional activity is necessary to establish coordination with environmental constraints.

Where the implementation of a decision takes place over a long period of time, the researcher may encounter the problem of existence: one can identify what action has been taken, and with what obvious effects, but one cannot be certain of the ways in which the environment would have evolved between the onset and termination of decision implementation had the decision not been made, and consequently the changes engendered by decision implementation do not exactly equal the differences between the environment at the onset and termination of the implementation process.

Résumé

Because of the significance of decision-making within our approach to political processes – and because of our introduction of some different models and argument – it is worth while to draw some conclusions from this discussion. Decisional analysis is appropriate to situations in which the researcher seeks detailed and comprehensive answers to questions concerning how particular interventions into the real world system have been formulated. It is essentially a dynamic (as opposed to static) form of analysis, and, in the words of Snyder, author of one of the most potentially geographically significant approaches '. . . dynamic analysis is *process* analysis. By process is meant here, briefly *time* plus *change* – change in relationships and conditions. Process analysis concerns a *sequence of events*, i.e. behavioural events'.[18] Snyder identified two forms of process analysis, interaction and decision-making; interaction analysis concerns patterns of interactions between individuals, groups, organizations and so on, but it 'does not and cannot yield answers to "why" questions. Thus interactions can be described and measured but the explanation of the patterns – why they evolved as they did – must rest on decision-making analysis'.[19]

The dogged pursuit of the question 'why' leads to the painstaking analysis of each stage in a decision process and requires an accurate assessment of the actors, their information and goals, the way that information is perceived and evaluated and interactions within and between the actors. For this reason the approach yields detailed insights. It is comprehensive because decisional analysis is of such breadth as to incorporate other analytical approaches which are fundamental to the understanding of 'why' questions which will be thrown up in the course of decision study. Particularly, these approaches include perception and power analysis, while structural functional analysis of institutions and their spheres of competence may be necessary as a foundation for dynamic analysis.

Decision-making approaches have been developed for use in several fields, for example management studies, economics and public administration. Probably the greatest potential for borrowing is from political science, but the geographer is unlikely to be able to adopt approaches which are custom-built for application to his problems. The majority of research by political scientists involves decisional analysis as a vehicle for the development of the rather formalized and uncomplicated models used in game theory, or as a means of identifying the locations of power by solving questions about 'who makes the decisions that matter?'[20] Generally speaking, the geographer will be interested in decision-making as a framework for analysis of problems which are empirical, involve interaction between several actors and involve decisions which are conditioned by and will affect elements of the geographical environment. Consequently, normative models of decision-making and the rather abstract models of the game theorists may be of limited value, while the answer to the question 'who rules?' constitutes a stage in, rather than the conclusion of investigation. Therefore in the development of approaches for decision study, the geographer will be as much a pioneer as a borrower.

In all decision-making analysis, the decision is viewed as the basic, stable unit of analysis; geographical approaches will tend to study decision-making in a broad context because of the concern with actors, goals and information as variables operating in the contexts of a particular empirical problem and a specific geographical environment, and this perspective constitutes a useful alternative to the existing tendency to focus attention on the allocative behaviour of one isolated decision-making body;

> If decision-making is to serve as the focus for the study of political behaviour, can we afford to ignore external influences? If we restrict our attention to the legally defined government we run the risk of assuming

that there are no individuals elsewhere who are concerned with decisional outcomes, and that they might not apply pressure to achieve their
ends . . . What function do they play, and how? Do pressure groups
facilitate or obstruct formation of public policy? These questions have
been asked and answered elsewhere, but decisional analysis has not this
far integrated these findings.[21]

By locating decisional activity firmly within its environment and
emphasizing the relationships between actor, decision and environment, the geographer can contribute to the fuller understanding
of decision processes.

Discussion points and further reading

For a long time political geographers have described examples of the ways
in which political decisions produce environmental change. This relationship between politics and environment, however, can only be fully under-
stood if the geographer is prepared to explain and explore the processes
which produce relevant political decisions. Within the geographic field
generally Chapman (1979) provides a readable account of the decision-
making mechanism, while Wolpert (1964) is a seminal article within the
decision-making area.

As case studies the decision-making processes underlying the siting of
facilities are of particular interest. Levin's (1976) of the New Towns in the
UK, Young and Kramer's (1978) analysis of the 'failure to open up the
suburbs', London-style, and Lowenthal's analysis of the siting of the capital
of the West Indies provide three interesting case-studies. Discussions of the
theoretical nature of power within society still revolve around concepts
introduced by Dahl, and his 1961 text, 'Who Governs?' remains an important introduction to questions concerning the distribution of decision-
making power in society. For descriptions of British cabinet decision-
making a political geographer could usefully read or refer to the Crossman
diaries.

Chapman, K., *People, Pattern and Process*, Edward Arnold, London, 1979,
    pp. 18–45.
Crossman, R. H., *Diaries of a Cabinet Minister*, Hamilton and Cape,
    London, 1977.
Dahl, R. A., *Who Governs?*, Yale University Press, New Haven, 1961.
Levin, P. H., *Government and the Planning Process*, Allen & Unwin,
    London, 1976.
Lowenthal, D., 'The West Indies Chooses a Capital', *Geographical Review*
    (1958), **XLVIII**.
Wolpert, J., 'The Decision Process in a Spatial Context', *Annals of the
    Association of American Geographers* (1958), **54**, 537–58.
Young, K. and Kramer, J. *Strategy and Conflict in Metropolitan Housing*,
    Heinemann, London, 1978.

Notes

1. S. D. Brunn, *Geography and Politics in America*, Harper and Row, New York, 1974, p. 100.
2. C.E. Lindblom, *The Policy Making Process*, Prentice-Hall, Englewood Cliffs, 1968, p. 12.
3. H. A. Simon, 'Theories of Decision-Making in Economics and Behavioral Science', *American Economic Review* (1959), **49**, (3), included in F. G. Castles, D. J. Murray, D. C. Potter and C. J. Pollitt (eds.), *Decisions, Organizations and Society*, Penguin, Harmondsworth, 2nd edn, 1976, p. 42.
4. F. E. I. Hamilton, *Yugoslavia*, Bell, London, 1968.
5. M. Conway and F. B. Feigert, *Political Analysis*, Allyn and Bacon, Boston, 2nd edn., 1976, p. 102.
6. Open University, *Decision Making in Britain*, pts 1–3, Open University Press, Milton Keynes (1972), p. 72.
7. Simon, 'Theories of Decision-Making', p. 36.
8. Conway and Feigert, *Political Analysis*, p. 241.
9. P. H. Levin, 'On Decisions and Decision Making', *Public Administration* (1972), p. 27.
10. G. D. Garson, *Handbook of Political Science Methods*, Holbrook Press, Boston, 2nd edn, 1976, p. 81.
11. R. H. S. Crossman, *Diaries of a Cabinet Minister*, vol. III, entry for 4 July 1968, Hamilton and Cape, London, 1977.
12. P. H. Levin, *Government and the Planning Process*, Allen & Unwin, London, 1976, p. 8.
13. T. Parsons, *The Structure of Social Action*, McGraw-Hill, New York, 1937, p. 44.
14. Levin, 'On Decisions', p. 26.
15. *Ibid.*
16. R. A. Dahl, 'Power', in *International Encyclopedia of the Social Sciences*, vol. XII, Macmillan, New York, 1968, p. 409.
17. R. A. Dahl, *Who Governs?*, Yale University Press, New Haven, 1961.
18. R. C. Snyder, 'A Decision-Making Approach to the Study of Political Phenomena', in R. Young (ed.), *Approaches to the Study of Politics*, Northwestern University Press, Evanston, Ill., 1958, p. 10.
19. Snyder, 'A Decision-Making Approach', p. 11.
20. Conway and Feigert, *Political Analysis*, p. 264.
21. M. Wise, 'Policy-making Studies in Political Geography', paper presented at the Institute of British Geographers' 1978 conference.

4 Voting and Elections

In democratic societies elections serve several purposes, the most important of which are the controlling and influencing of the process of governing. They provide governments with the necessary support enabling them to govern, while for the citizen voting provides a means of popular control. As such this is only consistent with Aristotle who argued that in a democracy sovereignty resides in the people. Notwithstanding this understanding of the nature of democracy, in the modern state the task of governing resides in an elected political elite rather than through direct forms of democracy. It is easy then to see why the study of voting and elections has become a major field of study in that the outcome of the process is the appointment of a representative who, regardless of the conflicting interpretations as to his precise role, whether merely a delegate or at the opposite extreme a trustee, becomes a key actor in the political process.

Increasingly, political geographers have contributed to the field of electoral study. This has followed several directions in which research effort has not been confined to or been spread equally between the three paths which Prescott[1] suggested more than 20 years ago, i.e. (1) the geographical factors underlying the adoption of a particular electoral method and set of constituencies; (2) the explanation of the differences in voting preferences between areas; (3) the methods by which governments influence electoral patterns. Despite Prescott's approach having a strong cartographic bias subsequent research effort brought electoral geography more firmly within the quantitative movement. The development was not surprising given the volumes of electoral results published by national and local governments. Much of the quantitative work was discussed within the ecological framework attempting to correlate environmentally derived variables with voting preferences. More recently in their wide-ranging study of elections Taylor and Johnston,[2] while eschewing the idea that electoral geographers study a proscribed and small number of well-defined items, discuss the field under three headings. These are the geography of voting patterns, geographical influences on voting, and the geographical influence on representation. Within the first are included those types of study, pioneered by French geographers seeking to establish causal links between voting preferences and ecological factors.

Our emphasis here is more deliberately focused on the behaviour of the political system to which voting acts primarily as a source of both support and demand. Within this the key questions for the political geographer become who votes, whether there are any systematic spatial variations in voting behaviour and the interrelationships between the methods used for electing representatives and for assessing voter behaviour and election outcomes. Within the first we include the analysis of the factors associated with voter preferences, a topic which has been a traditional concern of electoral geography. Besides casting his vote for a particular party it is important to recognize that what the voter is seeking to do is to vote a party into office. Here the focus turns more to the outcomes of elections and the influence of electoral systems on the effectiveness of the vote. Before looking at these we need to place voting within its context as part of the wider set of activities called political participation.

Methods of Participating

Participation is a term which has been used in a wide number of ways by political scientists.[3] Perhaps it is most frequently used to refer to acts of support for, as well as demands upon, governments; hence it is through participation that political leaders are selected and public policies influenced. The act of voting in elections, therefore, is a form of political participation or involvement. Clearly it is not the only method by which the citizen can become involved. Others open to him are joining a political party, endeavouring to convince other voters to elect a certain candidate ('canvassing'), and standing for political office.

In his stimulating analysis of political participation Milbrath[4] has suggested that there is a hierarchy of political involvement (Fig. 4.1). The activities in which citizens become engaged fall into three basic types: where he is not involved at all and is apathetic, where he is a spectator and only marginally involved, and finally where he is very active and, in Milbrath's terms, a gladiator. An intermediate range of activities exists between the spectator and gladiator roles. The analogy is drawn between the types of citizen activity and a Roman arena fight with a small number of gladiators actually engaged in combat, the outcome of which is decided by the spectators while outside the arena many people (the apathetics) fail to even go to the fight. What is apparent is that in nearly all countries only a very small proportion are willing to stand for office and while the majority are spectators in the sense that in most elections a majority will cast their vote, not insubstantial numbers do not participate at all.

Holding a political office Standing for a political office Soliciting political funds for a party Becoming an active member of a political party	Gladiatorial activities
Attending a meeting or rally Contributing to campaign funds Contacting a public official or politician	Transitional activities
Wearing a button and putting a sticker on the car Attempting to persuade a voter to vote alternatively Initiating a political discussion Voting	Spectator activities
Non-voting	Apathetics

Fig. 4.1. The hierarchy of political involvement.

Source: Adapted from L. W. Milbrath, *Political Participation*, Rand McNally, Chicago, 1965, p. 18.

Within the hierarchy of activities voting is a relatively 'low-order' activity. That is, amongst those who are going to participate voting will likely be an activity common to nearly all of them. Voting is, therefore, not the only nor probably the best activity by which to guage differences of participation. Many studies have indicated that the act of voting is a habit and that most citizens participate minimally between elections. In a later chapter on the politics of the environment other forms of participation will be discussed as they influence policy-making.

Explaining Variations in Voter Turnout

It is a common observation that in all countries where citizens are able to participate in, and thereby influence, the political process only a proportion actually do so. Not unexpectedly the extent of participation varies with the type of activity; many more citizens are willing to vote than are willing to stand for political office. Nevertheless, even within the relatively simple act of voting, undemanding in the sense of time or resources, the percentage of those eligible actually voting may be less than 50 per cent, and be at levels low enough in some countries (e.g. Australia) to have influenced the decision to introduce compulsory voting.

Structural variations in the extent to which people participate are matched by differences between geographical areas in political involvement. Table 4.1 shows some of the typical variations, illustrating the range in voting turnout in three different environments (urban/suburban and rural) in the United States, Canada, West Germany and the United Kingdom. Clearly voting turnout varies considerably between countries; even within a national election – the importance of an election correlates positively with turnout levels – the proportion voting in central cities of the northern United States can be as low as 25 per cent, while in West German urban constituencies the minimum is nearly three times this rate. In part such differences between countries can be explained by their differences of political culture, particularly of 'vote consciousness'. But there is also significance in that the American statistic refers to a minority population, principally to coloured groups, who have traditionally failed to vote in substantial numbers, in contrast to the types of population being surveyed in West Germany. The other, equally striking, result highlighted in the table is that turnout systematically varies according to the type of area under scrutiny, with

Table 4.1. **Voting turnout – recent elections in UK, USA, Canada, and West Germany.**

	Urban District low-income central city %	Suburban Districts affluent urban and suburban %	Rural (farm-oriented population) %
Northern US	25–55 (minority) 50–65 (white)	60–75	60–75
Canada	55–65 (French) 60–70 (Anglophone)	65–80	60–80
UK	40–55	60–75	65–75
West Germany	73–88	78–90	78–90

Source: K. P. Philips and P. H. Blackman, *Electoral Reform and Voter Participation*, American Enterprise Institute for Public Policy Research, Washington D.C., 1975, p. 41.

turnouts uniformly higher in the rural areas, a point to which we shall return later.

Before discussing what kinds of factors underlie such variations some of the limitations in the use of turnout should be made clear. Voting turnout is used as a measure of participation partly because of the widespread availability of published election statistics. However, it is not the best indicator of participation, partly because it relates to a single act rather than an ongoing form of involvement. As has been seen voting itself is a relatively minor activity within the spectrum of participation. Finally, some caution is necessary before concluding that a low turnout is bad for democracy in the sense that it fails to give the necessary support to the elected politicians. In fact non-voting may be as consistent with satisfaction as with apathy.[5]

There are also limitations which arise from the nature in which the data are collected. First, as with virtually all election data, the statistics are aggregated so that, as the argument of the ecological fallacy tells us, it is dangerous to extrapolate from the general to the individual case. Because, that is, the turnout data refer to a territorial area it is not possible to conclude directly that what is true for the area is also the case for the individuals which comprise the group. Secondly, there are difficulties in interpretation which arise from the way in which turnout is actually measured. To be an effective measure of participation turnout should be expressed as a proportion of the total eligible population. As eligibility to vote normally depends on a voter being registered and as registration methods vary widely care needs to be applied as to the basis upon which voting turnout is measured, the proportion of the voting age population or of those registered.

It is not so much that the methods of registering electors vary which is important but that these can be shown to influence the actual levels of voting participation. In countries such as Italy, where registration is automatic, the level of turnout is pushed upwards. In the United States by contrast the registration of voters is not automatic, though as registration is a task of the separate state governments practices vary widely. In some states (e.g. Idaho) it is virtually automatic, while in others registration is left to the citizen and can be a more onerous task than that of voting. Particularly in Southern states registration has been made a difficult process for the voter, involving in some cases literacy tests so as to discriminate against the black population. Because of the existence of the barriers to gaining eligibility – mainly those of the onus being placed on the citizen, residency qualifications and such like – Brunn[6] has shown how voter registration can be used to assess participation. In the north eastern states very high levels of registration, over 90 per cent in parts of New England, were associated with areas where 'local politics (town meetings) are popular and interest and awareness of political events is high'.[7] Economically poorer areas tended to have low registration rates.

Normally voting turnout differs between urban and rural areas, though the evidence as to in which it is higher is somewhat contradictory. In a comparative survey of the election turnouts in Norway and the United States Rokkan and Campbell[8] argued that the variations apparent were 'similar to those regularly found in official statistics – highest in the cities . . . lowest in the sparsely populated agricultural and other primary economy areas'.[9] In a subsequent study of the 1957 national election in Norway Rokkan and Valen[10] demonstrated that the turnout was lower in the more rural and peripheral communes. They devised an index of peripherality based on data measuring the importance of primary employment, farm size, population loss and physical accessibility. From this communes were classified as being within the extreme, moderate or non-periphery. Typically, participation in communes located in the extreme periphery was 8–10 per cent lower than those in the non-periphery.

Rokkan's study is important in illustrating how the 'position' of the voter, located relative to the centre–periphery axis, can be related to differences of participation. Political scientists have used the term 'mobilization' to suggest where levels of political activity will be greater, i.e. in urban rather than more rural areas. The reasoning behind this model is that

.persons close to the centre occupy an environmental position which naturally links them into the communications network involved in policy decisions for the society. They become identified with the body politic. They receive from and send more communications to other persons near the centre . . . (so that) . . . persons near the centre of society are more likely to participate in politics than persons near the periphery.[11]

Much depends on how the term centre–periphery is defined. When this is defined spatially as in the Norwegian study differences in participation between the two types of location are apparent. Studies of voting participation in Turkey in which the rural districts were classified by their isolation (this was measured by their accessibility and the frequency with which they were visited by government officials) revealed similar patterns. Centrality, though, can also be measured as a social attribute so that groups who feel that they are relatively isolated from the loci of power will feel more alienated, an explanation which might help to explain lower levels of participation among minority groups, especially where there is a sense of being discriminated against.

One of the problems of this centre–periphery model is that not all studies of electoral participation have found it to be higher in the more urban, centrally located areas. Table 4.2 shows the variations in turnout in the four different types of local government authority in the Irish Republic. These can be broadly divided between urban and rural authorities, and within the former the fourfold division into Dublin, other (all-purpose) county boroughs, urban districts, and municipal boroughs and town commissioners, roughly corresponds with population size. (The data refer to turnout at local elections and therefore, because each election is a separate contest with its own campaign, they may not be strictly comparable.) However, as a general trend what the variations clearly show is that voting turnout consistently declines with increasing urban size so that turnout in the capital in the earlier elections was 28–31 per cent lower than in the small towns. Figures for the county include the urban areas other than the county boroughs, so that it is not an exclusively rural electorate which is being counted.

Table 4.2. **Variations in local election turnouts – Irish Republic (1967).**

| | | Turnout (%) in | | |
| | Counties | County Boroughs | Boroughs/ urban districts | Town Commissioners |
	(n = 27)	(n = 4)	(n = 56)	(n = 23)
Average (mean)	72	56	69	73
Maximum	80	74	86	86
Minimum	58	52	55	66

Source: Personal survey.

The Irish data can be used to illustrate another general model developed to explain how the community environment interacts with voter participation, the 'decline of community' thesis (see Fig. 4.2). This model predicts that electoral participation, as indeed other forms of political involvement, will decline with the increasing size of the community in which the voter lives. Hence participation will decline as we move from

the smallness and intimacy of the town or village to the massive impersonality of the large city. In the small town social relations are more manageable, the sense of community more pronounced so that the voter will be more knowledgeable as to how the local political system operates and whom to contact.[12]

Added to this (the theory suggests) is that in the smaller political unit the citizen will have a more decisive influence on the political processes and be given more opportunities to operate. In Irish elections there is some evidence to suggest that personal factors influence voting decisions, particularly the 'friends and neighbourhood effect' (voting for the local candidate often personally known to the voters), which will tend to be more emphatic in the less urbanized constituencies.

+ Significant positive relationship

− Significant negative relationship

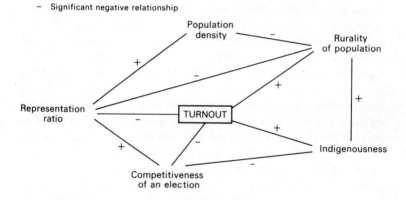

Fig. 4.2. Linkage analysis of factors influencing voting turnout – Irish local elections, 1967.

Note: + Significant positive relationship
      − Significant negative relationship

Source: Personal survey.

It is not possible to argue, however, that the decline of community thesis is applicable to elections generally. As far as the effects of population size on voting turnout are concerned the most comprehensive analysis to date concluded that from the available studies

within countries, among local (political) units . . . there is no general relationship between size and turnout. Thus in some democratic systems, election turnouts are somewhat higher in smaller than in larger municipalities. In others, it is the reverse. In still others, there appears to be no relationship between size and turnout.[13]

In their seven-nation study of political participation – that is, voting and other forms of involvement – Verba *et al.*[14] argued that particularly in the bigger cities there were fewer opportunities to participate. The survey, which included developing as well as developed world states, concluded that the variations apparent in political participation were broadly compatible with the decline of community thesis.

Looking more specifically at the factors which can be related to voting turnout it is convenient to group these under several headings, i.e. political, social and personal, and those relating to the effects of the electoral system itself. The latter have already been discussed under the different methods of registration. Personal factors – relating to age, sex, ethnic membership and the like – have frequently been correlated with voting turnout. In this respect membership of a minority group, as for example among the black population in the United States, has an effect on voting propensity. Individual factors too affect turnout, such as the distance separating the voter from his nearest polling booth. Taylor's[15] study of turnout at a local government election from a single ward in Swansea showed the strength of the relationship: 65 per cent of those living within a minute's walk from a polling station voted compared to only 35 per cent of those living 5–6 minutes away. Election campaigners are aware too of the importance of locating polling booths and its effect on 'getting out the vote'.

Relating more closely to the likely political and social factors, Lipset[16] has argued that the individual's decision to vote is determined by three main factors: (1) his access or proximity to the decision-making processes or, more generally, to information aiding the citizen in knowing how the political system operates; (2) the existence of group pressures to vote, e.g. the more socially cohesive the community the greater is the pressure to vote; (3) the existence of cross-pressures, e.g. the greater the party competition and the more intensely fought the election, the more involvement there is among electors. Clearly some of the arguments which Lipset is using can be traced to the centre-periphery and decline of community models discussed earlier.

Any evaluation of Lipset's model raises questions as to the measurement of such factors. In a study examining variations in county council electoral turnouts in the Irish Republic, Paddison[17] used six variables. Three variables were used to assess the proximity or access factor, a representation ratio (measured as the relationship of the number of registered electors to a councillor), the area of the county and its population density. (With the exception of a few counties the number of representatives is constant regardless of population size so that the less populous counties are the more densely represented.) The proportion of the population of each of the 27 counties defined as rural (resident in settlements of fewer than 20 inhabitants) and the ratio of the population resident in 1971 in the same county as they were born were used as surrogates of the social cohesiveness. Finally the incidence of cross-pressures was assessed by the competitiveness of the local election, i.e. the number of candidates in excess of the number of seats available.

In terms of their predictive power of voting turnout the variables measuring the representation ratio and the stability of the population were the most significant. Party competition was less important though this is contrary to the findings of other studies. Studies of British elections have suggested that the harder the election is fought in a constituency, particularly where the seat is marginal,[18] the higher the level of turnout will be. In the Irish case, however, candidates in the rural counties will generally be representatives of long standing. They will also be widely known and as Sacks[19] has found within a study of voting patterns in the rural county of Donegal – though in a general not a local election – the personality factor plays a prominent influence on voting behaviour and patterns of support.

Based on a comparison of local turnouts in two urban constituencies in Glasgow (Cathcart) and London (Clapham) Budge and Urwin[20] have identified the influence of other social and political factors. Among the social factors which they measured were the length of residence, participation rates in social organizations, the effect of religious membership, age, sex, occupational class, education and type of housing occupancy. Political factors included an assessment of the citizen's knowledge (gauged by asking voters to name their M.P., their local councillor and the party which enjoyed a majority on the city council) and the extent to which differences in political allegiance, such as membership of a party, affects turnout.

Table 4.3 summarizes the effects of the social and political factors. Length of residence and political knowledge were equally pronounced in both constituencies. In other cases voters in the two urban areas are differently affected by factors of their social environment. Indeed, church attendance, the second most important

Table 4.3. **Factors influencing non-voting: Clapham and Cathcart (UK).**

Factors related to turnout	Clapham	Cathcart
Residence of more than 5 years in area	+	+
General increase in age	+	−
Comparative youth of electors	+	+
Type of house-occupancy	+	−
Organization membership	+	−
Political knowledge	+	+
Strength of party allegiance	+	+
Education	−	−
Sex	−	−
Occupational class	−	−
Church attendance	n.e.	+

Notes: + positive relationship with voting and non-voting
     − no relationship with voting and non-voting
     n.e. not examined
Source: I. Budge and D. W. Urwin, *Scottish Political Behaviour*, Longman, London, 1966, p. 84.

predictive factor in the Glasgow constituency, was not even considered for inclusion within the Clapham survey.

Social Correlates of Voting

How people vote, choosing between rival candidates and more importantly the parties they represent, has been the focus of a great deal of research. Either implicitly or explicitly the suggestion of a majority of these studies is that voting is a reasonably predictable type of behaviour; that is, given a number of 'key' variables it is possible to predict the way in which most voters will choose. Economic influences – and the social class structure through which they are transmitted – are generally considered to be a major determinant of voting behaviour, though it is a relationship which varies in its incidence between, as well as within, countries. Besides the influence of class and differences of economic wealth there are other key factors which help explain voting behaviour, such as religious affiliation and ethnic membership whose effect can be to cross-cut or further reinforce the class-based differences. In seeking out the types of factors which influence voting the assumption is that the voter will vote for the party whose ideology is closest to those values and interests which he considers most important. In so far as political parties play a central role in this process it will be useful to look at their types and social origins before examining the factors underlying the spatial patterning of votes.

Social Cleavages and Party Systems

The social differences between groups of voters mentioned above constitute some of the cleavages which divide and subdivide society. Social class and the system of social stratification can be considered as a vertical cleavage; others, such as religious groups, neighbourhoods and the family, as horizontal cleavages differing in type in that they reflect divisions which are mutual equals. Some social cleavages are relatively minor (for example, the urban neighbourhood) while others, particularly those of class, ethnic or religious groups, are more pervasive. Not all social cleavages, then, become the foci of political conflict within a society.

How cleavages become the dominant foci of conflict within the state and how this relates to the system of political parties can be viewed as an historical process. Based on the experience of West European countries political scientists, notably Rokkan and Lipset,[21] have argued that the political parties of the state and the social cleavages they represent are in large part determined by the historical conditions within which the process of state-building took place. Four major conflicts have typified the development of the West European state:

(1) Core-periphery conflict. During the process of state-building peripheral cultures are dominated and frequently absorbed into that of the core national group. Generally the process will create its own conflict, often territorially based, where peripheral groups resist assimilation and even in historically long-established states (e.g. France, the UK) residual elements of 'peripheral nationalism', transmitted in some countries through the growth of regional parties, demonstrates the failure of total integration.

(2) Secularizing conflicts arising from the competing claims of church and state, particularly as to how social norms are to be defined. In some countries religion is less salient as a political issue than it was earlier in the development of the state while remaining as a passive determinant of voting behaviour, e.g. in France. In England, though less so in other parts of the United Kindgom, religious affiliations bear little relationship to voting behaviour. Although generally the influence of religion has waned Rose and Urwin, in reviewing the contemporary European scene, were still

able to demonstrate that 'contrary to popular belief religion, not class, is the main social bases of parties'.[22]

(3) Conflicts arising between the demands for protection by the primary economic producers against the urban-industrial interests. This has resulted in several European countries – though again the United Kingdom is a notable exception – in a marked political cleavage between the urban and rural areas and the emergence of parties specifically serving rural interests in an attempt to offset what is seen as urban domination.

(4) Class-based conflict which, it has been suggested previously, has become an increasingly important source of social and political conflict within industrial societies.

In Western Europe Rokkan and Lipset's argument is that the contemporary party systems of individual countries can be traced to the historical conditions under which these conflicts have occurred. It was argued (for example) that the existence of multi-party systems in Scandinavia in contrast to the two-party system in England arises from the historical sequencing of the conflicts. Thus in England rural–urban conflict, where it was important, had been resolved before the process of mobilizing the lower classes (itself a source of political party formation) began, whereas in Scandinavia both conflicts occurred within a short period of one another. This is not to deny, however, the role of other factors which have encouraged two-party and multi-party systems, notably the type of electoral system in operation.

Where it is possible to trace out the origins of different political parties to these types of social conflict those originating from the religious, urban-rural and class cleavages are electorally the more important. The classification of parties discussed earlier (in Fig. 2.3) can be used to illustrate the different types of party system. In the UK the stable two-party system polarizes around the single, dominant cleavage of class. In the Netherlands a complex, but also stable, multi-party system has evolved from the religious pluralism of the state and class-based conflict. A different pattern still is illustrated in the Scandinavian countries where in Norway the system of parties can be traced to a variety of cleavages – territorial, rural and class – which have been important in the state's development.

In contrast political parties based on the first cleavage type, i.e. the conflict between centre and periphery, are electorally less important in most developed states. In that the territorial integration of states is partly a time-dependent process political conflicts will tend to be 'deregionalized' and replaced by non-territorial, national ones, such as that of class. Nevertheless, regional parties have persisted or re-emerged in some industrial states and while the parliamentary representation of them tends to be small their importance is still real.

Social Cleavages and Voting Patterns

Since one of the roles of the political party is the articulation of interests it should be possible to follow through from looking at the origins of parties to particular voting patterns associated with the different types of social cleavage. The types of social factors frequently considered as determinants of voting behaviour include religious affiliation, social class, ethnicity and suchlike. Lijphart[23] has provided the evidence linking voting behaviour to the types of social conflict outlined above. Using a method devised earlier by Alford,[24] Lijphart was able to demonstrate the relative importance of the class, religious and rural-urban cleavages on voting in English-speaking and European countries (Table 4.4). Alford's method had been to find the difference between the percentage of non-manual workers voting for 'left' parties and the percentage of manual workers voting likewise; the derived index of class voting could vary between a value of zero, indicating no relationship between class and voting, and one hundred, measuring a perfect correspondence. Lijphart extended the method by looking at urban–rural voting (the number of rural residents choosing right-wing parties) and the importance of religion (the number of church attenders voting for right-wing parties).

Table 4.4. **Social cleavages and voting in selected European and North American Countries (1960)**

	Class	Religion	Rural/Urban
Belgium	25	72	7
Britain	37	7	10
Canada	8	22	—
Denmark	44	—	—
France	15	59	11
West Germany	27	40	17
Italy	19	51	12
Netherlands	26	73	10
USA	20	16	11

Source: Adapted from A. Lijphart, 'Class Voting and Religious Voting in European Democracies', *Acta Politica* (1971), **6**.

The importance of the three cleavages on voting patterns varies substantially between the countries. Voting on the basis of religious affiliation is strongest in continental Europe (outside Scandinavia) and particularly in the Netherlands and Belgium, located astride the geographical boundary separating Catholic and Protestant churches. In the English-speaking countries religion, by contrast, correlates only to a minor extent with voting. It recurs in Canada where the linguistic division is overlain by the Catholic–Protestant split.

The influence of social class on voting also differs between countries. In Alford's original study of the incidence of the voting determinants of class, region and religion, class-based voting was most marked in Britain and Australia and least developed in the United States and Canada. While, however, in Britain party support is strongly related to class it is not a relationship, as Pulzer put it, which is 'as high as it might be'.[25] In other words, there is some cross-class voting particularly among manual workers voting Tory and, to a lesser extent, among the middle-class electorate voting for leftist candidates.

Canada provides an interesting contrast in that, as a number of studies have shown, class-based voting is relatively unimportant. This conceals differences in the incidence of class voting within the country; of the five regions into which it is commonly divided class-based voting tends to be higher in Ontario, British Columbia and the Atlantic provinces and least in Quebec and the Prairie provinces. Overall, though, other cleavages – notably regional and sectional differences, religious and ethnic variations – have prevented the emergence of class interests as a nationally oriented focus for political loyalties. Political parties, then, do not appeal to different class groups nationally and in fact often tend to be associated with particular regions, notably in terms of their support. Support for the Conservative party is strongest among the Anglophone Protestant population, especially of Ontario. Conversely the other major party, the Liberals, while alone in being able to attract support from a wide spectrum, have traditionally relied on the Quebec vote, though within recent elections this support has been undermined by the development of the Quebeckan nationalist party. Elsewhere in Canada, particularly in the western provinces, support for the major parties has been less where agrarian protest, directed towards the perceived domination of urban–industrial interests within national politics, has underlain the support for third parties favouring sectional interests.

Ecological Analyses

Since it is a characteristic of all elections that the patterns of voting preference vary between constituencies, explaining these variations has been a major concern of electoral geography. This problem has been studied in two main ways: (1) by looking at the behaviour of the individual, particularly in terms of the influence of his local environment (see next section) and (2) by aggregate methods of analysis based on the pattern of voting preferences within territorial units. Busteed subdivides the latter into structural and ecological types, the former being a cartographic and essentially descriptive appreciation of the factors underlying differences in voting support. This approach has its roots in the early work of the French electoral geographers, notably André Siegfried, who attempted to trace out the way in which differences in the local physical and social environment explained variations in voting support for candidates of left and right parties.

Ecological methods of analysis, while similarly based on the patterns of voting support within territorially defined units, have sought to carry explanation further by identifying statistically the variables which strongly correlate, and indeed may act as determinants, of voting support. Generally such variables are selected so as to assess the social and economic character of the territorial area, together with a measurement of the historical pattern of voting support.

Studies of voting patterns within Italy illustrate the kinds of variables which are used in ecological models and how they are combined to help explain variations in voting support. Capecchi and Galli[26] examined the social bases underlying support for parties of the left and right, identifying the variables correlating positively and negatively with voting preferences. Table 4.5 presents part of their analysis, listing the range of variables which correlated with voting support for the Communist Party and for the Christian Democrats. Organizational factors, notably membership of the party and of the trade unions but also newspaper circulation, correlated strongly with support for the Communist Party. Provinces within which there was a tradition of left-wing voting – indicated by the proportion voting for the Republic in the referendum of 1946 – and in which sharecropping is significant correlate positively with support for the Communist Party. The latter in particular has been associated with Communist support in parts of central Italy (in Emilia, Tuscany and Umbria the Communists gain up to 40 per cent of the

Table 4.5. **Selected correlations with the Communist and Christian Democrat vote in Italy (1963).**

	Correlation with	
	Provincial Communist vote	Provincial Christian Democrat vote
Membership of Communist party (PCI)	·822	− ·688
Membership of Italian Trade Union Council (CGIL)	·722	− ·702
Circulation of *l'Unità*	·636	− ·675
Mezzadri (sharecropping)	·530	− ·367
Vote for the Republic, 1946	·449	− ·417
Spoiled (invalid) votes	− ·330	·359
Membership of Italian Employers Association (CISL)	− ·307	·312
Membership of Christian Democrat Party	− ·305	·496
Area of peasant small-holding	− ·296	·448[1]

[1] Figure for 1953, measuring correlation of Christian Democrat vote and the number of farmers working own land.

Source: Adapted from V. Capecchi and G. Galli, 'Determinants of Voting Behaviour in Italy', in M. Dogan and S. Rokkan (eds), *Quantitative Ecological Analysis in the Social Sciences*, MIT Press, Cambridge, Mass., 1969.

vote) as well as increasingly parts of the Mezzorgiono, which collectively Dogan[27] describes as areas of 'red peasants'.

While identifying the variables relating to voting preferences helps to explain the variations in party support what Capecchi and Galli were subsequently able to do was to unravel how these variables interacted with one another in influencing voting behaviour. Their method was to assess whether a variable had a direct or indirect influence on voting support, representing their results in a series of circuit diagrams for the Communist, Socialist and Christian Democrats first at provincial level for the entire country and secondly for within five regions. Fig 4.3 shows the circuit diagram relating to the 1963 Communist vote. From their analyses of the causal relationships at national and regional levels Capecchi and Galli were able to draw conclusions on the basic factors underlying voting behaviour; these were focused on the idea that while in Italy interregional differences in economic development are marked,

the process of industrialization influences the vote almost exclusively through the filter of the educational level. (Thus) the progression from illiteracy to elementary education tends to favour the Christian Democrats, to the disadvantage of the Communists and the Right.[28]

This progression, however, was modified by the influence of the

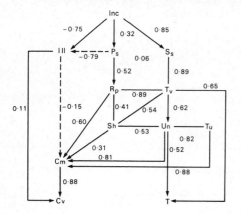

Inc	Income
Ill	Illiteracy
P_s	Primary Schooling
S_s	Secondary Schooling
R_p	Vote for Republic (1946)
T_v	TV Licences
Sh	Strike hours
Un	Circulation of L'Unita
Tu	Membership of Left Trade Unions
Cm	Communist Party Membership
Cv	Communist Party Vote
T	Electoral Turnout
—	Positive correlation
– –	Negative correlation

Fig. 4.3. Causal model of Communist vote at provincial level in Italy (1963). *Source*: as Table 4.5.

political tradition of the province or region; whether, for instance, there is a history of anti-clericalism or whether organizational factors (party membership and suchlike) are salient.

While, within limitations, ecological methods can help pinpoint the factors underpinning voting choice – and there is a sizable literature of other sophisticated studies – in Britain there have been relatively few attempts to build ecological models. Taylor and Johnston[29] cite several reasons for this: e.g. the apparent absence of regional patterns of voting and dominance of class voting, in contrast to the situation in continental Europe, implies that ecological explanations are less necessary. Crewe and Payne's[30] analysis of the Labour vote within the 1970 election is an interesting use of ecological methods applied to explaining the variations between constituencies. Their regression-based model is summarized in Table 4.6.

A combination of occupational variables and those relating to the previous electoral performance of the parties was sufficient to explain as much as 90 per cent of the variation of the Labour vote. Furthermore, Crewe and Payne were able to show that the model's findings were consistent with those generated from survey data,

Table 4.6. **The Labour share of the combined Labour and Conservative vote in any British constituency in the 1970 general election.**

= 30.7%
+ 0.24 × the percentage of manual workers
− 4.5% if the constituency is agricultural
+ 23.0% if the seat was 'very' Labour in 1966
+ 9.7% if the seat was 'fairly' Labour in 1966
− 7.3% if the seat was 'fairly' Conservative in 1966
− 16.2% if the seat was 'very' Conservative in 1966
− 3.3% if a Nationalist contested the seat in 1966
+ 3.6% if the seat is a mining constituency
+ 2.3% if the Conservatives lost in 1966 and captured less than 60% of the total vote of the losing parties
− 6.4% if Labour lost in 1966 and captured less than 60% of the total vote of the losing parties

thereby refuting the possibility that their aggregate analysis, through the argument of the ecological fallacy, contradicted the pattern of individual voting behaviour.

These two examples provide only a small sample of the ecological work that has been done on voting behaviour. In so far as ecological analyses attempt to look at the causal relations underlying patterns of voting support within spatial units they will rightly continue to occupy a central place within electoral geography. Nevertheless their emphasis is to look to the factors underlying voting support in terms of aggregate social and economic variables. Consequently they have been criticized for their lack of attention to the individual and the factors which might influence his voting behaviour.

The Influence of the Local Environment on Voting Behaviour

Most studies of voting behaviour assume that socialization is a major influence on how people vote. Such agents, as it has been seen in a different context, include the home, school, workplace and the community, their significance normally varying. As they affect voting each agent acts as a source and modifier of political information, providing the voter with cues by which to assess given situations; typically these cues will be biased, encouraging the individual to view political events through a partisan framework and vote in a particular way. The influence of trade union membership on voting preferences is a clear case in point. It has already been seen how this relates to voting support for the Communist Party in Italy, while in Britain one study[31] suggested that union members were approximately three times more likely to vote Labour than Conservative.

Because of its explicitly spatial nature it is the influence of the community environment (the 'neighbourhood effect') which is of special concern to the political geographer. Empirical studies of voting behaviour illustrate the influence of the place of residence. As an example Goldthorpe *et al.* in a study of the effect of social groups on voter preferences in Luton found that

> Workers owning houses in middle-class residential areas are more likely to be surrounded by persons for whom voting Conservative is the normal thing to do. Consequently, in so far as working-class newcomers to these areas are influenced by the standards of their neighbours, they will be subject to cross-pressures and will react by giving fewer of their votes to Labour than workers living in areas where the population is mainly in manual, wage-earning occupations.[32]

A small, though detectable, difference in voting preferences could be traced to this factor with 72 per cent of affluent workers living on middle- and lower-middle-class estates voting Labour compared to 79 per cent on the council estates.

Butler and Stokes,[33] in their study of voting behaviour in Britain, were also able to demonstrate that the social composition of the constituency had an influence on voting patterns. They compared two types of electoral area: mining constituencies (predominantly Labour) and seaside resorts (predominantly Conservative). In the mining seats it was shown that Labour was gaining votes from voters describing themselves as middle class, while working-class voters in the seaside resorts were voting for the Conservative party.

In the United States the role of the community influence on voting preferences has been linked to the apparent successes of the Republican Party, particularly during the 1950s, in the metropolitan suburbs through the conversion hypothesis. This hypothesis 'saw the suburb as a chrysalis, where men and women enter as Democrats and emerge as Republicans'.[34] The actual change, it was presumed, came about partly because of a wish to conform and partly because, as a new homeowner, the voter would be more anxious to support the Republican candidate given this party's greater sympathies with property rights.

The British survey results, and the conversion theory by which it is argued that Democrat supporters moving from the central city to the suburbs are converted to the Republican Party, argue for the importance of the local environment on voting behaviour. Assuming that this has some influence it will be through the network of formal and informal social contacts which the individual has within the local community that much of this information will be transmitted.[35] Orbell[36] suggested that individual voters will vary in their receptiveness to the cues which they are subjected but as his study of voters in Columbus suggested the stronger the messages in an area the more likely the voter will respond, while not unexpectedly the less committed voter tends to be more influenced by the partisan bias of his local environment.

A careful sociometric analysis of voting influences in Manchester by Fitton[37] has shown how the neighbourhood effect might operate. Fitton looked at the influence of the local street environment on voting, based on interviews with voters in three predominantly working-class streets. The street, then, would act as an arena within which social contacts were made and, at least during the period of a national election, within which political discussions would be held. Looking at the pattern of individual social contacts within the streets and the number of political conversions – that is, those people who switched their party allegiance from the previous election – Fitton was able to conclude that where such changes did take place 'it was generally towards that of the street sub-group to which the individual was attached'.[38]

In spite of the evidence which lends support to the influence of the local environment on voting behaviour much controversy has surrounded the hypothesized effects of the neighbourhood. The value of the conversion thesis in explaining support for the Republican Party in American suburbs has been questioned in several subsequent studies. Manis and Stine,[39] in their study of the predominantly Republican suburb of Kalamazoo, found that only 23 of 203 interviewees had switched affiliation and that in any case less than 50 per cent of the new arrivals were able to state the political affiliation of their immediate neighbours while a far smaller proportion (under 20 per cent) were able to state that they had discussed the 1956 presidential election with their neighbours. In another study[40] of a working-class suburb of San José most interviewees were unaware of what party their neighbours supported while the amount of political discussion between individuals was low. The study of the American voter by Campbell *et al*.[41] also cast doubt on the conversion thesis; their evidence supported an alternative explanation for the Republican voting – the migrants who had made the move from central city to suburb had been consistent voters of that party.

To the extent that the neighbourhood acts as an agent influencing the political socialization of the individual, and more specifically his voting perferences, it is only one of several influences. As Fitton expressed it of his interviewees, 'the orientation and behaviour of these individuals were structured by response to several primary and secondary reference groups of which the neighbourhood was one'.[42] Of the other influences studies of voting behaviour emphasize the role of the family in this respect. In their early classic study of Elmira (New York), Berelson[43] and his associates showed that 83 per cent of those who stated that their fathers voted for the Republican Party did so themselves. Even more striking were the results of Butler and Stokes's[44] sample surveys of the British electorate: in families in which both parents voted for right (Conservative) or left (Labour) parties approximately 90 per cent of the next generation did likewise.

Issue Voting

Our assumption underlying how people vote is that the voter will support that party which most closely meets his own interests. Because most elections are fought over a number of issues, albeit usually a small number, it is not always apparent how voting preferences relate to the attitudes electors have to specific questions. The nature of political parties accentuates this, for in most cases, though particularly in political systems in which there are only two or three major parties, each will represent itself, as comprising 'coalitions of interest'.

Because of its more specific nature issue voting – either in a general or local election in which the contest has become closely associated with a particular problem, or in referenda – shows more clearly how the voter uses the vote to meet his own needs or preferences. Political economists suggest that voting is a means by which the individual is able to increase his expected utility. If self-interest is a prime motivational force underlying voting behaviour, the value of issue voting is that governments will gain a reasonably accurate assessment of attitudes to specific problems.

The attitudes voters have towards particular issues will vary spatially where the issue imposes 'costs' and/or 'benefits' that themselves vary spatially. Not unexpectedly, then, issue voting over (for example) the siting of a noxious or dangerous facility will tend to reflect the fact that the negative externalities generated by the proposals will themselves vary geographically. The siting of a proposed nuclear power plant in south-east Scotland (Torness) provides a simple example, in which a sample poll conducted in the area to test attitudes to the proposal found that over 60 per cent of people in the county in which the plant is to be located objected while less than 50 per cent in the adjacent county held similar views. Other studies of issue voting reiterate the general relationship between the distance decay effects of the actual or perceived penalties or advantages and the distribution of voting preferences.

These spatial differences in voting reflect the use of the vote to protect self-interests or the interests of the voter's community. In Britain and also in the United States racist voting provides an opportunity to test the way in which voters directly choose parties which support their own attitudes. Racist voting is largely founded on the supposed threat the coloured minorities pose, either in cultural terms, or in the competition for scarce resources (such as housing) or as a general fear of 'invasion' to the national and/or local community. In Britain it was during the 1964 national elections that race first became an electoral issue and in several urbanized constituencies, notably in areas with high levels of immigrant populations, support polarized around the problem. Hence, while in the election nationally there was a marked swing in support favouring the Labour party, in Smethwick – a seat within the West Midlands conurbation – the swing was emphatically towards the Conservative candidate. This was the result partly of the local campaign which had highlighted the problems of the immigration phenomenon and partly of the way in which Labour party policies allegedly would tend to exacerbate the immigrant problem.

One of the general trends underlying racist voting, though not one that is always clearly traceable, is that support for racist candidates will be strong among the more 'threatened' electorate. Several studies have shown that voting support for George Wallace during elections in the 1960s varied spatially according to the potential threat of the black population. In a study[45] of the Wallace vote in Gary, Indiana, in the 1964 Indiana Presidential Preference Primary one major area of support was from southern, white, working-class homeowners and from homeowners of southern and eastern European origin who presumably felt their property values threatened by the possible 'invasion'. Furthermore, Rogin argued, 'the closer suburban whites lived to the ghetto, the more likely they were to vote for Wallace'.[46] Put alternatively, voting for Wallace was a kind of territorial defence.

Referenda are a direct means of gauging public opinion on specific issues giving direct support to government actions or giving rise to demands for particular action. Their use, however, has varied between countries so that in some (e.g. Switzerland, the United States) they are an accepted mechanism for measuring public opinion. In Britain conversely the first use of a referendum on a national issue – confined to Northern Ireland electors who were to decide whether or not to remain part of the United Kingdom – was in 1973. The result, an overwhelming proportion favouring the retention of links with the United Kingdom, illustrated the danger of relying on a simple majority rule as determining outcomes of elections. Thus the referendum attracted only 61 per cent of the possible turnout, the large Catholic minority largely abstaining. This problem raises questions of how voting preferences are actually translated into electoral outcomes which we shall turn to in the next section.

The Influence of the Electoral System

While voting is normally directed towards the election of a political representative whose responsibilities in part at least are to serve the local electorate, usually within a constituency, it is through the electoral system that voting preferences are translated into parliamentary representation. Different types of electoral systems behave in different ways directly impinging on how representatives are to be selected from the pattern of voting choices.

In the development of the modern state the demand for participation has been met by the implementation, although possibly gradually, of universal suffrage, giving 'one man one vote'. Parallel to these demands were those calling for the equalizing of the value of the vote, or 'one vote one value'. This is frequently considered one of the basic criteria by which the 'fairness' of an election should be judged. To be equitable an electoral system should reflect the different strands of opinion proportionately, avoiding any unwarranted biases in representation. Besides the influence of the type of electoral system inequitable practices and outcomes also arise from the way in which elections are organized spatially.

Because by definition the electoral system used affects the chances of a political candidate being elected and, thus logically, whether a party will be able to win sufficient seats to form the majority necessary to form a government or be an active member of a coalition, the whole question of the method of election is a politically sensitive issue. It is not surprising, therefore, that many more countries have been able to meet the demands for one man one vote than they have one vote one value.

Electoral Systems

The methods by which candidates are elected on the basis of voting preferences, what Rae[47] terms the electoral laws, vary substantially. Three major types can be recognized – plurality, majoritarian and proportional systems – on the basis of their influence on proportionality, the relationship between seats and votes. In a perfectly proportional system the number of seats gained by individual parties will exactly relate to their relative popularity at the polls; it is widely considered to be the fundamental criterion by which to assess the fairness of an electoral system.

The plurality system is the least equitable in terms of its proportionality effects. Normally organized in single-member constituencies, plurality elections translate votes into seats simply on the basis of the candidate who received the most votes regardless of whether that party gained a majority of the total vote. A candidate, then, may be elected from a constituency in which he has gained less than 50 per cent of the total poll and, by extension, it is not infrequent that governments are formed by a political party which has failed to attract a majority of national support. In Britain since 1945 no government has polled more than 50 per cent of the national vote, though all but one of the administrations have secured more than 50 per cent of the seats. The disparities between votes and seats are a well-known feature of plurality systems which has been formally stated in the 'cube law'.[48] This states that in two-party elections the number of seats a party wins is approximately proportional to the cube of the relative number of votes it attracts – where (for example) one party gains 53 per cent and the other party 47 per cent the cubic law predicts the share of seats as 59 per cent and 41 per cent respectively.

Majoritarian elections achieve a greater degree of proportionality by virtue of successful candidates only being elected where they have attracted a majority of the total vote. Elections based on this system (as in France and Australia) also give the voter greater choice in that he is able to rank order his preferences for candidates. Nevertheless representatives are usually selected within single-member constituencies so that even though they must have a majority to be elected votes cast for the losing party(ies) can be 'wasted'.

Elections based on proportional representation – of which there a number of variants – ensure that party political representation is more closely related to voting preferences. Candidates are normally elected within multi-member constituencies, and the larger the number of members that an electoral district returns the greater will be the proportionality achieved. In some systems such as the list method used in West Germany the voter has the opportunity to vote for both a candidate and a party – this is because half the representation to the Bundestag is elected from single-member constituencies while the remaining members are allocated among the parties proportionally to the votes the constituency candidates receive, calculated on a Land base. In the Single Transferable Vote system of proportional representation (used in Ireland, Malta and the Australian Senate) the voter is able to indicate his preference for candidates within multi-member constituencies, the votes being transferred between candidates not already elected in a complex manner until all the seats are filled.

A map showing in which countries these different types of electoral system are in operation would highlight a number of different areas. Plurality elections have been most favoured in the Anglo-American countries, though prior to the First World War plurality and majoritarian elections were used in the majority of democracies. Proportional methods of election, however, have become of increasing importance and in Western Europe only France and Britain do not use them, though even in the latter, as a measure to meet minority discrimination in Northern Ireland, proportionally based elections, using the single transferable vote, have been re-introduced. Political tradition plays a major part in the type of system in operation and in general countries are reluctant to change their voting methods.

As the case of Britain shows, the major political reasons why electoral reform, i.e. changing the method of election from a plurality to more proportional system, is resisted are because of the effect such change would have on the power base of the major parties. Plurality elections, as is well known, penalize minority parties and particularly those whose territorial support is widely distributed. In the 1974 (October) election the Liberal Party gained 19·2 per cent of the total vote but only 4·5 per cent of the seats while the two nationalist parties, the Scottish Nationalist and Plaid Cymru, with little more than 4 per cent of the vote gained 3·4 per cent of the seats. In Table 4.7 the disparities in the seat–vote relationships between the parties highlight differences in the value of the vote; what the table also shows is that with a proportional system of election coalition governments would become necessary; some implications of this are discussed in the last section of this chapter.

Table 4.7. **Seat–vote relationship in UK Parliament, October 1974.**

	% of votes	Actual seats	Seats on strict PR basis
Labour	39·2	319	249
Conservative	35·8	277	227
Liberal	18·3	13	116
Scottish Nationalist	2·9	11	18
Plaid Cymru	0·6	3	4
National Front	0·4	—	3
Communist	0·1	—	1
United Ulster Unionist	1·4	10	9
Social Democratic and Labour	0·5	1	3
Other Irish	0·5	1	3
Rest	0·3	—	2
TOTAL	100.0	635	635

Source: *Political Companion*, Winter 1974.

Territorial Biases in Electoral Systems

Besides the actual type of electoral system used, the way in which these are territorially organized also affects electoral outcomes. Because it is true that the majority of elections are organized within constituencies the way these are delimited can affect the results of an election. Two types of bias are commonly distinguished: malapportionment, in which the electoral districts have unequal populations or numbers of electors, and gerrymandering, in which the boundaries of the constituencies are deliberately manipulated so as to favour a political party.

Malapportionment is a bias common to nearly all legislatures. As with gerrymandering some cases of malapportionment are 'accidental' rather than intentional, arising out of the practical difficulties of using constituencies. In areas of high population movement, as in the dispersal of urban populations from central city to suburban areas, it is often impracticable for constituencies to meet the criterion of parity, particularly where they are single-member seats. Nevertheless, there are many other cases in which the malapportioned legislature is a deliberate bias in the system of representation. This can take the form of a rural bias, a practice common in American legislatures prior to the 'reapportionment revolution' of the 1960s and which in some notorious cases had meant that less than 40 per cent of a state's electorate could elect a majority. In

Australia, where the practice of rural over-representation is found in all states and in extreme cases means that the rural vote is worth 13 times that of the metropolitan vote,[49] malapportionment is argued as being necessary because of the geographical disabilities of the rural electorate though its origin, as elsewhere, is also to be sought in the conflict between the urban and rural areas.

While arguably the more difficult form of malpractice to prove, gerrymandering is a blatant form of political behaviour favouring one party against another. This is done either by maximizing the impact of one's own party and/or by minimizing the representation of other parties. As a practice it has been more widespread in American than it has in European elections with some noteworthy exceptions, such as Northern Ireland.

Both these types of spatial biasing of the electoral system are well known and it is in their 'solution' that we should pay more attention since this will help to show how the political system behaves. Central to this argument is the role of partisan forces. Partisan factors largely underlie the prevalence of such malpractices, for in their employment will lie potential advantages for the 'winning' party.

Given that both problems relate to the manner in which constituencies are devised, a crucial factor focuses on who or what body is responsible for devising the network of electoral areas. Broadly this can be either a duty of the existing government or devolved to an independent commission whose findings would be binding. In the case of the former it is clear that partisan factors will play a major part in how the boundaries are devised so as to give maximum advantage to the ruling party. The ease with which this is possible varies with the type of electoral system, being generally easier in plurality elections where the territorial patterns of support are more evident. Yet, as the Irish case shows,[50] it is possible to manipulate a proportional system to the potential advantage of a party by spatially manipulating the number of members a constituency returns.

The history of the parliamentary Boundary Commissioners in Britain provides an interesting case-study of the approach using an independent body because of the apparent difficulties in 'depoliticizing' the problem of defining constituencies. Several studies[51] have shown that non-partisan boundary drawing is an illusion, that regardless of the neutrality of the responsible body their recommendations cannot fail to have some political effects. In Britain, implementing the recommendations of the Boundary Commissioners has normally favoured the Conservative Party. As the ruling party has the option or not of actually introducing legislation adopting the Commissioner's recommendations, Labour governments (as in 1969) may be reluctant to introduce the changes; their failure to do so at that date, according to one estimate, gave them 11 extra seats. Recognizing, therefore, that even so-called neutral approaches act in a partisan way the solution to the problem may lie in adopting an approach which seeks a consensus among the political leaders. This is what is termed the bi-partisan approach in which constituencies will be arranged to give a more equitable representation among groups and parties.

Electoral Outcomes and Policy Outcomes

While it is clear that either fundamentally through the type of electoral system in operation or, more specifically, through its spatial organization there is a traceable effect on the pattern of electoral results it is less certain as to the implications of the latter on governments in their role as policy-makers. That is, where it is accepted that electoral systems discriminate, some more than others, how much does this affect how governments behave? Is it an influence which can be associated with different types of spatial outcome? These questions, while important to the political geographer examining behaviour, are complex and frequently difficult to evaluate in a rigorous fashion. We shall first discuss some implications arising from the electoral system in operation, before turning to look at the implications arising from the spatial organization of elections.

Most political scientists are agreed that there is a strong relationship between the type of electoral system and the party structure (i.e. the number of political parties), even if there is less consensus on whether there is a causative influence on the one by the other factor. Plurality elections are frequently associated with two-party systems, whose main advantages compared to the multi-party and coalition governments commonly met with in countries using a more proportional form of election, are alleged to be their strength and stability. Plurality elections are more likely to give a single party an outright majority so that it has the voting power to enable it to pass legislation without having to compromise on its preferences, as is more likely in cases where perforce there is a coalition government. In Britain especially, the two-party system has been linked to the idea of strong government and its converse, coalition government, with inherent weakness in that the major political parties are unable to govern effectively. These, however, are issues which for the most part belong more properly to political science than they do to geography.

It is where it can be argued (or shown) that single-party and coalition governments function differently that such variations might have an effect on the working of the state. Two contrasting models can be studied in this respect: the two-party system based on adversary politics and coalition government based on a more consensual approach. One 'cost' of the adversary style of politics will be the change of policies resulting from a change of government, since each government will be anxious to show that its programme visibly differs from that of the previous administration. Wilson[52] has demonstrated the effects this system has on regional economic policies – those designed to encourage the redistribution of industry and the economic regeneration of depressed areas – in Britain. Since their introduction in 1945, with the Distribution of Industry Act of that year laying down financial inducements available to industrialists within designated areas, the range of incentives has altered, sometimes substantially, with each change of government. The frequency with which these changes occurred, and therefore the uncertainty to which this gives rise, tended to undermine their value according to the views of industry. To a degree policy change is inevitable and desirable in some circumstances (where, for example, it is a response to a change in the economic environment). Nevertheless, changes for purely party political reasons tend to be less productive.

The illustration used to show the possible 'cost' imposed by adversary politics is not to suggest that coalition politics is not without its problems. Nevertheless, in the case of some European countries, a notable instance being West Germany, coalition government has 'encouraged a degree of policy continuity and the pragmatic modification of policy which the alternating one-party governments of Britain have not recently provided'.[53] In the case of others, such as Belgium, the ethnic configuration of the state supports, if not demands, the use of proportional representation because of the conflict between the groups, Flemish and Walloon. Yet the use of a proportionally based election system encourages the splitting of ethnic cleavages along party lines and contributes to the political instability arising from the need to rely upon coalition government. Generally though, in Western Europe, proportional representation has been associated with relatively stable coalition government in which alliances between the parties, once struck, tend to be lasting.

Looking more specifically at the spatial organization of elections, the division into constituencies and its spatial biasing through electoral malpractices will also influence the policy-making process. In terms of their voting support for a particular party constituencies can be described as safe, marginal or hopeless. Constituencies which have supported the ruling party, including especially those marginal ones which could easily prove important to the government's survival in the next election, will tend to curry more favour among the politicians.[54] In Britain and Australia then, where Labour support is in large part an urban vote, financial programmes will be biased in favour of the urban electorate, while a change to a right-wing government will bring greater rewards to the rural, and especially farming population. Cultivating the vote, something which can be spatially specific because of the manner in which constituencies pinpoint patterns of party support, is a political expedient which, as political behaviour, is likely to recur as long as there will be beneficial payoffs for the politician and his party.

Perhaps more difficult to demonstrate is whether electoral malpractices affect, in a substantive manner, policy-making. In extreme cases, such as in Northern Ireland prior to the civil disturbances of 1969, the effects will tend to be more obvious: it was because of the way in which the gerrymandered councils of towns such as Londonderry, Omagh and Dungannon discriminated against the locally dominant Catholic population in terms of housing, jobs and suchlike that demands for civil rights were raised.

The effects of reapportionment in the United States have been closely examined in a number of studies.[55] Presumably in a malapportioned legislature, in which the rural areas were overrepresented, policy-making would be biased to the interests of rural conservatism so that per capita spending on welfare programmes, education and the like would be lower. Several studies have indeed shown that policies have been altered since reapportionment, though most writers have suggested that reapportionment has had less effect on policy outcomes than expected. (Equally few if any have claimed that reapportionment has had no effect.) At least one reason has been suggested as the greater solidarity of the rural representatives in the state legislatures, whereas by contrast the urban members find it difficult to agree among themselves so that central city representatives may be pitted against the suburbs as well as the rural areas. Dye cites the following graphic example from Floridan experience:

> The fellows from the upstate counties control the state's politics no matter what happens with the one-man one-vote law. Those fellows work together . . . They can stop the big cities cold whenever they want to . . .[56]

Representatives of the metropolitan areas were often divided whereas the 'Porkchoppers' (rural legislators) acted as a more united voting bloc.

Discussion Points and Further Reading

Voting provides one of the more widely acknowledged methods by which the citizen can lend support to the political system. Taylor and Johnston (1979) present the most detailed discussion of the factors underlying voting behaviour; their important analyses of the social bases of voting using Rokkan's conceptual framework differentially to individual countries, and the spatial patterning of electoral preferences within them, and the differential significance of socializing factors on voting choice (family, peers, neighbourhood) provide major areas for discussion and further research. Other forms of participation have been more neglected by political geographers, notably voting turnout and 'higher-order' forms (in Milbrath's typology). The question of participation, for example, on a neighbourhood basis closely relates to demand-making (see Chapter 7).

The relationship between election systems, electoral outcomes and policy outcomes can be studied from two main viewpoints. The first (discussed here) is the possible effect of different methods of electoral organization on allocations. The edited volume of readings by Finer (1975) and the research papers on malapportionment (note 55) provide relevant case-study material. An alternative viewpoint is to ask how votes are bought, of which examples are discussed in Johnston (1979).

Finer, S. E. (ed.), *Adversary Politics and Electoral Reform*, Wigram, London, 1975.

Fitton, M., 'Neighbourhood and Voting', *British Journal of Political Science* (1973), **3**, 445–72.

Johnston, R. J., *Political, Electoral and Spatial System*, Clarendon, Oxford, 1979.

Taylor, P. J., and Johnston, R. J., *Geography of Elections*, Penguin, Harmondsworth, 1979.

Notes

1. J. R. V. Prescott, 'The Functions and Methods of Electoral Geography', *Annals of the Association of American Geographers* (1959), **49**, 296–304.

2. P. J. Taylor and R. J. Johnston, *Geography of Elections*, Penguin, Harmondsworth, 1979.
3. M. Weiner, 'Political Participation: Crisis of the Political Process', in L. Binder, *et al.*, *Crises and Sequences in Political Development*, Princeton University Press, Princeton, 1971, p. 161.
4. L. W. Milbrath, *Political Participation*, Rand McNally, Chicago, 1965.
5. W. H. Morris-Jones, 'In Defence of Apathy', *Political Studies* (1954), 2 (1).
6. S. D. Brunn, *Geography and Politics in America*, Harper and Row, New York, 1974.
7. *Ibid*. p. 312.
8. S. Rokkan and A. Campbell, 'Citizen Participation in Political Life; Norway and the Unites States of America', *International Social Science Journal* (1960), 12, 69–99.
9. *Ibid*. p. 82.
10. S. Rokkan and H. Valen, 'Regional Contrasts in Norwegian Politics', in E. Allardt and S. Rokkan (eds.), *Mass Politics,* Free Press, New York, 1970, pp. 190–250.
11. Milbrath, *Political Participation*, pp. 113–14.
12. S. Verba and N. H. Nie, *Participation in America: Social Equality and Political Democracy*, Harper and Row, New York, 1972, p. 231.
13. R. A. Dahl and E. R. Tufte, *Size and Democracy*, Stanford University Press, Stanford, 1973, p. 61.
14. S. Verba, N. H. Nie and J. Kim, *Participation and Political Equality*, Cambridge University Press, Cambridge, 1978.
15. A. H. Taylor, 'Journey Time, Perceived Distance and Electoral Turnout – Victoria Ward, Swansea', *Area* (1973), 5, 59–63.
16. S. M. Lipset, *Political Man*, Doubleday, New York, 1960.
17. R. Paddison, 'Factors underlying Variations in Local Electoral Turnouts', unpublished paper, Department of Geography, University of Glasgow, 1976.
18. P. Fletcher, 'The Results Analysed', in L. J. Sharpe (ed.), *Voting in Cities*, Macmillan, London, 1967, pp. 290–321.
19. P. Sacks, 'Bailiwicks, Locality and Religion: Three Elements in an Irish Dail Constituency Election', *Economic and Social Review* (1970), 1, 531–54.
20. I. Budge and D. W. Urwin, *Scottish Political Behaviour*, Longman, London, 1966.
21. S. M. Lipset and S. Rokkan, 'Cleavage Structures, Party Systems and Voter Alignments: an Introduction', in S. M. Lipset and S. Rokkan (eds.), *Party Systems and Voter Alignments*, Free Press, New York, 1967, pp. 1–64.
22. R. Rose and D. Urwin, 'Social Cohesion, Political Parties and Strains in Regimes', in M. Dogan and R. Rose (ed.), *European Politics: A Reader*, Macmillan, London, 1971, p. 220.
23. A. Lijphart, 'Class Voting and Religions Voting in European Democracies', *Acta Politica* (1971), 6, 158–71.
24. R. R. Alford, *Party and Society*, Rand McNally, Chicago, 1963.
25. P. G. Pulzer, *Political Representation and Elections in Britain*, Allen & Unwin, London, 1972, p. 107.

26. V. Capecchi and G. Galli, 'Determinants of Voting Behaviour in Italy: a Linear Causal Model of Analysis', in M. Dogan and S. Rokkan (eds.), *Quantitative Ecological Analysis in the Social Sciences*, M.I.T. Press, Cambridge, Mass., pp. 235–84.
27. M. Dogan, 'Political Cleavage and Social Stratification in France and Italy', in S. M. Lipset and S. Rokkan (eds.), *Party Systems and Voter Alignments*, Free Press, New York, 1967, pp. 129–95.
28. Capecchi and Galli, 'Determinants of Voting Behaviour', p. 283.
29. Taylor and Johnston, *Geography of Elections*.
30. I. Crewe and C. Payne 'Another Game with Nature: an Ecological Regression Model of the British Two-Party Vote Ratio in 1970', *British Journal of Political Science* (1976), **6**, 43–81.
31. Quoted by J. Blondel, *Voters, Parties and Leaders*, Penguin, Harmondsworth, 1965, p. 67.
32. J. H. Goldthorpe, *et al.*, *The Affluent Worker: Political Attitudes and Behaviour*, Cambridge University Press, Cambridge, 1968, p. 59.
33. D. E. Butler, and D. E. Stokes, *Political Change in Britain: Forces Shaping Electoral Choice*, Macmillan, London, 1974.
34. F. M. Wirt, *et al.*, *On the City's Rim: Politics and Policy in Suburbia*, Heath, Lexington, 1972, p. 51.
35. K. R. Cox, 'The Spatial Structuring of Information Flows and Partisan Attitudes', in M. Dogan and S. Rokkan *Quantitative Ecological Analysis*, pp. 157–85.
36. J. M. Orbell, 'An Information-Flow Theory of Community Influence', *Journal of Politics* (1970), **32**, 322–38.
37. M. Fitton, 'Neighbourhood and Voting: a Sociometric Explanation', *British Journal of Political Science* (1973), **3**, 445–72.
38. *Ibid.* p. 471.
39. J. C. Manis and L. C. Stine, 'Suburban Residence and Political Behaviour', *Public Opinion Quarterly*, Winter 1958, 485–9.
40. B. M. Berger, *Working-class Suburb: A Study of Auto Workers in Suburbia*, University of California Press, Berkeley, 1960.
41. A. Campbell, *et al.*, *The American Voter*, Wiley, New York, 1960.
42. Fitton, 'Neighbourhood and Voting', p. 471.
43. B. R. Berelson, *et al.*, *Voting*, University of Chicago Press, Chicago, 1954.
44. Butler and Stokes, *Political Change in Britain*.
45. M. Rogin, 'Politics, Emotion and the Wallace Vote', *British Journal of Sociology* (1969), **20**, 27–49.
46. *Ibid.* p. 30.
47. D. W. Rae, *The Political Consequences of Electoral Laws*, Yale University Press, New Haven, 1971.
48. M. G. Kendall and A. Stuart, 'The Law of Cubic Proportions in Election Results', *British Journal of Sociology* (1950), **1**, 183–97.
49. N. Blewett, 'Redistribution Procedures', in H. Mayer and H. Nelson (eds.), *Australian Politics: A Third Reader*, Cheshire, Melbourne, pp. 295–300.
50. R. Paddison, 'Spatial Bias and Redistricting in Proportional Representation Systems: a Case Study of the Republic of Ireland', *Tijdschrift voor Economische en Social Geografie* (1976), **67**, 230–40.

51. P. J. Taylor and G. Gudgin, 'The Myth of Non-Partisan Cartography: a Study of Electoral Biases in the English Boundary Commissions Redistribution for 1955–70', *Urban Studies* (1976), **13**, 13–25.

52. T. Wilson, 'The Economic Costs of the Adversary System', in S. E. Finer (ed.), *Adversary Politics and Electoral Reform*, Wigram, London, pp. 99–116.

53. G. K. Roberts, 'The Federal Republic of Germany', in Finer, *Adversary Politics*, p. 221.

54. For further examples see R. J. Johnston, *Political, Electoral and Spatial Systems*, Clarendon Press, Oxford, 1979.

55. T. R. Dye, 'Malapportionment and Public Policy in the States', *Journal of Politics* (1965), **27**, 586–601; H. Jacob, 'The Consequences of Malapportionment: A Note of Caution', *Social Forces* (1965), 256–61; D. Brady and D. Edmonds, *The Effect of Malapportionment on Policy Output in the American States*, Laboratory for Political Research, Iowa City, 1966.

56. *Tallahassee Democrat*, 26 October 1969. Quoted in T. R. Dye, *Politics in States and Communities*, Prentice-Hall, Englewood Cliffs, 2nd edn, 1973, p. 134.

5 Politics and 'The Environment'

As the sensitive and changeable medium within which the dramas of human behaviour, large and trivial, are enacted, man's environment is central to his survival. With its land, sea and resources the targets of wars of territorial conquest it has been a permanent focus of political activity, but it is only within the last fifteen years or so that 'the environment', its quality and its future, have emerged as major issues in a public debate which has generated a multitude of pressure groups and engaged the attention and efforts of numerous politicians and public servants. The discovery by the news media of 'the environment' as the source of a consistent flow of issues, and the ensuing publicity given to environmental questions, might foster the assumption that government concern with environmental questions is a recent phenomenon. Though priorities may have been upset in the recent era, when issues of pollution and conservation have received headline coverage, environmental legislation in fact has a long history. Johnson catalogues the execution of a Londoner in the early fourteenth century for causing excessive smoke through the burning of coal, the introduction of the first English laws on water quality in 1388, and an Act for wildfowl conservation of 1534.[1] According to Kennet the first democratically framed environmental legislation, which controls the taking of turtles, was passed by the Assembly of Bermuda in the first half of the seventeenth century.[2] The first modern anti-pollution law in the UK was the clean water legislation of 1848, passed in response to a London cholera outbreak, and it was followed by the Alkali etc. Works Act of 1863. The important Town and Country Planning Act of 1947 and the Clean Air Act of 1956 both predate the period when the term 'the environment' was much used or much comprehended other than by geographers and ecologists. Nevertheless, if river pollution is newsworthy today, it certainly was not so twenty, thirty or forty years ago; and the 'environmental debate' is the product of much more than the specific issues of pollution, planning and conservation upon which the media focuses.

Public Opinion and the Environment

Though many definitions of geography exist, the relationship between man and his environment is the established core of the subject, and although the political aspects of this relationship have been less fully explored than the economic and social ones, the relevance of questions concerning human attitudes and behaviour relating to environmental modification or disruption hardly needs to be stressed. In order to gain an understanding of why environmental issues have come to command a central position in the arena of public and institutional concern, analytical concepts, frameworks and interpretations are required. A reasonably coherent analysis has been developed by Solesbury.[3] He states that

> There is at any point in time a public agenda of issues to which political debate is addressing itself, a list of the most important matters on which action is called for. Over time the agenda changes as matters get dealt with or no further action is required and new issues arise to take their place on the agenda for consideration.[4]

For almost two decades 'the environment' has held a high position on the public agenda, not only as a result of concern over particular changes in the environment, but also because of changes in attitudes towards the environment. If the community environment is regarded as consisting of a multitude of changing situations, it can be said that a situation becomes transformed into an issue when by common consent the situation is bad and should be improved – thus effluent discharge is a situation and pollution an issue. Once identified, an issue will call for a response from government, for 'responses are just what government decides to do or is urged to do. The principal responses are policies which are designed to change the environmental situation giving rise to the issue'.[5]

The political system is not a perfectly functioning machine producing a suitable response to every emerging issue. The vast majority of issues fail the tests of recognition and response, and while the institutions of government largely exist to process issues, public resources of time, money, support and commitment are in short supply, and issues compete for them. According to Solesbury, to proceed through the policy process the nascent issue must pass three separate tests: to command attention, to claim legitimacy, and to invoke action. Each issue has its own innate qualities which will assist or inhibit its passage, and these qualities can be examined in relation to environmental issues.

Solesbury identifies one valuable attribute as that of particularity, that is the ability to be exemplified by particular events, since this will assist the public and political identification of the issue. The intimacy of the human relationship with the environment is advantageous in this respect. Many environmental events have tangible outputs and thus usually fail to respect privilege, which makes it difficult to purchase immunity from issues such as pesticide effects or radioactive fallout, while their largely physical manifestation suggests simple causal explanations and simple allocations of responsibility. Thus events like the Torrey Canyon oil tanker disaster of 1967 or the crash of the nuclear-powered Soviet satellite in Canada in 1978, by the nature of their particularity are likely to make more effective impact upon public consciousness than less visible problems such as the mutation of a virus or the gradual weakening of a currency, both of which might be more serious.

A second desirable attribute is that of generalization, concerning the degree to which an issue can be related to a more general system of values and thereby become legitimized as a proper matter for political concern. For example political parties are likely to be attracted to issues to which their ideologies appear to offer ready responses. Although environmental issues clearly relate to fundamental ideological attitudes concerning resources, growth, property rights and the past and future, Solesbury is unconvinced that the major British parties have been able to formulate distinctive environmental ideologies, thereby reducing the force of environmental issues. In general he relates particularization to the ability of an issue to raise public support and generalization as being more significant as a means of attracting political institutions to a problem.

However, it would seem to us that a major factor in the promotion of 'the environment' to a high position on the public agenda has concerned the generalization attributes of environmental issues within the domain of public opinion. A wide range of public preoccupations, some fashionable and some serious, which have arisen during the last two decades can clearly be related to environmental dimensions. They include 'the bomb', overpopulation, the depletion of energy resources, planning and conservation, 'health foods' versus 'junk foods' and most of the tenets of the 'alternative society'. Furthermore, the liberalization of society and the discernible

rise in cynicism in attitudes towards authority have helped to produce a socio-political milieu in which individuals, communities and
organizations are prepared to challenge authority (very frequently
on environmental issues), with some confidence in the outcome.

Although an issue may succeed in commanding attention and be
accepted as legitimate, action by governments may not be assured.
In the course of policy-making processes, issues progress from the
public arenas to the internal black boxes of the governmental system. Here they may be overtaken by external events such as expenditure cuts, transformed into other issues in the way that an
environmental issue concerning an energy source might be
absorbed into an energy policy with different priorities, or, in the
absence of sufficient levels of interdepartmental integration or
commitment or agreement, be effectively dismissed in a partial
response, a loose statement of principle or an inconsequential
administrative reorganization. Although no reference is made by
Solesbury to the Easton model of the political system, his emphasis
upon the means by which demands (issues) obtain sufficient levels
of support to achieve their acceptance by the political system
as potential causes for action appears highly compatible with the
Eastonian approach. In the context of environmental politics
Solesbury's analysis provides useful insights into the potentialities
of 'the environment' as a source of issues for the public agenda.

Pressure Groups

Paralleling and partly arising out of the increase in public awareness
of environmental problems has been a proliferation of pressure
groups, the majority of which are in some way closely associated
with environmental issues. While the disorganized forces of public
opinion may on occasions obtain victory through the sheer weight of
reaction on issues which generate widespread commitment, pressure groups, whether operating at the state or at more local levels,
are able to provide the generalship to organize the forces of opinion,
the intelligence service which gathers information and discovers
critical points for attack, and also recruitment and propaganda to
enlist support and magnify its dimensions and resolve. Thus,
'Legitimate popular power . . . is likely to be nebulous without the
opportunity to mobilize and organize, including the formation of
pressure groups, and to create clienteles or attentive publics.[6]
Pressure groups have probably existed as long as there have been

collective interests to defend and principles to uphold, but it is their multiplication, particularly in the field of environmental conflict and conservation, that characterizes the recent period. For example, in 1976 1,250 local amenity societies were registered with the Civic Trust in the UK, while in America the environmental lobby has also spawned a multiplicity of pressure groups.

The influence of pressure groups on policy-making is considerable and by no means confined to the environmental arena. Nevertheless, their numbers and performance in this field suggest that this chapter is a convenient location within which to consider pressure groups in terms of their general characteristics as well as their effects upon environmental policy-making.

Attempts at the definition and classification of pressure groups by political scientists have produced a copious literature embodying 'the almost total confusion of terminology which reigns in the field'.[7] If we define a pressure group as 'any organized group which attempts to influence the decisions of government or other public bodies without itself being a political party or seeking to exercise the formal powers of government', at least we will be in reasonable harmony with most authoritative definitions, though the question of classification is more factious and divisive. Most authorities seem to recognize a basic twofold classification between what are variously termed interest, spokesman, functional or sectional groups on the one hand and principle, attitude, promotional or cause groups on the other. Having reviewed the literature, and not seeking to become deeply involved in what is in part a semantic argument, we will adopt the categorization used by Allison and recognize a distinction between interests as privately oriented wants not logically dependent on public benefits, and principles as publicly oriented wants inseparable from a widespread public effect.[8] For example, a neighbourhood amenity society as an interest group might resist the location of a factory in its vicinity, not caring whether, or perhaps hoping that, it will be located in some similar but more distant neighbourhood, while a principle group might seek to resist factory location in all residential neighbourhoods as a point of principle.

This basic distinction seems reasonably appropriate to most conflict contexts. Referring to the USA, Henning writes that

A broad generalization concerning interest groups (the British would say 'pressure groups') is that they can be divided into broad categories: (a) those associated with clientele and their consequent economic interests, e.g. National Woolgrowers Association (grazing on federal land), and (b) those associated with ideological conservation including memberships of private individuals without economic interests, e.g. The Wilderness Society (wilderness) and National Wildlife Federation (wildlife). Generally speaking, the former are registered lobbyists while the latter are considered as educational organizations although they seek to influence policy.[9]

Allison also provides a useful subdivision of the two main groups: interest groups being divided into major economic interest groups like the Confederation of British Industry, representing broad production-based interests; minor economic interest groups such as individual trade unions, firms and professional associations which represent more narrowly defined production-based interests; and non-financial interest groups which include local amenity associations and organizations such as the Royal National Institute for the Blind. Principle groups are subdivided into programmatic groups such as the British Humanist Association or the Conservation Society, associated with broad social policies; promotional groups, whose attention and efforts focus upon a single definable policy reform, such as the old Anti-Corn Law League; and emphasis groups, concerned with vigilant support for certain principles which are widely current if not so strongly held within society at large. The latter category would include organizations such as the Royal Society for the Prevention of Cruelty to Animals and the Council for the Preservation of Rural England.

National principle groups appear to have exerted a more prolonged influence in the field of environmental politics than have local interest groups, and the following table summarizes the dates of formation of the major UK environmental principle groups.

1865 Commons Preservation Society	1926 Council for the Preservation of Rural England
1877 Society for the Protection of Ancient Buildings	1937 Georgian Group
1889 Society for the Protection of Birds	1939 Central Council of Civic Societies
1895 National Trust	1944 Council for British Archaeology
1899 Garden Cities Association Coal Smoke Abatement Society	1957 Civic Trust
1924 Ancient Monuments Society	1967 Conservation Society
	1970 Friends of the Earth

Although the earliest local amenity society in the UK, the Sidmouth Improvement Committee, formed in 1846, predated the earliest environmental principle group, from information on 635 local amenity societies compiled by the Civic Trust it emerges that only 1 per cent of the sample originated before 1900, only 6 per cent in the period 1900–41, while 75 per cent of the societies were formed after 1961 and 37 per cent after 1969.[10] Surges in the emergence of such societies followed the formation of the Civic Trust as a national co-ordinating organization in 1957 and the report of the Skeffington Committee in 1969 with its encouragement of public participation in environmental planning, though the recent explosion in the birth rate of amenity societies is closely related to the emergence of the environment as an issue, as discussed above.

Fundamentally, political geography focuses on the political causes of geographical change. The most significant aspect of pressure groups, therefore, is their effectiveness in the primary task of influencing the policy-making process. In absolute terms, the effectiveness of a group will be measured by the degree to which relevant decisions would have been made differently, or not at all, if the group concerned had not acted. Investigation however is likely to yield only incomplete measurements of effectiveness, partly because of the effects of the arch enemy of political–geographical research, the problem of existence (uncertainty of knowing what would have been if x had not occurred), and partly because of difficulties in knowing exactly how much a particular decision reflects a response by officialdom to pressure imposed upon it by the group as opposed to pressures from other sources or initiatives from within the institution. In any event, the effectiveness of a pressure group will be conditioned by two factors: the quantitative and qualitative nature of its political resources, and the efficiency with which these resources are mobilized and deployed. Political resources are diverse, each group being characterized by its own particular bundle of resources; for example, a police association gains strength from its potential ability to resist the imposition of laws of which it does not approve while the powerful transport union derives power from its ability to influence the voting behaviour of its membership and to withdraw labour if affronted.

These resources can be divided into two types: sanctional resources which include the ability to resist the implementation of policy, impose an economic burden on the state, and vote swinging, and non-sanctional resources, which are varied, with the possession of information and sometimes expertise which is desired by public bodies frequently being the most valuable resource. At the national level, only the major economic interest groups and conceivably a few of the largest principle groups can threaten vote-swinging sanctions, but at the local level even the smaller interest groups can be credited with this power. With information as a valuable commodity, the existence of some pressure groups is welcomed rather than feared by public bodies while the exchange of information may provide access to public officers and a basis for bargaining. Other non-sanctional resources include established channels of communication with public bodies, wealth, the moral force of a just cause which makes public opposition an unattractive proposition (an important factor where environmental issues are concerned), and the abilities, status and prestige of the membership.

A variety of factors will determine the amount of mobilized resources that will be necessary to elicit the desired governmental response. Compatibility of group aims and institutional policy constitutes a fundamental constraint, and it is difficult to imagine government being induced to abandon a policy crucial to party ideology regardless of the weight of pressure group opposition. Since pressure groups exist to influence public bodies, access to policy-makers is also crucial, and for a group to develop its role it must be perceived by those in authority as having some significance. Access can be obtained through the formal channels of government, routeways which are particularly likely to be open if the group is a repository of valuable information or the representative of a numerous or influential constituency. Access is assisted by the shared membership by group leaders and public officials of class, social, educational, cultural or recreational groups, or, in the case of trade unions for example, where the group has strong affiliations with the party or government which it seeks to influence. Deprived of any form of access, the group must dissolve or work against the established political order.

A third constraint concerns the existence of countervailing pressures, and one group may negate the endeavours of another. At the same time, government may be reluctant to oppose a pressure group which has no articulate opposition; for example the UK Lord's Day Observance Society, though only representative of a minority of opinion for a long time, successfully resisted government action to liberalize the British Sunday, assisted by the absence of coherently organized extra-governmental opposition to the aims of the society.

Each pressure group exists within a particular political, social and economic environment. Eckstein has provided numerous examples which show that the scope, nature and effectiveness of pressure groups is greatly affected by the character of their environment.[11] He argues that in the USA with a political system in which the assent of numerous bodies is normally necessary to produce change, defensive pressure groups are favoured, while positive decisions are more easily obtainable under the unitary cabinet government system of the UK. He also suggests that pressure groups come more and more to resemble the departments with which they deal. For example, as long as Parliament was the real focus of power in the UK, pressure groups tended to be ephemeral, one-purpose organizations whose activities were concentrated on the lobbying of sympathetic M.P.s. The bureaucratization of government and transfer of power to a vastly expanded Civil Service, however, has been paralleled by changes in the nature of the major pressure groups which are now permanent, bureaucratic and engaged in continuous dialogue with government officials.

The nature and effectiveness of sanctional pressure group activity, particularly where environmental issues are concerned, can be considered within the context of Kasperson's model of stress and strain and the political system.[12] The natural resource management system is seen as a subsystem of the larger political system, one of several such subsystems which are in competition with each other for allocations of scarce resources. These allocations are needed to reduce 'stresses', and the managers in the political system attempt to alleviate stress according to rules and constraints governing their particular roles within the system, and in view of the goals and policies to which they are committed. 'Stress' is defined as 'noxious or potentially noxious environmental forces upon the individual',[13] while 'strain' is introduced to refer to the individual's perception, evaluation and reaction to the stimulus, and involves the notion of threat to the political actor or to the system within which he operates.

Stress may originate in the physical or in the man-made environment and be produced by a traumatic event or the gradual worsening of a situation; thus flooding, pollution, riot or weaknesses in an educational system may all produce stress. The political actor concerned will perceive and evaluate the stress within the context of other stresses acting upon the political system, attempt to assign relative priorities and, within the context of his managerial goals and values, assess the various alternative strategies for coping with the stress-inducing situation. Various vehicles may articulate the stress to the managers of the system, and these will vary in their potency; 'Stress articulated by a major urban newspaper or a racial interest group, for example, may exert more strain than stress communicated within the administrative framework since the former is much more capable of inducing threat into the political environment of the decision-maker'.[14] Therefore the effectiveness of sanctional pressure group activity can, in a sense, be judged in terms of the additional levels of stress and strain that the group's actions bring to bear upon the relevant political actors.

Principle Group Activity

Gregory's study of principle group activity in relation to the proposed Cow Green reservoir in north-east England is of particular interest because it demonstrates how matters of considerable environmental and public amenity concern are likely to lead to the formation of confederations of groups. This is partly because of the nature of the physical environment as a focus for a wide range of sectional interests, and partly because a high degree of sharing of membership exists between groups having a common focus on the physical environment.[15] For example, a botanist may be a member of different groups active in botany, conservation, rambling and access to the countryside.

The conflict developed from the promotion by the Water Resources Board of a Private Bill which would enable the construction of a reservoir at the Cow Green site in Upper Teeside which was needed largely as a result of planned industrial expansion by ICI, one of the main consumers of water in Teeside. Opposition came from botanical, conservation and amenity interests and mainly concerned the belief that the site to be affected contained the last surviving British assemblages of species of post-glacial flora. The initial catalyst which was to lead to the emergence of an opposition confederation which included most major British environmental principle groups is found in a statement by the Nature Conservancy (the government-sponsored conservation body). This body had been consulted by the water interests, that it would agree without prejudice to test borings at the proposed site. This apparent resignation by the official conservation body alarmed four botanists, members of the Botanical Society of the British Isles, two of them professionals and two amateurs, who formed a nucleus for opposition. The tactics adopted included writing to *The Times* and appealing to the council of their organization to institute a committee which would launch an appeal for funds and mobilize opposition within the scientific community. The letter to *The Times*, signed by fourteen eminent botanists, duly appeared and elicited the desired response. Three weeks later the Council of the BSBI established a Teesdale Defence Committee which included representatives from the locally active Northumberland and Durham Naturalists' Trust. Support from the general public was not greatly forthcoming from the Teeside area despite an efficient programme of leafletting, lobbying and attracting the attention of the local news media. The main response achieved by the Teesdale Defence Committee was in obtaining support from the scientific community.

Most of the earliest organizations to mobilize their resources alongside those of the Teesdale Defence Committee were scientific societies associated with local and national botanical and ecological interests. In due course, and to a large extent stimulated by the Committee's distribution of 40,000 copies of the illustrated booklet 'The Threat to Upper Teesdale', the main national amenity societies and leisure organizations came to realize that they might have interests at stake and aligned themselves with the scientific objectors. They included the Council for the Preservation of Rural England, the Commons Open Spaces and Footpaths Preservation Society, the Countrywide Holidays Association, the Cyclists' Touring Club, the Holiday Fellowship, the Ramblers' Association, and the Youth Hostels Association. As the opposition gathered momentum even government institutions took the side of the protestors; the Nature Conservancy announced its support for the designation of the area under dispute as a nature reserve and made clear its fears that the reservoir would have severe repercussions for the rare plant assemblages, and its successor, the Natural Environment Research Council, was to adopt a similar stance. Furthermore, the National Parks Commission advanced the case for designating Upper Teesdale as a national park and lent its support to the protestors. As priorities were clarified, the powerful Department of Education and Science, with its responsibilities for scientific research, found itself at odds with the Ministry of Housing and Local Government and the Ministry of Land and Natural Resources, which favoured the reservoir.

Through the use of effective pressure group strategies involving the exploitation of the news media, professional and personal contacts, lobbying and the distribution of publicity material, within the space of little more than a year opposition to the Cow Green reservoir had expanded from a small nucleus of private individuals to embrace an impressive confederation of prestigious organizations which even included a major government department and several lesser official institutions. Opposition was undoubtedly favoured by the multifarious nature of environmental interests, and by the overlapping of membership of environmental organizations, particularly between scientific, conservational and recreational organizations. As Gregory points out:

> There are certain interests that go naturally together; individuals who are members of one society are likely to belong to other organizations concerned with similar and related activities. Through these multiple and interlocking memberships and affiliations, a small but dedicated group of energetic people may be able to activate centres of opposition across a whole range of institutions.[16]

In the event, the opposition campaign failed, for on 22 March 1967, following more than two years of fervent campaigning, the Tees Valley and Cleveland Water Bill received the Royal Assent. It had been thoroughly debated in both Houses of Parliament, and while both the conservation and industrial points of view were well represented, it appears that Members of both Houses, having been exposed to the considerable evidence amassed by each contestant, and unrestricted by the operation of party whips (members ensuring that representatives vote with the party) or greatly affected by the weight of powerful vested interests involved, assessed the evidence according to its relationship to their individual value systems and perceptions of priorities.

Although the case is well recorded, a variety of explanations for the failure of the principle group case is possible. In terms of the Kasperson model, it might be decided that the perceived stresses and experienced strains resulting from the ecological loss and associated pressure group action were less than those associated with the damage that the rejection of the reservoir Bill and consequent loss of employment and export production on Teesside, or the tripling of costs and loss of valuable agricultural land at the alternative Middleton site, would impose.

Alternatively, or additionally, it can be argued that the forces arrayed against the conservationists and their sympathizers were superior. The supporters of the Cow Green scheme included two major government departments, a large nationalized industry and the Water Resources Board. Significantly, the local elected councils, the local landowners and tenants did not join the protestors and efforts to enlist general public opinion in the north-east largely failed. Moreover, the North-East Development Council, the

Northumbrian River Authority and the local branches of the National Farmers' Union (an extremely influential interest group) were all in favour of the reservoir.

Both the Kasperson and the 'balance of forces' approaches heavily involve the important concept of power, with decisional outcomes being considerably dependent on the power in the form of stress or the outweighing of opposition which is brought to bear on or experienced by the decision-makers (a topic which is more fully explored in the chapter on decision-making). The analytical approach employed by Gregory depends more on detailed empirical observation than on concepts, and he does not offer any general thesis concerning the outcome of the Cow Green episode, though he mentions a host of factors which may have been influential at particular stages in the complicated passage of the issue through the political system. As examples, university professors such as those called as witnesses by the conservationists find difficulty in adjusting their style of presentation to a situation in which their authority might be questioned by expert counsel, while the production by the reservoir lobby of an academic botanist prepared to deflate the conservation case before the Select Committee of the House of Lords at a crucial stage in the decisional process may have been decisive. The advantage of the detailed empirical approach as exemplified by Gregory's work is that it emphasizes the intricacies of the political process which the theorist might overlook, indicates how many different interests may be involved in a dispute, allows for factors such as personality, circumstance and fortuitous accident, and reveals the legal, institutional and procedural complexities of real world political systems. For example, the fact that the Cow Green reservoir issue was resolved through the processes of a Private Bill was the result of interaction between modern and nineteenth-century legislation; the need for a speedy decision argued against using the procedures of a public inquiry, and the fact that common land was involved ruled out the normal procedures of compulsory purchase. Merely in order to understand the choice of routeway through the political system requires the researcher to obtain familiarity with the Acts of 1876, 1899, 1945, 1946 and 1948.

Again, the case could be interpreted in terms of one of the political decision-making models of society. The fact that the production interest was upheld could be interpreted as further confirmation for their views by Marxist adherents of the ruling-class model, though on the other hand it could be said that the labour interest emerged supreme because politicians were more concerned about the loss of employment that shortage of industrial water supplies could cause than they were about the loss of some plant communities. Equally, supporters of the pluralist model of society could point to the number of influential groups involved and the relative narrowness of the defeat of the conservation coalition (by 112 votes to 82 in the House of Commons) as endorsement for their outlooks. The ultimate decision was made after thorough consideration of the evidence by the elected decision-makers and according to the proper constitutional procedures, and although the coalition of principle groups exerted considerable pressure at least M.P.s were unrestricted by party ties.

In fact, under the circumstances it would have been as impossible to reach an optimal decision as it is for us to evaluate the quality of the decision made, largely because of the limited effectiveness of cost/benefit analysis. For example, it could be calculated that the Cow Green reservoir would destroy $0·1 \times 10^6 \text{m}^2$ of the vegetation, while associated constructional work might damage a further $0·4 \times 10^6 \text{m}^2$ of valuable land; the alternative Middleton reservoir proposal would not affect important plant communities but would inundate $4·1 \times 10^6 \text{m}^2$ of farmland, affect 39 holdings which supported 2,050 head of livestock and 2,500 head of poultry, be more than twice as costly, and take much longer to complete. A third alternative, suggested as a compromise by the conservation lobby was the Upper Cow Green site, three times as expensive as Cow Green in terms of construction costs. Drought arising before the completion dates for the Middleton and Upper Cow Green sites, which would take an estimated two to three years longer than the Cow Green site to complete, might involve costs of £8·5 million to £35 million in lost production, of which up to 25 per cent would be lost export output. Obviously, the scientific and amenity value of the lost plant communities could not be calculated, and neither could the possibility of drought during the additional constructional period for the Middleton or Upper Cow Green sites be accurately foreseen. Consequently the decision was based upon subjective evaluations, with the majority of Members in both Houses of Parliament apparently deciding that potential losses of industrial output and employment could be less easily borne than definite losses of valuable plant communities. In the words of Allison, '"Experts" are asked to make choices, on society's behalf, between beauty, peace and quiet on the one hand and economic efficiency on the other. Incomparable goods perhaps, but in administering a country decisions must be made and to rationalize such decisions, comparisons must be made'.[17]

Interest Group Activity

Interest group activity associated with the environment concerns numerous dispersed localized conflicts. Although alliances with principle groups may be forged in situations where the facet of the environment at risk is considered to have a national conservational or scientific value, interest groups are motivated by the privately oriented wants of their membership. Therefore, while many local amenity groups exist on a permanent or semi-permanent basis, numerous interest groups such as residents' associations are born out of a specific challenge to their amenity, and exist only so long as there is a prospect of conflict being resolved in their favour; their association with place and issue is consequently much more specific than is the case with principle groups. Conflicts involving principle groups tend to produce clashes between interest and principle, those involving interest groups, clashes between interest and interest.

The number of cases for potential study is vast, but that of the conflict concerning the Glyn Glas opencast coal mining site near Blaenau in Dyfed reveals many characteristic features.[18] The conflict was initiated by an application by the Opencast Executive of the Coal Board for authorization to undertake mining at the Glyn Glas Extension, south site. Although excavations had taken place previously without controversy, in this case objections were raised by local authorities, interests and residents, and the conflict culminated in the ministerial reversal of a public inquiry finding against the application.

In cases such as this, analysis can involve a chronological survey of the main events; an identification of the actors in the conflict, their goals and the tactics and strategies employed in the pursuit of these goals, and an analysis of the outcome, which should clarify the contribution of power, principle, personality and the decisional structure and contexts to the resolution of the conflict. Space does not permit us to present a coverage of the historical development of the conflict, which involved considerable activity by a number of actors between the application in October 1972 and the ministerial allocation in July 1976. The actors, goals and tactics involved in the Glyn Glas dispute can be displayed as follows:

Actor	Goal(s)	Tactics
Actors in Support of the Application		
National Coal Board	Economical production of coal, taking advantage of sites such as Glyn Glas.	Exploiting the powers of a major nationalized industry to influence the appropriate governmental decision-makers. Bargaining with local residents, e.g. the offer of an alternative ground to the rugby club; the proposal to institute a liaison committee between the Board, contractors and residents. The employment of landscape architects and the production of their evidence to the Public Inquiry.
Transport and General Workers' Union	Reduction of unemployment in the Blaenau area. Support for developments such as Glyn Glas which would create constructional employment.	Counter-petitioning. Presentation of evidence to the Public Inquiry.
County Planning Committee of Dyfed C.C.	To support the application because the development would result in the construction of improved communications.	Statement of support. Influence upon councillors.
Actors Opposed to the Application		
Blaenau and District Community Action Group	To protect the amenity enjoyed by the membership. To resist further opencast mining development in the vicinity of the villages of Blaenau, Cae'r Bryn and Llandybie.	The stimulation, organization and articulation of local opposition. Petitioning; arousal of media interest; demonstration at the Public Inquiry; presentation of evidence to the Inquiry.
Blaenau and District Local Welfare Association	Goals were similar to those of the Community Action Group, but specific interest concerned with Association land threatened by mining.	Support for the activities of the Community Action Group.
Farmers' Union of Wales	To resist the loss of agricultural land owned by members to mining.	Statement of opposition.
Dyfed County Council; Llandeilo RDC; Llandybie Parish Council	Llandeilo RDC and Blaenau Parish Council were influenced (a) by the amenity implications of the	Public statements of opposition.

Actor	Goal(s)	Tactics
	Actors Opposed to the Application	
	scheme; (b) by the considerable strength of local opposition, and (c) by doubts that the Coal Board could offer many more inducements to offset the negative externalities of further mining. The County Council stance reflected the advice of the lower-order authorities and the views of individual councillors, one a member of the Action Group.	
	Unaligned Actor	
South West Wales River Authority	To enforce strict regulations concerning water purity. To protect spawning grounds on the River Lash. To satisfy the demands of the industrial users of water.	Stipulation of points to be observed in the event of a successful application.

Some points of general interest emerge from the dispute. First, the readiness of the NCE to engage in conciliation and bargaining with the interest groups at an early stage in the conflict. The effectiveness of pressure group activity in recent years is testified by the adoption of bargaining strategies by powerful interests when confronted by organized local protest. In the case of the Cow Green reservoir mentioned above, ICI made an offer of a grant of £100,000 for intensive research prior to the inundation of the Cow Green site, and even before the resources of the opposition pressure groups had been thoroughly mobilized. In the case of the Cottage Hall mining site near Glyn Glas, the NCB provided a new church to replace an original one affected by mining operations. Secondly, there is evidence of how interest groups with conflicting goals can partially cancel out each other's effectiveness.

The Action Group's petition was met with a counter-petition organized by the TGWU, while demonstrations at the Inquiry against mining were met with counter-demonstrations. The behaviour of the local authorities is also interesting, first because they found themselves opposed to the 'establishment' interest as represented by the NCB, and secondly because of their opposition to the planning committee of the County Council. Though opposed to the NCB application, the councillors appear to have allowed the initiative for the mobilization of opposition to remain with the Action Group, which may be seen as testimony to a pluralistic society.

The outcome is less amenable to analysis because while the public debate culminated in a recommendation by the Inspector against further mining, the decision was reversed by the Secretary of State for Energy. Such decisions, quite frequently made in relation to environmental conflicts, have considerably undermined public and pressure group confidence in the adjudicatory apparatus of government. One can only conclude that the Minister was party to information, or subject to pressures not witnessed at the Public Inquiry, and/or that he considered the national need for anthracite to outweigh the conflicting needs of Blaenau residents.

Interest groups associated with the community action movement are of a variety of kinds, and include tenants' associations, medical service users' associations, ethnic associations, ratepayers' associations and others. Those connected with environmental and planning concerns fall under the broad heading of local amenity groups, and a sample of half of the 1,250 such groups registered with the Civic Trust was surveyed by that organization.[19] While the size of the membership may be constrained by the size of the environmental unit concerned (as with village amenity societies), the survey revealed that 45 per cent of societies have memberships of between 100 and 299 individuals, and only 6 per cent have more than 900 members. The information on the class structure of memberships may not be entirely reliable, being based on the perceptions of questionnaire respondents, but it is nevertheless significant that 87 per cent of respondents agreed that 'most of our members are white collar or professional managerial people and their spouses', and four-fifths of the respondents considered that less than a third of their membership consisted of members of manual occupational groups. The middle-class domination of rural and Greater London societies appeared to exist to a lesser degree than in the provincial city societies. However, the nature of the sample frame was such that many of the smaller urban neighbourhood action groups with very high levels of working-class membership will have been excluded from the sample since such groups are unlikely to register with the Civic Trust. Two-thirds of the respondents agreed with the statement that 'our members generally tend to live in neighbourhoods with the best standards of layout and amenity'. On the whole it can be assumed that environmental interest groups have a disproportionately middle-class membership, and that within each society the active leadership is again disproportionately representative of the middle classes, a phenomenon which is easily explained by reference to middle-class values relating to property and amenity, and aquired professional techniques of organization and influence. With the latter point in mind, 43 per cent of respondents reported having 'relevant' professions such as planning, law and architecture strongly represented within their memberships. This figure rose to 70 per cent amongst the Greater London societies but declined to around one-third in the case of rural English and Welsh societies.

Six out of ten of the societies sampled came into existence in response to a particular issue, the most common being opposition to a major planned development, the motive to oppose proposals being much more frequent than the intent to initiate conservation policies. Thus the protection of the amenity enjoyed by the membership emerges as a more potent formative influence than the enhancement of existing amenity, and only 7 per cent of respondents listed practical voluntary service such as restoration or tree planting as being the main aim of their society.

In the pursuit of amenity goals, the picture that emerges involves the use of formal rather than informal techniques and a preference for bargaining rather than confrontation. Therefore the model of the interest group as being effective through its ability to impose sanctions and stress upon public officials is not supported by the evidence of the sampled amenity groups. Indeed, during the period 1972–4, society members more often appeared at local public inquiries to support the positions of their local authorities than to oppose them. No less than 85 per cent of respondents considered that the local planning officers were sympathetic to their societies views and values, though only half of the respondents regarded traffic and engineering officials as sympathetic.

If we are to form a stereotype of the typical British amenity society based upon the copious information compiled by the Civic Trust (bearing in mind the regional and urban/rural variation in the data, the imperfections of the sample base and the fact that responses came from the leadership rather than the general membership of the groups), an image emerges of a society composed of a largely middle-class membership, which is concerned to protect enjoyed environmental amenity and which operates through formal processes of letter-writing and arranged meetings with an official-dom that is generally sympathetic if not always wholly responsive to the views and objectives of the society.

The Institutional Response

The institutional response consists of the actions taken by those institutions with statutory responsibilities in the fields of environmental policy and management, in order to anticipate or reduce the stresses imposed by environmental problems and to reduce or eliminate the stresses resulting from public and pressure group activity that such problems may create. Decisions are made at a variety of levels, ranging from international agreements and government policy to local officials with responsibility for some aspect of environmental management. On the broad scale, at the government level, policy generally consists of attempts to reinternalize the externalities caused by environmental disruption and the formulation of general planning and conservation policies providing mechanisms for influencing the nature and form of land-use.

The reinternalization of externalities involves placing the cost and responsibility for unpolluted soil, water and air upon the creators of negative externalities. Ultimately these costs will be borne by the consumer in the form of higher prices for the industrial or agricultural products whose uncontrolled production would produce the negative spillovers, the alternative to this being to impose the costs for pollution control upon the taxpayer and so subsidize the controls from public funds. As Kennet points out,

> any decision which increases the internal costs of private industry in one place without equally increasing them in all places distorts the framework of competition in general, and reduces the short-term efficiency of enterprises in the places concerned, thus risking local unemployment . . . The politician has therefore to seek to relate the rate at which he transfers costs away from the public and on to the enterprises in question to the rate at which they are being transferred on to other, comparable competitive enterprises.[20]

Thus in a sense, the politicians responsible must seek some equilibrium between the stresses imposed by the negative externalities of the production process and the potential stresses imposed by reduced production and unemployment. The nature of the international system, however, is such as to impose severe economic sanctions upon economies subject to effective environmental controls because within a sovereign state system there can be no supranational agency with the power to formulate standards and synchronize the imposition of universal controls. Consequently the state which adopts a far-reaching and responsible policy of pollution control will be penalized in international competition as its additional costs of production are passed on to the international consumer and export earnings will fall.

The second thrust of state environmental policy concerns the formation of planning and conservational regulations which intervene against natural economic processes. If land-use competition is unregulated then the uses to which land is put will be determined by the intentions of the highest bidders in the land market. To varying degrees governments attempt to regulate land-use through the creation of planning controls, the designation of areas for conservational or recreational use and the subsidization of certain forms of agriculture. Since conservation is seldom an economically competitive form of land-use, 'conservationists must look to their defences within the planning system'.[21]

The fundamental problem of government policy formation in relation to the environment is therefore one of determining the optimal level of state regulation of production and land-use. Unfortunately, this optimal level is usually impossible to determine, first because of the inability of cost/benefit analysis to ascribe quantitative relative values to the incomparable goods of economic efficiency and environmental quality, and secondly because the 'public will' can seldom be ascertained with any clarity and generally consists of a complex of vague and conflicting values. Thus, 'without some committed public consensus as to what constitutes a desirable environment it is impossible to develop the necessary guidelines against which to weigh incoming proposals for the use of air, land, and water, and within which to evaluate future strategy . . .'[22]

The nature of the environmental policy adopted in any state will obviously be influenced greatly both by the environments involved and by the nature of the political system. Under a mixed economy one may expect to find a somewhat piecemeal process of government intervention to regulate the excesses of environmental degradation by production interests, while under a state-planned economy one might anticipate a more comprehensive integration of productive, amenity and conservation interests; in either case the characteristics of the environments concerned would dictate the type of environmental problem encountered. As an example, the Soviet Union has a state-planned economy and a system of government organized on the basis of rigid ministerial hierarchies. The superimposition of this decision-making structure upon the flood plain environments of European Russia has produced specific problems even though the possession of a state-planned economy provides the potential ability to reconcile productive and environmental interests and the adoption of comprehensive conservation policies. Generally in the Soviet Union, the ecological interest is subordinated to the higher state aim of expanding production to achieve economic superiority over the USA, while the vertical ministerial hierarchies obstruct the development of horizontal interministerial linkages necessary for the co-ordination of development policies at local and regional levels. Consequently, in the environment mentioned above the construction of barrages, primarily for the generation of hydro-electricity, have resulted in the inundation of vast areas of agricultural land and have produced conflicts between the sectional interests of the ministries of power and of agriculture.[23]

Under a federal system of government, responsibility for environmental policy is likely to be divided between the federal and state levels of government, and difficulties may arise in the allocation of spheres of competence. This was the case with the Federal Water Pollution Control Act Amendments of 1972, described by Lieber.[24] In this instance, stress on the Nixon administration came from three main sources: from the environment, where stronger anti-pollution controls were necessary; from public demands for radical approaches to a range of environmental problems, among which that of water pollution was prominent, and from the need to be seen to act in accordance with the President's often expressed intent to devolve power from the federal to the state level of government.

In the event, the institutional response favoured the two former challenges, at the expense of the latter. The legislative processes were complex, but Lieber attributes the victory of the federal over the state level in obtaining responsibilities for pollution control under the amendments to a number of factors: the states' lack of a recognizable and influential lobbying organization to represent their case, coupled with the divergence of objectives between and within the state administrations; the poorly developed communication channels between state environmental managers and state politicians; the wooing of governors and local officials with promises of generous federal construction grants, and the loss of credibility concerning the ability of states to take effective action in the light of the past experience of state environmental management.

The legislative process revealed the inflexibility of the federal response. and demonstrated

the difficulty and, in many cases, the inappropriateness of applying one single national act, no matter how detailed, to fifty different states. For example, as a result of the Act's uniform requirements, Wyoming will be forced to needlessly install (*sic*) sophisticated monitoring devices and Texas, which already has a well-developed planning program, will have to unnecessarily reshuffle (*sic*) this function.[25]

A well-documented illustration of the institutional response of the UK government to an environmental disaster concerns the case of the Torrey Canyon, which grounded on the Seven Stones reef between the Isles of Scilly and Land's End in March 1967, shedding its cargo of 117,000 tons of crude oil into the sea, and subsequently onto 100 miles of the British coast. The ill-preparedness of government became swiftly apparent and the institutional machinery to handle such a disaster had not been developed. Although the seriousness of the incident was never in doubt, four days elapsed before a committee to advise on technical and scientific aspects was convened under the government's chief scientific advisor, Sir Solly Zuckerman, the committee being retained following the belated decision to destroy the remaining cargo by bombing. The question of formulating measures for application in cases of oil pollution was passed to a committee of back-bench M.P.s, the Select Committee on Science and Technology, which was 'quite ill-prepared, understaffed and lacking adequate resources for the particular task'.[26] The SCST formed a sub-committee on coastal pollution and called on Zuckerman's committee, which had reported the need for administrative reforms and for research into a number of aspects of coastal pollution, to present evidence regarding progress made on these proposals. The SCST then expressed its grave concern and proposed the delegation of responsibility for supervision and co-ordination on environmental matters to a senior minister, and the integration of research. It was not until sixteen months after the disaster that the SCST report appeared, and although the majority of its proposals were accepted by the government, the crucial one for a co-ordinating minister was not.

In the meantime public opinion, aroused by the Torrey Canyon incident, had been further excited by subsequent smaller oil spillages and the parliamentary opposition had recognized the political potential of the pollution issue. An opposition censure motion was launched with Sir Harry Legge-Bourke, chairman of the SCST, opening the debate for the opposition. As a result of this pressure and further urging from Zuckerman's Advisory Council for Science and Technology (whose report of July 1969 had advised further co-ordination of departments concerned with environmental matters), changes in the structure of the relevant government departments were announced in October 1969, more than 30 months after the Torrey Canyon disaster. In December that year a permanent Central Scientific Unit on Pollution was established within the office of the Secretary of State for Local Government and Planning and a standing Royal Commission on Environmental Pollution was established. Then, under a Conservative government, a Department of the Environment was created in 1970, assuming the role for the ministerial co-ordination of environmental pollution problems.

A purposeful institutional response to problems of environmental disruption involves the creation of suitable institutional structures to permit prompt and effective reactions, coupled with action by the responsible agencies. In some cases administrative reform may be introduced as a palliative to public disquiet, but without the resolve to use the reformed structures as a mechanism for a forceful attack on the central problem. In the case reviewed, it is clear that there was considerable reluctance on the part of government to undertake even the necessary structural reforms. This was due partly to governmental inertia. and partly to the opposition of vested interests within the Ministries of Housing, Transport and Works, all of which had responsibilities in the field of environmental policy. The administrative aspect of the pollution problem concerned this dispersion of responsibility and the absence of an authoritative minister with co-ordinating responsibility. Only sustained public discontent, the forceful representations of scientific advisors, pressure from the SCST, and probably most significantly, the exploitation of the political potential of the environmental issue by the Opposition, resulted in the creation of appropriate governmental structures, if not the guarantee of effective, future action. Eleven years after the Torrey Canyon incident, in 1978, the oil tanker Amoco Cadiz began to break-up off the Brittany coast, and a similar pattern of public outrage, governmental confusion and scientific uncertainty and ill-preparedness was replicated, the event coinciding with a national election in France. The effect of the event upon voting patterns was probably slight since confusion concerning the allocation of responsibility was as widespread outside government as within, and public demonstrations at naval installations were more an expression of frustration than an allocation of guilt.

The day-to-day operation of environmental policy is largely the responsibility of environmental managers. Few if any of these officials are endowed with such independence of spirit or freedom of action as to be able to formulate decisions without considering pressures other than those issuing from the physical environment, while their spheres of responsibility are seldom defined with a clarity that will reduce the decision to the level of an automatic and optimizing response. They operate in an environment which is political, economic and social as well as physical, and the absence of a general consensus concerning the priorities of environmental policy makes them susceptible to pressure and often inclined towards satisficing allocations. Although the manager might prefer to be regarded as a professional technical expert, guided only by rationality and scientific principles, the natural resources with which he works are as much matters for public concern as resources such as transport, hospitals and weapons, and are equally subjects for political debate. As in other fields of decision-making, the range of alternatives reviewed will be largely determined by information received, and according to White, the presentation of information will be influenced by 'social guides' of two kinds.[27] First, there are the guides represented by legislation and directives concerning specific standards and policies, which may or may not be ambiguous or conflicting, but have greater clarity than the second class of guides which consists of partisan statements by pressure groups, officials, politicians and individuals. Upon this information, the environmental manager will bring to bear his professional expertise, his individual attitudes, and also his perception of 'the degree of threat presented by the problems in relation to other stresses in the community'.[28] Also, as an employee, he will be prudent to ensure the compatibility of his decisions with the policies, priorities and traditions of the agency for which he works, a process which Kaufman termed 'the internalization of agency values and policies'.[29] The specialist agency employee will be subordinate to administrators, and

> with job security in mind, specialists hesitate to make recommendations which might offend their superiors. For example Rocky Mountain National Park Rangers, from a period 1931 to 1944 hesitated to recommend direct reduction or the shooting of overpopulations of elk and deer although the problem was recognized in almost every report.[30]

Clearly then, political pressures are involved both in the manner of the presentation of information, which may be distorted by interested parties, and in the anticipation of reactions to the various alternative actions reviewed. A model of municipal stress management developed by O'Riordan from work by Kasperson and MacIver symbolizes the role played by political pressure in the arena of environmental decision-making.

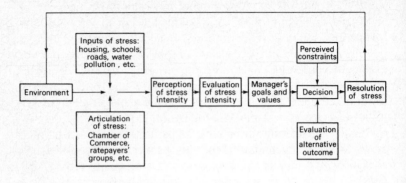

Fig. 5.1. Municipal stress management model.
Source: T. O'Riordan, *Perspectives on Resource Management*, Pion, London, 1971, p. 116.

Even the best professional advice may prove unacceptable to the political policy-maker. Kasperson has described the case of a water shortage crisis occurring in the early 1960s in the city of Brockton, Mass.[31] Though warned by consultants of an impending water supply crisis, the city officials failed to take timely action. This was attributed to two causes: first, an inability of the elected officials to comprehend the specialist advice they had received, and secondly, the political nature of the office of Mayor; the incumbent faced a re-election campaign and was anxious to project a reassuring image of a stable and smoothly-running administration to the electorate. This led to the relaxation rather than the intensification of the town's water conservation policy. The combination of these factors led officials to encourage public faith in mythical alternative water sources from rock wells and bogs.

The pervasiveness of conflicts of interest and the lack of agreed priorities in the field of environmental policy make the environmental manager vulnerable to pressures, and to quote again from O'Riordan,

The traditional, seemingly reliable, 'quick fix' technological solutions of the past are increasingly being called into question by a broadening base of sincere public opinion, both informed and uninformed . . . political and technical judgements are not infrequently based on flimsy assumptions as to what the public wants and should get. It is no wonder that in situations where aims are vague and ambiguous political expendiency and economic opportunism is (*sic*) rife.[32]

Land-use Conflict

The goal of the environmental manager concerns the reduction of stress and the resolution of conflict. While the sociologist may interpret environmental conflict in terms of contrasting value systems, to the geographer these stresses and conflicts exist in part because space is a finite resource and because of the friction imposed upon human mobility by distance; one can neither light-heartedly escape the pollution caused by a neighbouring enterprise by moving house, nor indulge a love of rambling in a landscape populated by arable farmers. We have already suggested that environmental conflicts are the products of external diseconomies and land-use competition, and attention in this section is focused upon the latter group of causes.

Outside the most centralized of the state planned economies one does not widely encounter the direct determination of land-use by government, though the *laissez faire* system of land development will usually be considerably modified by interventions such as agricultural subsidies and environmental planning legislation and policy. However the apparent lowness of the governmental profile does not reflect an absence of conflict or of intense competition for the control of land but, at least in the democracies, a general communal will concerning the extent to which government should affect the property-owning rights of the individual.

Only rarely can the human utilization of a landscape be interpreted by reference to a specific act of policy. Thus, within a three-mile radius of the strangely-named village of Blubberhouses, on the western flanks of the Pennines between the dales of the Rivers Nidd and Wharfe, one may find the following land-uses represented: upland sheep grazing, grouse moors, forestry, US army and Royal Navy bases, reservoirs, and recreation. These forms of land-use do not exist because they constitute part of an overall plan for the area, because they are complementary, or even because they are all necessarily well adjusted to their particular environmental locations. Rather, the landscape mirrors a piecemeal and gradual accumulation of items of private and public decision-making, decisions taken not solely in relation to the environment of a Dales watershed, but in relation to a range of environments contrasted in their character, scale and temporal location. These include the local physical and national economic environment of the farmer; the social environment of the grouse-shooting host; the post-war European strategical environment of the military, and the West Yorkshire urban industrial environment of the reservoir authority. Wherever land exists, interests compete for its utilization; sometimes adjacent or superimposed uses are complementary, as may be the case with forestry and water storage or recreation and conservation, but frequently they are apparently incompatible, as with military training and conservation or recreation and grouse shooting.

The effects of political institutions in regulating and conditioning land-use involve the effects of specific environmental policy, including the designation of recreational areas and the accretion of a corpus of environmental planning legislation, the indirect effects of policy concerning the rights of property owners, the stimulation of favoured forms of agricultural production, the construction and expansion of towns and the establishment of industry. Finally, there are the effects which stem from the activities of public officials acting as arbiters in the resolution of conflict and reduction of environmental stress.

Many land-use conflicts can be resolved through the application of a multiple-use concept: for example the UK Forestry Commission has become increasingly sensitive to public demands for access to the countryside, and in addition to various efforts to landscape its plantations, a series of controlled nature trails have been introduced into some plantations, permitting a tolerable symbiosis between foresty and recreational uses. The introduction of a multiple-use policy will depend upon the environmental resources concerned and the attitudes of the appropriate decision-makers, though the concept itself is poorly defined, and Henning has noted the confusion concerning whether multiple use involves allowing other uses to the extent that they do not interfere with the 'best' use, or whether it involves introducing as many uses as possible into an area.[33] He also points out that agencies may tend to favour certain uses which are central to their interests to the disadvantage of alternative uses; examples quoted include the US Forest Service's predisposition towards the lumber industry and the US Bureau of Reclamation's favouring of irrigation and power.

The primary US legislation in relation to forestry states that

'multiple-use' means: the management of all the various renewable surface resources of the national forests so that they are utilized in the combination that will best meet the needs of the American people . . . with consideration being given to the relative values of the various resources, and not necessarily the combination of uses that will give the greatest dollar return or the greatest unit output.[34]

The interpretation of the legislation is a matter for the US Forest Service, and both Henning and Reich[35] have suggested that the Service unduly favours certain users. Hall considered that the concept as applied by the Service encouraged bureaucracy and would not resolve conflicts concerning incompatible uses, and he recommended the development of decision-making based upon a more sophisticated cost/benefit analysis.[36] Martin, however considered that the multiple-use concept as applied by the Service could resolve conflict, and both integrate and decentralize authority within the Service as a result of discussion and debate between field and administrative officers over the acceptability of proposed uses.[37]

Whichever view prevails, at least in the case of US state forests there exists an organization with the capacity and responsibility for making informed allocations. In cases of land-use conflict where such an institution is less immediately available, the process of conflict resolution may be tortuous and inefficient. Such a situation was evident from Kasperson's study of the Brockton water supply crisis, mentioned above. In 1952, acting on the advice of water consultants, the Brockton civic authorities formulated legislation to augment its water supplies by tapping streams and ponds a few miles to the south-east of the town, in the Silver Lakes area. The Bill was killed in committee as a result of determined opposition from the settlements adjacent to the proposed catchment, summer residents and the local cranberry industry. The threat posed by rapidly rising levels of water consumption was masked to Brockton residents by a period of abnormally high precipitation but the consultants alerted the Brockton officials to the impending crisis in 1957, and urged the reintroduction of the 1952 Bill. The public hearings in Boston were overwhelmed by 1,800 protestors and the Bill was withdrawn. In 1962, with Brockton's reservoir drained to half its capacity and with water consumption continuing to rise at a rapid rate, the consultants warned that the situation had reached crisis dimensions. A modified Bill was submitted to the state legislature in 1963, guaranteed to protect the recreational potential and the cranberry industry in the proposed source area. Again the opposition staged powerful demonstrations at the hearings on the Bill, though the situation was saved for Brockton with the intervention of the House Committee on Water Supply and Water Resources in support of the formation of a special legislative commission to study the problem, and the subsequent call for a State Water Resources Commission investigation into the water supply situation in south-eastern Massachusetts by the state governor. The special commission, composed of a cross-section of interested parties, swiftly recognized the need for the water Bill and a concession by Brockton to construct a filtration plant to ensure that recreational use was included. The Bill became effective in 1964.

The case reveals the inefficiency which may ensue from the absence of the appropriate decisional mechanisms for the resolution of environmental conflict. Kasperson points out that the ultimate investigation led to the recognition that society was not prepared to let a town go dry. This was always the case, but twelve years elapsed between the drafting of the orginal Bill and the resolution of the conflict. The explanation of this delay concerns conditions in the political rather than in the physical environment, the opponents of the Bill being much more effectively organized and committed than were its proponents. It also concerns the failure to develop an information system (see Fig. 5.2) which would allow for the formulation of balanced overall views of the situation by the parties involved. The Brockton officials failed to comprehend or act consistently on specialist advice, the protestors misconstrued the contents of the proposed legislation and the ownership of the resources in question, while, partly as a result of the vacillation of their officials, the Brockton residents were misinformed and inadequately motivated. When an efficient information system was belatedly created in the form of the special commission, the problem was swiftly comprehended and resolved.

In cases of environmental conflict where the machinery for conflict resolution neither exists nor is developed, the problem will either continue unabated or produce its own outcome. An interesting example concerns the recreational conflict between anglers and boat users which has been investigated by Owens.[38] The setting is the wetlands recreational environment of the Norfolk Broads, which accommodates tens of thousands of anglers, along with 7,800 private craft and 4,100 hire craft. The conflict concerns the partial incompatibility of the two forms of recreation and exists largely in a psycho-social rather than a physical form; it probably arises from cumulative rather than transient experience, which has the effect of reducing the quality of recreational experience enjoyed by the angler or the boat user. This occurs for example when an angler is repeatedly obliged to reel in his fishing tackle to allow a boat to pass,

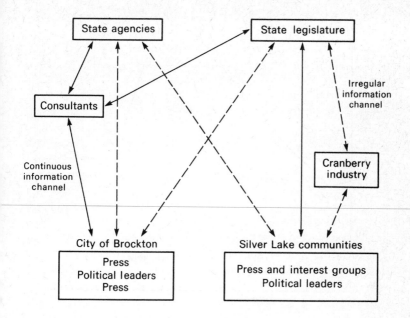

Fig. 5.2. Information system in the Brockton water supply dispute.

Source: Kasperson, 'Political Behaviour and the Decision-making Process', *Natn. Resources J.* (1969), **9**, 176–211.

or when a boat user is frequently obliged to dislodge an angler from intended moorings.

In the absence of a mediating mechanism, such conflicts may develop *laissez faire* solutions. The increase in the number of private craft using the Broads in recent years has been paralleled by a decline in the number of rod licences issued; of the anglers interviewed by Owens, 72·8 per cent believed that their chances of catching fish had decreased compared with five years previously, and 76·2 per cent of those making this claim attributed the blame to some aspect of boat use, involving the disturbance of fish or damage to fisheries.

Owens argues that rather than allowing the *laissez faire* solution to develop, a managerial authority should be created, with powers to oversee and integrate all forms of recreation. The problem is made difficult by the statutory rights of boat users to navigate on the rivers concerned, and the most forceful response from the River Commissioners came in the form of a request that boat users should voluntarily avoid a stretch which amounted to 7 per cent of the total

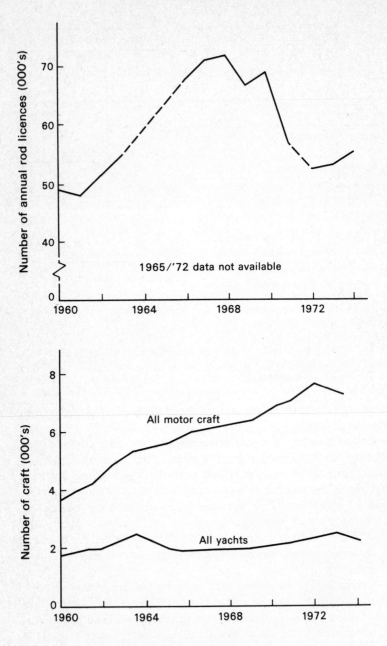

Fig. 5.3. Recreational conflict in Broadland, Norfolk.

Source: P. L. Owens, 'A Managerial Issue', in M. J. Moseley (ed), *Social Issues in Rural Norfolk*, CEAS, Norwich, 1978, p. 2.

water mileage during daytime on Sundays during the angling season.

It is evident that land-use conflicts come in many shapes and forms, and as well as the particular uses and environments concerned, the nature of conflict resolution depends upon the presence, creation or absence of appropriate mediating mechanisms, the distribution of power and the relationship between policy legislation and property rights, the concepts and outlooks currently in favour (such as 'multiple-use'), and the attitudes of those with responsibilities in the environmental field.

Discussion points and further reading

In the course of recent years, 'the environment', its quality, exploitation and abuses have emerged as important public issues. The general theme of the politics of the environment, while vital in itself, also provides a useful framework for the introduction of other important behavioural themes in political geography. These include the formation and impact of public opinion on decision-making, the behavioural aspects of pressure group activity and the ways in which institutions may react and respond to pressures originating in both the political and physical environments. It is likely that these responses are conditioned as much by the nature of the existing political system as by the characteristics of the problems which are faced.

One of the very few political geographers to study the decisional processes which condition the nature of the politics of the environment is R. E. Kasperson, and his chapter in *The Structure of Political Geography* (1969) is strongly recommended. The various publications on the subject by T. O'Riordan also demonstrate the relevance of the behavioural approach, while a more descriptive but very thorough series of British case studies is provided in Gregory (1977).

Gregory, R., *The Price of Amenity*, Macmillan, London, 1977.

Kasperson, R. E., 'Environmental Stress, and the Municipal Political System', in Kasperson, R. E., and Minghi, J. V., *The Structure of Political Geography*, The University of London Press, 1969, pp. 481–96.

O'Riordan, T., *Perspectives on Resource Management*, Pion, London, 1971.

Smith, P. J.(ed.), *The Politics of Physical Resources*, Penguin, Harmondsworth, 1975.

Notes

1. S. P. Johnson, *The Politics of Environment*, Stacey, London, 1973, p. 1.
2. W. Kennet, 'The Politics of Conservation', in A. Warren and F. B.

Goldsmith (eds.), *Conservation In Practice*, Wiley, London, 1974, p. 466.

3. W. Solesbury, 'The Environmental Agenda', *Public Administration* (1976), **54**, 379–97.
4. *Ibid.* p. 380.
5. *Ibid.* p. 381.
6. G. C. Moodie and G. Studdert-Kennedy, *Opinions, Publics and Pressure Groups*, Allen & Unwin, London, 1970, p. 60.
7. F. G. Castles, *Pressure Groups and Political Culture*, Routledge and Kegan Paul, London, 1967, p. 1.
8. L. Allison, *Environmental Planning, A Political and Philosophical Analysis*, Allen & Unwin, London, 1975, pp. 110–12.
9. D. H. Henning, 'The Politics of National Resources Administration', *Annals of Regional Science*, (1968), **2**, 245.
10. The Civic Trust, *The Local Amenity Movement*, London, 1976.
11. M. Eckstein, *Pressure Group Politics: The Case of the British Medical Association*, Allen & Unwin, London, 1960.
12. R. E. Kasperson, 'Environmental Stress and the Municipal Political System', in R. E. Kasperson and J. V. Minghi, *The Structure of Political Geography*, London, 1969.
13. *Ibid.* p. 484.
14. *Ibid.*
15. R. Gregory, *The Price of Amenity*, Macmillan, London, 1971.
16. R. Gregory, in P. J. Smith (ed.), *The Politics of Physical Resources*, Penguin, Harmondsworth, 1975, p. 166.
17. L. Allison, 'Politics, Welfare and Conservation; A Study of Meta-Planning', *British Journal of Political Science* (1971), **1**, 438–9.
18. I am indebted to one of my students, D. Hywel Williams, for detailed background information on this dispute. (R. M.)
19. Civic Trust, *Local Amenity Movement*.
20. Kennet, 'Politics of Conservation', p. 472.
21. *Ibid.* p. 474.
22. T. O'Riordan, *Perspectives on Resource Management*, Pion, London, 1971, p. 112.
23. K. Bush, 'Environmental Problems in the USSR', *Problems of Communism* (July–Aug. 1972), pp. 27–9.
24. H. Lieber, *Federalism and Clean Waters*, Lexington Books, Lexington, Mass., 1975.
25. *Ibid.* p. 191.
26. P. D. Lowe, 'Science and Government: The Case of Pollution', *Public Administration* (1975), p. 288.
27. G. F. White, 'The Choice of Use in Resource Management', *Natural Resources Journal* (1961), **1**, pp. 23–40.
28. O'Riordan, *Resource Management*, p. 115.
29. H. Kaufman, *The Forest Ranger: A Study in Administrative Behaviour*, John Hopkins Press, Baltimore, 1960.
30. Henning, *National Resources Administration*, p. 241.
31. R. E. Kasperson, 'Political Behaviour and the Decision-Making Process in the Allocation of Water Resources Between Recreational and Municipal Use', *Natural Resources Journal* (1969), **9**, 176–211.

32. O'Riordan, *Resource Management*, p. 111.
33. Henning, *National Resources Administration*, p. 244.
34. 74 Stat. 215, 1960.
35. C. A. C. Reich, *Bureaucracy and the Forests*, Center for the Study of Democratic Institutions, Santa Barbara, Calif., 1962.
36. G. H. Hall, 'The Myth and Reality of Multiple-Use Forestry', *Natural Resources Journal* (1963), **3**, 287.
37. P. Martin, 'Conflict Resolution Through the Multiple-Use Concept in Forest Service Decision-Making', *Natural Resources Journal* (1969), **9**, 228–36.
38. P. L. Owens, 'A Managerial Issue: Conflict Between Norfolk Broads Coarse Anglers and Boat Users', in M. J. Moseley (ed.), *Social Issues in Rural Norfolk*, CEAS, Norwich, 1978.

6 Political Processes and Territorial Integration

Political processes, the making of decisions and the allocation of public goods and other values, do not take place within a spatial vacuum but are adapted to, structured within and constrained by space. This is because governments, and the task of governing, are organized into territorial units. Decisions therefore, except those of foreign policy, apply only to those areas lying within the territory controlled by a specific government, whether one serving the whole or only a portion of the national territory. Looking at the outputs of the political system the salience of the territorial organization of government, particularly at the intranational scale, is most obvious from the variations between jurisdictions in the way in which public goods are provided. Territory is important also as an input providing through its partitioning, besides the arena in and sometimes over which conflicts take place, the framework within which the political system operates.

The analysis of the spatial structures within which political processes operate has been a continuing theme amongst political geographers. Most emphasis has been placed on the state and, particularly within early work, to its morphology. Describing such characteristics as the size and shape of political territories, their internal features – their physical and cultural make-up, for example – constitutes the kernel of what Hartshorne termed the morphological approach.[1] Such 'measurements', however, though they help to define the broad characteristics of the political unit, do not relate easily to the task of showing how political processes and space interact.

Functionalist approaches to the analysis of how space is partitioned into political units come closer to this question. In its classic formulation the functional approach argued that the political region should be seen as the complex interaction between a set of ideas, and political institutions and environmental forces. Viewed in this context, the central question for the state was that of countering those forces tending to encourage its disintegration while fostering those which promoted cohesion. In this chapter our main focus of study concerns the mutual interactions between political processes and the jurisdictions in which they take place, particularly that of the state.

The Role of Territory

Space is a basic factor underlying and influencing the operation of political systems. Initially the reason for this importance can be attributed to the use of territory as the prime basis upon which political processes are organized. Although not the only principle by which organization is possible – functional differentiation is another possibility – it is certainly one of the most prominent.

The advantage to governments in using territory as the basis for defining the boundaries of the polity is that they can claim to represent and serve the interests of citizens within a defined area. Although there have been cases, particularly in pre-state societies, of political units being organized along blood or tribal lines – in which, therefore, the spatial definition of the social groups entered as a secondary factor – the overwhelming trend has been towards the primary recognition of territorial divisions. This is especially true in the modern state in which the notions of territory and sovereignty are inextricably linked. Similarly, in regard to that other major form underlying contemporary socio-political organization, the nation, a territorial base is considered essential to its survival.

Within states the only way in which modern governments (to which the role of the production of public goods has become a major activity) can function effectively is by the organization of public goods to be provided territorially through a network of subnational governments. This is not true for all allocations: some will be provided nationally. Nevertheless in most countries a great many services, such as the maintenance of law and order and the provision of educational, social and cultural services, will be met by local or other substate forms of governments operating within what Cox has termed 'legally bounded spaces.'[2]

A third way in which territory is important is in its relations with political conflicts. By their nature political conflicts tend frequently to be fought within territorial arenas. Decisions on the location of a new airport, the closure of a railway, the establishment of fisheries limits are the kinds of commonplace conflict which, if not always directly associated with the control of space, are fought over it. The implication of the latter is that such conflicts will bring governments into competition with one another.

Underpinning the process of partitioning space into political territories is the argument that man, in so organizing his political arrangements, is only fulfilling a basic need, that of territoriality. As it has been developed among studies of animal behaviour, territoriality is the means by which certain animals lay claim to a specific area, which they need for life-support purposes, and which they are willing to defend. We have suggested earlier that amongst humans at least, it is not possible to prove territoriality to be an instinctive pattern of behaviour. From our viewpoint, however, territoriality has two aspects of importance to the political geographer, i.e. (1) space providing for the group and the individual an identity and a medium for action; (2) the space which for the individual and the group is utilized and modified to accord with basic needs.[3]

Linking this to Easton's systems framework space is related to both the inputs and outputs of the political system. As an input it provides the framework for the operation of governments as well as a factor further distinguishing social and economic differences within the political unit. As an output governments will need to regulate their policies to meet the demands and needs of different areas. Finally one other facet of the system is important: to recall the existence of a feedback relationship. From this it is feasible to see how well the outputs of governments meet or conflict with those of the differently expressed needs of individuals and groups within the polity, together with the extent to which the decisions of governments continue to maintain and build up levels of support necessary for their own survival.

Types of Political Unit

Political units operate at a number of levels, representing different spatial scales. Frequently these are described as a hierarchy, extending from the supranational body to the local jurisdiction serving a parish or other local community. Hierarchy, in this sense, is being used to refer to the scale of activity rather than to the ordering of the units in a power ('pecking order') capacity. Part of the controversy surrounding Britain's entry to the European Common Market followed from the losses of sovereignty incurred by joining, yet the individual states rather than the supranational body remain the supreme units.

The actual range of political units serving the citizens of individual countries varies considerably. In the United States the citizen is simultaneously governed by the federal, federated state, county, city or township, and school boards besides a whole host of special districts. In Ireland (the Irish Republic) comparable levels include the national, county and urban governments, above which are those largely social and economic matters controlled by the EEC. Finally in India political units are represented at federal, federated state, district, subdistrict and village levels. The basic distinction to be made is between national and subnational units, recognizing that within the latter are subsumed a series of different levels.

National and subnational political units (and their respective governments) vary in importance. In contemporary affairs it is the state, or nation-state as some political scientists designate it, which is the pre-eminent actor. In large part this is attributable to the link between statehood and sovereignty, the idea that the ultimate power resides in the state. The ascendancy of the state is apparent in other ways, not least in the increase in their number. Currently there are more than 180 sovereign states, considerably more than twice the number at the beginning of the century. The general reasons underlying the 'explosion' in their numbers are easily traced, particularly as most are Third World countries which gained independence following the dissolution of the colonial systems. The appeal of nationalism as a politically organizing ideology underlies the popularity of the concept of the nation-state in which the national group gains control over its own affairs. Furthermore, nationalism has proved a resilient and adaptable ideology, able to adapt itself or be moulded to the other major 'isms' of the twentieth century, fascism and socialism. Were all those political groups currently seeking secession to succeed there would be a further major rise in the number of sovereign states. However, any prediction of the likely future number of sovereign states is a hazardous task, partly because of what Smith has termed the 'Shetland effect',[4] i.e. the process where a yet more localized movement for secession takes place within a larger one, and indeed often because of the latter, as with the Shetland Islands in Scotland. On the other hand, certainly when compared to the two previous centuries, separatism, for a variety of reasons, is markedly less successful than has formerly been the case.[5]

By way of contrast the number of local governments in many

countries has been falling within the post-war period. Exceptions can be cited in the case of some developing countries in which new local governments are being established as the effective state area (the territory over which central government control effectively applies) is extended. Generally, though, the pattern has been one of a reduction in the number of subnational governments, often for similar kinds of reason. These include the need to co-ordinate, plan and finance public services over wider geographical areas and the need to realign boundaries to changed patterns of circulation.[6] Nevertheless substantial variations remain between countries – and, in the case of federal countries, within them – in even such a basic characteristic as the number of subnational governments.[7]

The State – its Basis for Integration

Within the hierarchy of political territories, from local to supranational, the sovereign state is the dominant actor. Sovereignty is usually taken to imply two elements.[8] Externally, it refers to the state's legal right to a separate existence and its expectation that the decisions it makes to apply within its own territories will not suffer interference from any foreign power. Internally, sovereignty is an indication of the vesting of supreme authority in the state, and by implication in the organs of national government. Hence sovereignty can be linked to the territorial stability of the state through (*a*) the doctrine of territorial integrity, the right to resist any externally-borne threat to its existence and (*b*) the doctrine of territorial supremacy, by which the state government has the legal authority and power to make decisions at will within its own jurisdiction.

Such definitions, in emphasizing the legal aspects of sovereign statehood, outline the basic attributes as they should be. In practice, such absolute acceptance of state sovereignty may be a chimera. History and present-day events can document many cases to show that states which are legally sovereign do not enjoy a similar status when it comes to their political and economic dealings with other states. Small states, in particular, are often heavily reliant, or influenced by, the actions of larger neighbouring powers even though in the contemporary world, given the concentration of international economic and political power, they have shown a remarkable ability to survive. Nevertheless the demise of the three Latvian states and the enforced neutrality of Finland illustrate the effect political inequalities can have on the relationships between theoretically equal states. Internally, conflicts undermining state sovereignty are also commonplace. In absolute terms total acceptance of the doctrine by the state population is probably unattainable, though again substantial differences occur between countries.

As history amply demonstrates political territories are not static features. Through processes of fission and fusion existing states have been subdivided, while others amalgamated into larger entities. To earlier political geographers[9] such processes were part of the 'natural' order of things; their models contrived to show how through patterns of territorial growth and life-cycle changes states grew and declined relative to one another. Processes of territorial growth and political integration, however, are countered by those leading to disintegration. To Hartshorne this was the central question underlying the existence of the state, namely how to 'bind together more or less separate areas into an effective whole.'[10] Broadly the answer was that the stability of the state depended on its ability to counter those centrifugal forces tending to undermine its existence, such as physical barriers and differences in cultural and ethnic makeup, and to stimulate those centripetal forces, notably the 'state idea', which foster integration.

As part of their goal-seeking behaviour the task of integrating the state is a major item on the agenda of national politicians and one demanding the management and reconciliation of diverse interests and expectations. Such demands for improved services, the implementation of agricultural subsidies and so forth are catered for by the policies of central government.

State and Nation

The process of political integration of the state has become closely tied to the concepts of the nation and nationalism. It is important, however, to distinguish between the state and nation in that though both are forms of socio-political organization they are not interchangeable concepts. The state is a legal and political organization by which citizens living within a defined jurisdiction are governed and controlled. The nation, on the other hand, is a cultural and social entity. As discussed earlier (Chapter 2) it refers to a territorial social group united by a common culture and history.

Underpinning the recognition of separate nations is the national ideal. By this creed groups which enjoy a common pattern of descent and set of cultural symbols will want to be autonomous within their own homelands. The idea that the nation, and not a dynasty, should be the font of sovereignty and that it was to the nation that the citizen's primary loyalties should lie perhaps first came to prominence during the French Revolution. The natural outcome of this belief was that each nation should strive (and have the right) to gain political control over its own affairs.[11] The concept of the nation, therefore, developed alongside that of the modern state, giving as the ideal the establishment of the nation-state.

In one respect use of the term nation-state is confusing. This is because few states comprise a single nation and in that sense justify the label nation-state. Some scholars use the term to describe those countries in which the state is dominated by a particular (national) group, recognizing that minorities exist; e.g. within Spain, Spanish speakers form the group which has been in the more favoured position politically, particularly by comparison with minority national groups in Catalonia, Galicia and the Basque provinces. In spite of the objections that can be levelled against the term, 'nation-statism' is important in that it forms part of the goal-seeking behaviour of a large number, if not most, states.

Political Integration

Political integration can be loosely defined as the process by which smaller political territories are subsumed into larger ones which are able to secure the loyalty and support of citizens. Integration is a factor which underwrites the effective functioning of the state; only when it is more or less fully integrated will its sovereignty be accepted internally.

In spite of the definition suggested above political integration is neither an easy term to define nor one over which political scientists have been able to reach agreement. One source of difficulty arises because the term can be used to refer to both an end-state and a process. As an end-state countries can be described as more or less integrated in relation to varying degrees of political cohesiveness. Hence countries such as Denmark, New Zealand and the Netherlands would be described (qualitatively) as more integrated than Canada, Nigeria or Belgium in so far as in the former internal conflicts do not threaten to undermine the polity or form deep-seated territorial cleavages which affect the way in which the political process operates.

In behavioural terms one feature which clearly underlies the act of political integration is that of co-operation. It will be through co-operative behaviour that a consensus on the broad goals of the political unit will be established. This is implicit in Jacob and Jeune's definition of political integration which to them 'implies a relationship of community among people within the same political entity . . . (that is, they are) . . . held together by mutual ties of one kind or another which give the group a feeling of identity and self-awareness'.[12] The basis of any community, social or political, is the commonality of group values and attitudes which are established through the co-operative actions of individuals. In his comparison of integration at national and international levels Hayward[13] summarizes the processes by emphasizing two factors both related to the co-operative behaviour of the actors within the political unit, i.e. (1) the willingness of individuals to adapt to the laws and rules issued by governments, and (2) their orientation, or measure of identification, with the political structure.

Underpinning the willingness of individuals to adapt and orient themselves to a new political unit – whether a state amongst those to whom some smaller political unit, such as a tribe, was their primary unit of government, or a group of states electing to join a larger union – will be the perceived benefits likely to follow from association in the wider unit. Where there are mutual interests individuals will be willing to act co-operatively, though these will be balanced against the perceived losses joint action will incur. One of the common benefits associated with membership of a larger politico-territorial unit will be the greater security it affords. At the same time, however, such association may incur a penalty arising from the loss of autonomy of the individual members.

As integration is such a central theme to the state, as well as to governments at local and international levels, the kinds of factors which stimulate integrative behaviour have been extensively discussed by political scientists. Jacob and Jeune list ten factors as having an influence on the integrative process (Table 6.1). Several points raised by the table need further explanation. Jacob and Jeune discussed the factors as a number of hypotheses, which while considered as related to the integration of political territories, would vary in their individual importance. A record of failure in previous attempts at integration is likely to outweigh other factors more conducive to integration because of the events which precipitated disintegration. Any proposal (for example) for the re-federation of the West Indies would be likely to be doomed because of the balance of factors which had led to its earlier failure. Secondly, it does not follow that in any particular example of integration all the factors will be in play, though this begs the question as to the 'necessary combination or "mix" of variables to produce integration'. One further proviso is that only some of these variables have been empirically evaluated or easily facilitate such analysis.

Table 6.1. **Factors Underlying Political Integration.**

Spatial proximity
Social homogeneity
Transaction/interactions
Mutual knowledge
Functional interests, e.g. over
  economic or defence matters
Communal character, the presence of
  a common culture, 'national
  interest', etc.
Previous integrative experience (if
  any)
Political structure, i.e. structural
  influences/impediments to
  integration, e.g. mass participation
  as a factor encouraging consensus
Sovereignty–dependence, e.g. the
  extent of real autonomy among
  political units/actors
Governmental effectiveness, i.e. the
  more effective a government in
  meeting demands the more likely
  will integration be achieved

Source: Adapted from P. E. Jacob and H. Jeune, 'The Integrative Process: Guidelines for analysis of the bases of political community', in P. E. Jacob and J. V. Toscano (eds.), *The Integration of Political Communities*, Lippincott, Philadelphia, 1964.

One factor which has been empirically tested under a variety of situations and which is of special interest to the political geographer is the influence of individual and group transactions or interaction.[14] Transactions are contacts or dealings taking place between different actors' political areas. These might be flows of mail, the number of telephone calls or interactions representing trade or movements, especially of migrants. In terms of trade much more examination has been made of the patterns of interaction between rather than within states, in which indices have been constructed to measure the relative geographical concentration of flows.

Transaction flow analysis properly belongs to the study of communications behaviour. Any transaction can be considered as an information flow which by its nature will relay messages between two parties. What scholars of the 'transactionalist school', notably Karl Deutsch among current political scientists, have subsequently argued is that 'cohesiveness among individuals and among communities of individuals can be measured by – and is probably promoted by – the extent of mutual relationships or interaction among them'. In an important application of transaction flow analysis to political integration Soja[15] argues that from the intensity of action there inevitably comes a threshold point at which 'two units become solidly locked together in a chain of interreactive behaviour'.[16] Transactionalists identify this critical level as indicative of the salience of the relationship. Using telephone traffic data collected for individual exchanges within Kenya, Uganda and Tanzania Soja mapped the pattern of salient interactions. As earlier studies of transnational interactions – notably Mackay's[17] analysis of telephone traffic within and between Canada and the United States – demonstrated, the effect of the international boundary is to compartmentalize communication. Because of the compartmentalization, which appeared to increase within the time-span studied by Soja, the author concluded that 'in a behavioural sense, there are virtually no "East Africans", just Kenyans, Ugandans and Tanzanians'.[18]

Spatial influences on the integration process are both direct and indirect. Directly, they are inferred by the argument that proximity *per se* fosters integration. As a very large number of studies have shown, distance has a pronounced effect on spatial interactions of a wide variety. However, as in the case of transaction flow analysis it is assumed that interaction fosters integration, an argument which overlooks the more fundamental idea that the perceptions of the individual actors as to the likely benefits of integration may be much more important than the mere establishment of contact.

Geographical influences on political integration, where they are traceable, tend to be more important where they are qualified by the inclusion of intervening variables. Integrative factors, such as social homogeneity, can often be defined spatially giving rise to differing potentials for integration between different areas of the political territory. In states in which one or a few regions have pronounced differences of ethnic or cultural makeup from the population as a whole the dissimilarities may be sufficient to act as the catalyst for conflict and secession.

One morphological characteristic of states which is frequently cited as influencing integrative behaviour is that of contiguity. Territorial contiguity, the establishment of governments over lands which are in physical contact, is usually considered as preferable from the viewpoint of the cohesion of the state. Among the reasons given are the difficulties in administering discontiguous areas, the problems in establishing adequate transport facilities and the obvious vulnerability of such areas to external aggression, particularly where transport difficulties pose obstacles to the ease of movement of military units. West Berlin exemplifies the problems, though its 'ideological' position sandwiched between Eastern and Western powers greatly exaggerates the mere fact of discontiguity.[19]

While noncontiguity is often related to physical difficulties in ensuring the effectiveness of the central authority it is less clear what its effect is on patterns of political behaviour. In the case of island polities physical separation leaves its imprint historically through the development of distinct ways of life. One reason underlying the failure of the short-lived West Indies Federation (1958–62) was what might be called the 'natural parochialism' of the islands provoking competition and conflict between the members of the federation.[20] However, it was only one factor – the weakness of the constitution itself – which left the federal government the weak partner; others included the imbalances created by the existence of the large units of Jamaica and Trinidad, and it is difficult to 'partial out' the effect of these other variables.

Integrative Crises and Policies Promoting Integration

Building nation-states, and ensuring their survival, is a long-term process. In many states the process has become intertwined with that of modernization, so that simultaneously with the social and economic changes the state itself develops politically, and through its own policies in turn becomes increasingly involved in the development programmes. Political scientists[21] have identified a number of 'crisis areas' which all nation-states will need to meet and overcome if they are to survive, the incidence of which will be 'controlled' by the policies of the national government, as follows.

(1) Identity. Citizens must be willing to accept the supremacy of the state as the territorial jurisdiction in preference to any previously held territorial identities. Identity crises arise from several sources, including the barriers raised by social class and ethnic differences and the conflict between new and previous associations arising out of social change. Modernization itself can pose severe strains on traditional values and because of the rapidity of social

change (as in Iran) conflict may arise threatening the stability of the state.

(2) Legitimacy, definable as 'the degree to which the decisions of government are accepted by the populace of a society because of (generally held) normative beliefs . . . as to the rightness of the ways in which decision are made'.[22] Legitimacy, therefore, acts as a support of the political system – at least a substantial proportion of the state's population must be willing to accept its authority – and one which is closely linked to what governments do. In other words legitimacy is linked to the way in which material benefits are distributed within society, though this does not mean that all policies will (or could) meet individual wants. As Rabushka and Shepsle have expressed it, 'individuals remain loyal to a regime so long as they expect the regime to implement some of their preferences in the future, despite their unhappiness with current policy outcomes'.[23] Indeed in the case of unpopular measures (such as decisions on energy-saving questions in the United States) their palatability depends on their general recognition as being in the 'national interest'. Similarly regional development programmes, the earmarking of financial aid for some areas at the expense of others, may only be acceptable because they are recognized as a legitimate concern of central government and because of a broad acceptance of the need to reduce interregional differences of economic prosperity.

(3) Distribution. Questions of this nature – who benefits from the political system, who pays, etc. – are tied, as has been seen, to the search for legitimacy. Increasingly government policies have sought to redistribute values within society among individuals and, as the example above suggested, between geographical areas. Distributive and redistributive issues are a continuing source of political conflict, the sensitivity of which is raised by the differing ideologies which are brought to bear on their resolution. Revolutionary ideologies, in particular, challenge the view that inequalities are an inherent character of human society and where they have been applied in socialist states repercussions are apparent in their socio-economic makeup with states in the nonsocialist world.

(4) Penetration. Central governments will seek to ensure that their authority is recognized throughout the national territory, so that the desires of central rulers will in fact be executed in all parts of the political territory. Penetration is important: for one thing all governments rely on dependable sources of revenue so that efficient centrally organized tax collection agencies depend on a network of

outstationed officials. Also, the ability of central authorities to penetrate the national territory is a measure of their effectiveness. Where opposition groups (e.g. revolutionary insurgent groups) are able to claim administrative control of part of the state this not only obviously illustrates the ineffectiveness of the central authority, it also raises questions about the viability of it. Nevertheless, it is likely that no state has or will attain total penetration; differences in political preferences between territorial collectivities, national and local, for example, underline the difficulties confronted by central authorities in establishing their own policies.

(5) Participation. Under this heading are asked some of the key questions about the political process, notably who participates in the decision-making process and what are the mechanisms available to ensure that minority opinions are taken into account, issues which have in part been discussed in an earlier chapter. As far as the task of national integration is concerned the assumption is that mass participation is the ideal in assuring common access to the decision-making processes. Crises of participation, 'when the governing elite views the demands or behaviour of individuals and groups seeking to participate in the political system as illegitimate',[24] occur in all states and under a variety of situations. Spatially one of the important sources of such crises is where an organized group (ethnic association, political party and the like) demand greater control over local affairs or advocate secession, aims which are normally considered inimical to the governing elites.

Although crises of these types characterize the development and functioning of all states their incidence will obviously differ between countries. Among political scientists there has been some speculation as to the sequencing of the crises: that is, given that central authorities within the state are able to manipulate its integration what should be the ideal sequencing of the different types of crisis? Verba and Rustow,[25] two workers in the field, have suggested the ordering of identity, legitimacy, penetration, participation and distribution (in Rustow's terms unity, authority and equality) as one sequence facilitating the integration and survival of the state. Thus once a sense of identity is established, through the inculcation of a national identity, this will ease the problem of legitimacy in so far as the governing elites will be seen as belonging to the same national group. Similarly, a common identity will reduce the likelihood of any regional groups demanding communal autonomy or secession. Finally, where crises of distribution and redistribution are endemic to all polities the importance of identity is that it provides an overarching influence, reducing the disintegrative potential of such problems.

Where the establishment of a common sense of identity is so fundamental it is not surprising to find that among the new states of the Third World this issue has been considered as one of the more pressing. Usually this has been interpreted as a question of establishing a national identity. However, it has not proved an easy objective to meet, particularly because of the colonial legacy. During the colonial period national loyalties were not actively sought. Rather the colonial rulers were more concerned to build a class loyal to the colonial power so that the means for territorially socializing the population, especially the education systems, were geared to alien rather than indigenous needs.

Most African governments and their leaders, recognizing the role that political socialization can have in the inculcation of national identity and awareness, have acknowledged the need to build up the educational system. In some countries over 25 per cent of all public expenditure is devoted to education alone. In Ghana Kwame Nkrumah attempted a number of reforms and in 1960 established the Young Pioneer Movement whose aims were civic training – 'to foster the spirit of voluntarism, love and devotion to the welfare of the Ghana nation' – and fostering Nkrumahism.[26] However, as in a number of other African countries using the educational system for this purpose has met with only limited success, partly because of the colonial inheritance and partly because of their multi-ethnic composition. The existence of ethnic fragmentation in states such as Uganda or Ghana is a sensitive issue educationally; should the educational curriculum attempt to convey the cultural characteristics of each separate group, of only the dominant group(s) or just of their shared features?

Singapore presents an interesting case study of the problems of building a national identity within a developing state, partly because of its ethnic diversity and partly because of the way in which the identity has been socially engineered in the period following the territory's expulsion from the Malaysian federation.[27] In multi-ethnic societies there are two general public policy strategies available which seek national integration, i.e. (1) incorporation – the establishment of a national identity while not eliminating the subordinate cultures; (2) assimilation, in which the minority groups are assimilated usually within the framework of the dominant groups.

In Singapore the ruling People's Action Party sought a policy of ethnic democracy (an incorporationist policy) while actively pursuing the establishment of a Singaporean identity. Thus all communities were to be treated equally (in 1970 the population was 76 per cent Chinese, 15 per cent Malay and 7 per cent Indian) in contrast to the policy of cultural hegemony developed in Malaysia. One of the more significant policies of the People's Action Party was the creation of integrated schools bringing together students from different ethnic and linguistic backgrounds, the outcome of which has been to raise the level of bilingualism. The success of these policies was assessed in a survey in the early 1970s, which showed that majorities, overall and in the three ethnic groups separately, preferred a national identification over a communal one and indicated positive associations with the symbols of the state (Table 6.2). Significantly though, smaller proportions considered that Singapore's secession from Malaysia was advantageous, while a plurality thought that reunification would be beneficial. While social engineering has been able to achieve progress towards the inculcation of a national identification it has not been able to counter attitudes, partly derived from historical experience, as to the optimum destiny for the nation-state.

Table 6.2. **Levels of positive affective involvement with patriotic symbols – Singapore.**

Patriotic symbols	Total %	Chinese %	Malays %	Indians %
National day parade	77	71	83	66
Prime Minister	68	68	72	74
National flag	67	66	74	70
National anthem	67	65	83	72

Source: Adapted from J. A. MacDougall, 'National Identification in Singapore', *Asian Studies*, **16**, 1976.

Conflicts – the Case of Multi-ethnic States and Political Integration

So far the emphasis in this chapter has been on the co-operative aspect of political integration. It is clear, however, that the political system, sometimes in order to actually survive, will need to be able to cope with internal conflicts.

In the simplest case conflicts arise wherever two people or groups are intent on pursuing objectives which are mutually incompatible. Either each party can continue to pursue its own preference and accept that the inevitable conflict will impose its own penalties, or agree to compromise through some form of 'conflict resolution' or co-operative agreement.

Conflicts arise from a wide variety of sources. Each of the crisis areas discussed in the previous section generates conflicts of various types. Distributive policies, for instance, by their nature will be selective as to who benefits, though the selectivity itself may not become a sensitive issue where the policy has been widely discussed (and possibly influenced by) the interested parties. Financial allocations by central governments to local governments provide a case in point. In a number of countries (e.g. UK, USA, West Germany) how the grants are distributed geographically is the subject of discussion between national and local governments, and to a certain extent its basis is open to bargaining between the parties. In the case of the Rate Support Grant (UK) such discussions lessen, but by no means eliminate, the severity of the conflict.

Conflicts whose origins stem from the multi-ethnic composition of the state are among the more intractable with which governments have to contend. In contrast to the great majority of conflicts within states their severity can be great enough to threaten the territorial integrity of the state. This is particularly so in those cases where minority groups are advocating secession. Conflicts of this type, to use game theory terminology, describe zero-sum games, in which the gains of one party are a direct loss to the other. Control over territory or the acquisition of many other scarce resources are not activities which can be easily shared.

Ethnic differences are measurable along several dimensions, notably those of race, language, religion and tribe. Using these as criteria to assess ethnicity very few states can be described as mono-ethnic. Walker Connor[28] has suggested that only a handful of countries can be described as effectively mono-ethnic. In Western Europe these include West Germany, Iceland and the Irish Republic. However, within the larger number of multi-ethnic states the political significance of ethnicity varies. Political scientists have drawn the distinction between ethnically plural states in which the ethnic factor is the dominant, if not the exclusive, factor dominating political behaviour and pluralistic societies (such as the United States) in which it is only one of a number of factors. Ethnically plural states (which we discuss here) harbour the danger of territorial balkanization because of their frequently weak sense of national identity, an essential prop to the state's stability. The key question focuses on reducing what Geertz[29] describes the 'primordial loyalties', around which discontent tends to crystallize.

The patterns of inter-ethnic behaviour within states strongly reflect their relative numerical balance. On the basis of the relative size of the groups Rabushka and Shepsle identify four types of behaviour patterns:[30]

(1) The dominant majority, e.g. Cyprus, Northern Ireland and Sri Lanka. Typically the majority group, by weight of numbers, dominates the political machine and may use it to actively discriminate against the minority whose interests may only be safeguarded by adopting nondemocratic tactics.

(2) States in which the groups are more or less balanced, e.g. Belgium, Guyana and Malaya. Attempts to establish inter-ethnic co-operation have generally proved short-lived, resulting in increasing competition between the communities. In Belgium the increasing dominance of ethnic politics has led to demands for the replacement of the unitary state by a federal government.

(3) The dominant minority, e.g. South Africa, in which one ethnic group behaves in the belief that it has a 'natural' right to govern.

(4) Fragmented states, in which there are a large number of separate ethnic groups with a smaller number being numerically dominant, a pattern common within black African states.

One of the hallmarks of the ethnically divided society is that each group views issues through its own (ethnic) frame of reference. Much of the foundation of this bias is determined (as has been argued earlier) by the partisan nature of the information flows to which group members are exposed, a factor which is reinforced by the common pattern of residential segregation within ethnically conscious populations. The outcome is that consensual approaches to the resolution of conflicts become extremely difficult.

Communal relations in Cyprus illustrate some of the territorial implications of ethnic conflict. Numerically the Greek population is four times the size of the Turkish Cypriot population. Intercommunal relations in the period leading up to and since independence (1960) have been marked by conflict, culminating in the 'stalemate' following the Turkish invasion of the island. In essence the problem stems from the frequently expressed goal of the Greek Cypriot population for enosis (union with Greece) and the opposition to this by the minority Turkish population, who are already sensitive to their political domination but consider enosis would be a more decisive threat to their identity. Solutions to the crisis by the Turkish population – the partitioning of the island or its federalizing – are opposed by the majority on the ground that dividing the island, quite apart from the sensitive question as to how this would be achieved, would impose unnecessary political and economic penalties.

Ethnic conflicts arise mainly over issues of participation and distribution. Those of participation are the more fundamental in dictating how the different groups have access to power. The hallmark of some multi-ethnic states is that only the dominant group(s) have disproportionate power, leaving minority groups in a relatively weak position. There are several methods by which the state can help ensure that the various ethnic groups are able to participate politically, three of which will be discussed here. These are: ensuring through the electoral system that there is fair or adequate representation of the minority groups in particular, the territorial decentralization of power to meet ethnic demands, and the mode of decision-making between the ethnic groups.

As was argued in Chapter 4 electoral systems vary in their fairness in representing adequately the different strands of opinion among the electors. In the ethnically plural society this property of electoral laws has obvious implications given that each ethnic group will want to ensure that it has reasonable (proportionate, for example) representation within the national legislature. In fact few multi-ethnic states have adopted proportional representation, one of the exceptions being Guyana in which elections are organized on the basis of a single constituency for the whole country. The effect of its introduction was to weaken the power base of the (East) Indian community which constitutes more than 50 per cent of the population. In other cases while not using proportional representation some guarantees of representation particularly to minority groups can be given, e.g. in Sri Lanka a minimum number of seats is reserved for the minority Tamil population.

Electoral arrangements can be engineered to obviate possible sources of conflict within the plural state. The guarantee of minimum levels of representation is one possible method. An interesting adaptation of the plurality electoral system was devised in Uganda by Milton Obote to overcome the twin problems of regionalism and tribalism (the system was never actually implemented because of the military coup led by Idi Amin in 1971). Obote's scheme was to get each candidate to the 82-seat Assembly to stand not only in his 'home' constituency but also in three other seats, one being located in each of the other three administrative regions covering the country. This novel system of election would ensure that only those candidates who had wide (inter-tribal and inter-regional) appeal would be elected.

It is in those plural states in which there is a dominant majority that the electoral methods are most likely to be manipulated for partisan advantages. We have noted how the Protestant majority in Northern Ireland used the electoral system in its favour (first by replacing the system of proportional representation which came into being at Partition). The effect on the minority groups of their being denied the right to exercise political power (as in Sri Lanka, Cyprus) is their resort to extra-legal methods.   IRA

Within the multi-ethnic state the decentralizing of power, and its distribution within some federal framework, potentially offers the possibility for reducing conflict. Through a federal constitution it is possible to ensure that at least some of the ethnically more sensitive kinds of issues (e.g. education) are dealt with by subnational governments. Federalism is commonly linked with ethnicity as a means of accommodating minority demands within a territorially larger ethnically diverse state, though the evidence as to its actual achievements within such states is mixed.

The case of Nigeria presents an interesting case-study of how the spatial structure of federalism, matched with the strength of tribal feeling, can combine to exacerbate, rather than reduce, inter-ethnic conflict. During the period of the First Republic (1959–65) the country was divided into three federal states very unequal in size (Fig. 6.1), each of which was dominated and most associated with one of the federation's three major tribal groups. The diversity of the country was such that during the colonial period it had been run along 'federal lines', so that federalism, once independence was granted, was inevitable. As Okpu[31] has shown the pattern of ethnic conflict generated its own behaviour interaction – beginning with the basic incompatibility between the groups this leads on to various responses and confrontation. The responses could be the formation of a separate ethnically founded interest group or political party or the establishment of alliances with existing political parties, while the confrontation generally took the form of physical violence, or other hostilities. It was this incompatibility which generated the frequent demands for the creation of new federal states within the early period of Nigeria's post-independence history, moves which in all but one case were resisted.

The working of the federation strongly reflected its division into three states. Each was closely identified with three major political parties and for much of the period there was a complex switching of coalition arrangements between the regionally based parties. The effect was that whereas we argued earlier that in ethnically divided societies one of their distinguishing features is that issues are seen along ethnic lines, this also became associated with the regional division so that the threat of territorial integration became more obvious. Issues which highlighted differences between the ethnic groups and which might be seen to favour one group against the other(s) were likely to lead to confrontation. The fiasco of the 1963 Census (see Table 6.3), which enumerated population growth within the Northern Region, already the dominant region, far above the levels expected illustrated the kind of problem arising when each group views a problem through its own rather than a more embracing framework. Because both the regional representation within the national assembly and its financial allocations from the federal government were related to its enumerated population size it is understandable why the smaller regions should have been so concerned.

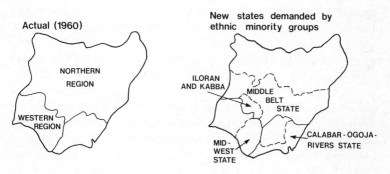

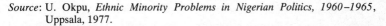

Fig. 6.1. Alternative federal configurations – Nigeria.

Source: U. Okpu, *Ethnic Minority Problems in Nigerian Politics, 1960–1965*, Uppsala, 1977.

Where ethnically divided societies present central governments with formidable problems of integration one other method by which each group can be seen to be being dealt with equitably is through some formula of 'power-sharing'. The engineering of the electoral system to suit the pattern of electoral diversity will give results not unrelated to the idea of giving each group access to power, though by itself it is unlikely to be sufficient. In some countries the constitution has stipulated in what ways key positions of power within the government and its agencies (notably the security forces) will be divided among the ethnic groups. In Cyprus, prior to the Turkish invasion, the constitution agreed at independence stipulated how

Table 6.3. **Population data of Nigerian regions. Population (thousands).**

Region	1931 Census	1952/3 Census	1963 Census
Northern	11,434	16,840	29,809
Western	2,743	4,595	10,266
Mid-Western	986	1,493	2,536
Eastern	4,266	7,218	12,395
Lagos (township)	126	272	665
Totals	19,555	30,417	55,671

Source: H. K. Hicks, *Federalism: Failure and Success*, Macmillan, London, 1978.

such positions were to be divided between the Turkish and Cypriot populations.

One interesting model of collective decision-making within ethnically divided societies is that of consociationalism. The consociational model is based on the idea that political elites representing each of the state's subcultures are able to arrive at decisions through accommodation, the outcome of which is that each group will benefit. Majoritarian, 'imposed', solutions are avoided. The model was developed by Lijphart[32] in an analysis of Dutch politics. Dutch society is deeply divided along ideological and religious lines (as is apparent from the complex structure of political parties) yet has remained politically stable because the 'subcultural leaders are committed to bargaining with each other and to keeping political controversy from reaching explosive proportions'. While the model has been linked to the operation of other European countries (Austria, Switzerland and Belgium, though the latter is more doubtful) its applicability to developing nations is more problematic.

The question of access to power is of importance because of what this can potentially mean for the safeguarding of the group's interests. In the ethnic society political allocations are even more sensitive issues than in more homogeneous societies. This is because, as Furnivall recognized, plural societies lack consensus; services then which are provided for public consumption tend to refer to only one group. To the others rather than being a public good such services, and the decisions on which they were based, are 'public bads'. In Guyana Despres[33] quotes the example of the problem of where to locate a new health centre, which because of its 'indivisibility' must be located in either an African or an Indian village. Its location bestows an obvious advantage but politically its importance is that where it is located becomes a more highly charged issue because of the salience of ethnicity.

Biases in how public goods are allocated within ethnically divided societies, while to a certain extent inevitable because of the problem of indivisibility and the prominence of ethnicity in the operation of the political system, give rise to feelings of relative deprivation. This in turn is a force which is potentially divisive to the state. Gurr[34] has suggested a formulation linking deprivation to its political outcome as relative deprivation $\rightarrow$ frustration $\rightarrow$ discontent $\rightarrow$ violence, to which in some cases it has been possible to add territorial secession. How much individuals, groups and regions gain from the political system will obviously be of importance in regard to the legitimacy which they are willing to assign to it. It is to these important questions of allocation, therefore, that we turn in the next chapter.

Discussion Points and Further Reading

This chapter has sought to examine some of the political processes underlying the integration (and possible disintegration) of one type of political unit, the state. The problems of defining integration and its measurement, major tasks in their own right, are comprehensively discussed in the volume of edited readings by Jacob and Toscano (1964). Deutsch (1979) provides a stimulating discussion of national integration. Another promising line for further inquiry is provided by cross-national comparisons of the experience of promoting integration and the overcoming of crisis issues: the volumes by Binder *et al.* (1971) and Grew *et al.* (1978) furnish case material.

Rabushka and Shepsle (1972) give a number of case-studies of countries affected by ethnic conflict, while Gurr's (1970) theory of relative deprivation provides a conceptual model to explain regional secessionist movements.

Binder, L. *et al.*, *Crises and Sequences in Political Development*, Princeton University Press, Princeton, 1971.

Deutsch, K., 'National Integration: A Summary of Some Concepts and Research Approaches', in K. Deutsch (ed.), *Tides Among Nations*, Free Press, New York, 1979.

Grew, R. *et al.*, *Crises of Political Development in Europe and the United States*, Princeton University Press, Princeton, 1978.

Gurr, T. R., *Why Men Rebel*, Princeton University Press, Princeton, 1970, esp. chs. 1–3.

Jacob, P. E., and Toscano, J. R. (eds.), *The Integration of Political Communities*, Lippincott, Philadelphia, 1964.

Rabushka, A., and Shepsle, K. A., *Politics in Plural Societies*, Charles E. Merrill, Columbus, 1972.

Tapper, T., 'The Prerequisites of Political Conflict: Divided Ulster as a Case Study', in ch. 10 of T. Tapper, *Political Education and Stability*, Wiley, London, 1976, pp. 209–37.

Notes

1. R. Hartshorne, 'The Functional Approach in Political Geography', *Annals of the Association of American Geographers* (1950), **40**, 95–130.
2. K. R. Cox, *Conflict, Power and Politics in the City*, McGraw-Hill, New York, 1973.
3. R. A. Patrick, *Political Geography and the Cyprus Conflict, 1963–1971*, University of Waterloo, Department of Geography, Publications Series no. 4, Waterloo, 1976 p. 407.
4. A. D. Smith, *Nationalism in the Twentieth Century*, Martin Robertson, Oxford, 1979, p. 182.
5. C. H. Enloe, 'Central Governments' Strategies for Coping with Separatist Movements', in W. H. Morris-Jones (ed.) *The Politics of Separatism*, Institute of Commonwealth Studies, Seminar Papers, London, 1974.
6. See the arguments used by D. Senior in his Memorandum of Dissent, vol. 2 of the *Royal Commission on Local Government*, HMSO, London, Cmnd, 4040-I, 1969.
7. For a detailed comparison see S. Humes, and E. Martin, *The Structure of Local Government: A Comparative Survey of 81 Countries*, IULA, The Hague, 1970.
8. P. E. Jacob and H. Jeune, 'The Integrative process: Guidelines for the Analysis of the Bases of Political Community', in P. E. Jacob and J. R. Toscano, *The Integration of Political Communities* Lippincott, Philadelphia, 1964.
9. E.g. F. Ratzel, 'The Laws of the Spatial Growth of States', in R. E. Kasperson and J. V. Minghi (eds.), *The Structure of Political Geography*, University of London Press, 1970.
10. R. Hartshorne, 'The Functional Approach in Political Geography', *Annals, Association of Geographers,* (1950), **40** (2), 105.
11. A. Cobban, *National Self-Determination*, Oxford University Press, London, 1944.
12. Jacob and Jeune, 'The Integrative Process'.
13. F. M. Hayward, 'Continuities and Discontinuities between studies of National and International Political Integration: some implications for future research efforts', in L. N. Lindberg and S. A. Scheingold (eds.), *Regional Integration: Theory and Research*, Harvard University Press, Harvard, 1971, pp. 313–37.
14. For a review of transactional studies see D. J. Puchala, 'International Transactions and Regional Integration', in *ibid.* pp. 128–59.
15. E. W. Soja, 'Communications and Territorial Integration in East Africa: An Introduction to Transaction Flow analysis', *The East Lakes Geographer* (1968), **4**, 39–57.
16. *Ibid.* p. 43.
17. J. R. Mackay, 'The Interactance Hypothesis and Boundaries in Canada', *Canadian Geographer* (1958), **11**, 1–8.
18. Soja, 'Communications and Territorial Integration', p. 55.
19. R. L. Merritt, 'Noncontiguity and Political Integration', in J. N.

Rosenau (ed.), *Linkage Politics*, Free Press, New York, 1969, pp. 237–72.

20. E. H. Dale, 'The State-Idea: Missing Prop of the West Indies Federation', *Scottish Geographical Magazine* (1962), LXXVIII, 166–76.

21. L. Binder, *et al.*, *Crises and Sequences in Political Development*, Princeton University Press, Princeton, 1971.

22. S. Verba, 'Sequences and Development', in Binder *et al.*, *ibid.*, p. 299.

23. A. Rabushka, and K. A. Shepsle, *Politics in Plural Societies*, Merrill, Columbus, 1972, p. 32.

24. M. Weiner, 'Political Participation: Crisis of the Political Process', in Binder *et al.*, *Crises and Sequences in Political Development*, p. 187.

25. Verba, 'Sequences and Development'; D. A. Rustow, *A World of Nations*, Brookings Institution, Washington, 1967.

26. A. C. Smock, 'Education and National Integration in Ghana', in D. R. Smock and K. Bentsi-Enchill, *The Search for National Integration in Africa*, Free Press, New York, 1975, pp. 117–38.

27. J. A. MacDougall, 'Birth of a Nation: National Identification in Singapore', *Asian Studies* (1976), **16**, 510–24.

28. W. Connor, 'Self-determination: The New Phase', *World Politics* (1967), **20**.

29. C. Geertz, 'The Integrative Revolution: Primordial Sentiments and Civil Politics in the New States', in C. Geertz (ed.), *Old Societies and New States: The Quest for Modernity in Asia and Africa*, Free Press, New York, 1963, pp. 105–57.

30. Rabushka and Shepsle, *Politics in Plural Societies*, pp. 88ff.

31. U. Okpu, *Ethnic Minority Problems in Nigerian Politics, 1960–65*, Almquist, Uppsala, 1977.

32. A. Lijphart, *The Politics of Accommodation: Pluralism and Democracy in the Netherlands*, University of California Press, Berkeley, 1968.

33. A. Despres, *Cultural Pluralism and Nationalist Politics in British Guiana*, Rand McNally, Chicago, 1967.

34. T. R. Gurr, *Why Men Rebel*, Princeton University Press, Princeton, 1970.

7 The Allocation of Public Goods

One of the most frequently quoted phrases in the social sciences is Harold Lasswell's definition in 1936 of political science as the study of 'who gets what when and how'. If we substitute the temporal 'when' by the spatial 'where' we have created a topic which many modern socially and politically oriented geographers would consider to be the most central in the study of geography. While the subject is multi-faceted and cannot be organized around a single central question (and in any event the definition would only be a variant of the traditional view of the subject as the study of man in relation to his environment) the problem of the processes by which societies reallocate their unevenly distributed resources is fundamental – not least in the political branch of the discipline.

Particularly in the developed world, the role of government as the protective state has, in the course of the last century, been joined and to some extent overtaken by that of the productive state (although a reversal of priorities seemed to be a hallmark of the newly elected right-wing Conservative party in the UK). The productive state is involved in the provision of public goods and services to a population which would be unsupplied or undersupplied were their production left to private enterprise. Relevant geographical questions concern the magnitude of this provision, the breadth of the range and relative emphases within the range of public goods supplied and, particularly, the spatial characteristics of the pattern of goods allocation. Many of the features of this allocation are determined by the wealth and resource endowment of the governmental unit concerned and each must to some extent tailor a particular coat of public goods to the economic cloth available. Some of the aspects of the goods and services provision relate to historical and psychological factors, with expectation of what justly should be received conditioning many allocations; the concept of expectation has strong political undertones as we shall show, while political perceptions, behaviour and values as well as ideological priorities may greatly colour the process.

A considerable proportion of the geographers who research the allocation process do so from positions of political commitment, and in some cases research and publication are extensions of political life according to one of the varieties of Marxist belief. The objective study of the allocation process would not seem to be precluded and indeed, it would be impossible to establish or obtain consensus regarding what a morally or socially optimal allocation would amount to; as Professor W. Kirk said in his presidential address to the 1978 conference of the Institute of British Geographers, 'I know what social justice is, but what is spatial justice?' [1]

In the course of this address, which reviewed the philosophical influence on the career of perhaps the most perceptive pioneer of the behavioural movement in geography, problems relating to the allocation process were succinctly reviewed:

> structural transformations are perceived and ranked according to the criterion of operational *possibility* – what is technically possible, for example, in physical or social engineering; and secondly, according to the criterion of *desirability* – which hypothesized structures would produce the greatest (or least) satisfaction in terms of the sets of values of the decision maker, or indeed the decision-making situation, for example profitability, survival, reduction of stress, power harmony, development of knowledge. In analysing such play-off situations we are further assisted by the knowledge that the framework of ranking is to a large measure socially or culturally determined and that at the heart of the process is a learning model. For an individual or a society the structural analysis of behaviour according to criteria of the possible or the desirable is constrained by the stage reached in the cognition of the environment, i.e. the accepted cosmology, in Popper's usage of the word. [2]

Demand-Making

As we shall see, it would be ridiculous to suppose that even in the most elitist society, the allocation of public goods is the exclusive prerogative of those wielding concentrated power, or that in the most pluralistic societies the political perspectives of the most dominant group do not significantly influence the allocations. Fundamental to any political philosophy is a judgement on the proper relationship between privately provided and state provided goods and services and, in the age of the productive state, such a judgement cannot be anywhere but at the heart of ideology. Even so, no socialist state has succeeded in the total elimination of private production (Soviet citizens would starve without the crucial horticultural and small livestock production of the farm workers' private plots), and no modern regime of the most conservative complexion has eliminated the public sector. Were one so to succeed, there would be no government as such, only a diplomatic service and armed forces. Whatever the political stance of a government, demand-making is a crucial input of the political system while it is of fundamental geographical significance that the nature and volume of demands and expectations will vary according to spatial, social and political circumstances.

Perhaps the highest level of neglect of demands in the allocation of resources occurred in Stalin's Russia when the edict of 'guns not butter' was rigidly imposed and enforced. Demand-making certainly exists in contemporary Soviet society although the political system has managed to condition and structure the forms which it takes. First it should be noted that the provision of public goods is relatively high in the Leninist (or state capitalist?) economy.

> While trailing US cities in the supply of consumer services and certain municipal services as well, Soviet cities are generally better supplied with inexpensive public transportation, with medical clinics, and with such recreational and educational facilities as parks and child-care centres. Between 1956 and 1970 more housing was erected in the USSR than in any other country in the world . . . Nonetheless Soviet municipal governments have lacked needed resources because central authorities concentrating their efforts on industry have not provided sufficient assistance. Such neglect is doubly damaging: it shortchanges city-run services directly, and it forces the city to beg aid from industrial enterprises, which, in return, may demand the right to continue the practices that aggravate urban ills in the first place. Answerable for housing and services, mayors preside over shortage; responsible for the law, soviets countenance its violation; guardian of the city interest, the *ispolkom* fails at city planning . . . Cities may seek more authority and more funds but non-city agencies and higher authorities, reluctant anyway to yield scarce resources, are even more chary of giving them to ineffective municipal administrations.[3]

Taubman goes on to criticize the crude elitist approach to the question of 'who governs?' in Soviet politics and states that 'the Party *apparat* power has been exaggerated, (and) what is needed for the analysis of Soviet politics is a more pluralistic approach'. City government is virtually dominated by the urban Party and higher-level government authorities on matters of municipal administration but they do not dominate the political process in which non-city industrial agencies play a part and on questions of industrial growth industrial interests come the closest to constituting a ruling elite.

What scope then is there for demand-making by the citizen in the street?

Both Friedgut[4] and Oliver[5] show that within certain fields citizen demand-making is not only tolerated, but necessary to the political life of the state.

> The bodies which supplement the limited resources of the administrative structure also aid the citizen in reaching that structure. Organized both functionally and territorially and reinforced with volunteers recruited on the basis of both work and residence, these bodies transmit authoritative pressures which keep local politics alive, evoking socialized, supportive inputs from citizens while informing the executive of the needs for relevant policy outputs.[6]

Oliver points out that

> Not all demands need be given actual material satisfaction. The mere acceptance of a demand by local officials of some expression or indication of interest and concern (even if this amounts to nothing more than helpless thrashing about) can create support. The citizen is able to vent his grievances and make his wishes known. He may derive some release of hostility merely from seeing the discomfort of local officials as they struggle to meet his demands and suffer the criticisms of higher authorities. Even this useless effort may make the regime seem more human and interested in the welfare of the ordinary citizen. The more limited, the more private the demand and the more personal its handling by local officials, perhaps the greater the support generated for the regime, even though the regime persists in the policies that created the conditions that gave rise to demand.[7]

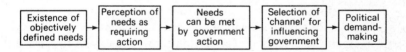

Fig. 7.1. A Schedule for Demand-Making.

Source: Adapted from W. A. Cornelius, *Politics and the Migrant Poor in Mexico City*, Stanford University Press, Stanford, 1975, p. 170.

In any system with a modicum of political sophistication, the provision of some framework for demand-making seems essential to political life. In the Soviet Union the proper fields for demand-making are known and circumscribed and the launching of unacceptable demands requires courage and may carry dire consequences.

The norms governing acceptable demand expression, although not nearly as restrictive and inhibiting as some in the West seem to think, effectively restrict the citizen's expression of demands. His awareness of these limitations has the effect of reducing the number of demand inputs flowing into the system and, even more important, of restricting their content. The regime is thus protected from the possible consequences of a divisive public debate on basic policy questions.[8]

While Easton considered that the main differences between demand-making in totalitarian systems and developed democracies concerned the severe restrictions on demand-making and on the number of those considered competent to make demands, and the fact that demands from the citizens are of little importance in the former system, on the whole it seems that the main characteristics of demand-making in the Soviet Union do not concern the blanket discouragement of demand-making – which can be of assistance to the regime – but the constriction of demands within certain acceptable arenas, the absence of alternative vehicles other than those of the state for the aggregation of demands and the apparent impossibility of using demands to create alternatives to the policies produced by the party.

The curtailment of demand-making in the Soviet Union need not in itself constitute a cause of political instability and when, under Stalin, the influence of citizen preferences on the allocation of goods and services was almost non-existent, the political system was monolithic and – at least outwardly – stable. More complicated psychological associations concerning government policy towards public goods seem to determine the relationship between allocations, stability and discontent. Here, the concept of relative deprivation developed by Runciman may offer a suitable framework for analysis.[9] Relative deprivation concerns a discrepancy between a community's perception of what it is entitled to expect to receive and what is actually obtained. When the gap between the value expectations – the group's perception of what it is entitled to expect the system to deliver – and value capabilities – what the system, according to its resource constraints and preferences, is able to provide – reaches a critical width, then political unrest can be expected to result. According to this concept a system in which the levels of demand-making along with those of expectation and resource delivery, were low, might be expected to be politically stable. However, when the community has high expectations of receiving or maintaining a particular output of public goods but finds these aspirations denied, then unrest or even revolution may occur. The 'food riots' in Poland during the Christmas of 1970 which resulted from rises in the price and limitations on the supply of foodstuffs for domestic consumption may provide an example, with the riots being caused by the failure of the regime to maintain an acceptable provision. Meanwhile, in China where the standard of the provision was lower, so too was the level of expectation and the system was undisturbed by consumer dissatisfaction.

A useful development of the concept relating it to the problems of multi-national states has been developed by Bertsch, using the relative deprivation of Croats and Serbs as examples of the causes of discontent.[10] A further development which would relate the concept of relative deprivation to the current vogue for the catastrophe curve might merit some attention. At a point where frustrated expectations and demands or perceived deprivation reach the crucial level, the community might be faced with a choice between a precipitous fall into unrest and revolution or a reappraisal of the basis for the allocation of resources, leading to progress along a gentler gradient. In a very general sense, the aftermaths of the events in Paris in 1968 or of the UK election in February 1974 seem to have resulted in a sufficient alleviation of frustrated demands to restore stability, while in Iran in 1979 the existing system was unable to assuage popular frustration and the result was a form of revolution which some may regard as retrogression and the basis for a more severe crisis of demand frustration.

The general absence of political constraints upon demand-making in the West does not result in demand inputs to political systems which provide accurate indications of resource priorities for needful communities or areas and neither does it ensure that decisions regarding the allocation of public goods will not be heavily filtered by the vested interests and personal preferences of the decision-makers. The discrepancy between demand and need is as significant in the fields of allocation and demand-making as it is in that of Marxist economics. The correlation between the need for public goods and the ability to articulate effective demands may be negative rather than positive, with the provision of goods being strongly biased in favour of elements in the community whose needs are relatively few but whose calls for action are the loudest and the most difficult to ignore. The narrow pavements or sidewalks of the inner city backstreets may be the most needful of clearing during a snowstorm but the broad avenues of commuterdom may be the first to feel the shovel.

The case of the Barnsbury Association in Islington has been described by Ferris.[11] Formed by young professional immigrants engaged in the gentrification of an area of rented working-class housing, the society mobilized its considerable resources to oppose a council redevelopment plan and sponsored a traffic management scheme which deflected traffic away from the areas of improved housing but into areas populated by working-class tenants. In situations where, as is frequently the case, the ability to organize demand-making is unevenly distributed between different social groups, the rich man's meat may prove to be the poor man's poison. Gregory points out that the poorer sections of society 'are obliged to pay more for what everyone needs in order to preserve amenities from which they derive no more (and sometimes less) benefit than the rich'.[12] In a wide-ranging review of the consequences of inequalities in the ability to organize and articulate demands, Lowe writes that

> With growing emphasis on public participation in statutory planning, serious problems arise because certain areas and sections of society are not effectively organized to protect their interests in the environment; certain sections of the community lack the available resources to sustain effective pressure group activity, and some local political cultures are unreceptive to group activity.[13]

He goes on to add 'the equity and political neutrality of planning are questioned, and whether planning fundamentally serves a public interest, which is variously defined; and, if not, whether it does or should serve the needs of particular propertied and commercial interests of the poor and deprived'. If the spatial intensities of demand-making were a straightforward indicator of degree and distribution of the need for allocations of public goods, the task of the social scientist would be much simpler. In fact, to a certain extent the ability to launch a demand in a manner likely to elicit the desired response may reflect a disassociation from the areas of greatest need on the part of the demand-maker.

Behavioural Aspects of Allocation

Those groups in society which participate least in the process of demand-making lack the wherewithal for its effective pursuit and are devoid of more powerful allies within the community as a whole, may often expect to obtain the least in way of social justice from the allocations of the political system. This view is supported by the example of the gypsies in Hull, as documented by Sibley.[14] This small minority group neither plays an active or influential role in the political life of the community nor finds ready supporters amongst those which do. Culturally separate from the mainstreams of communal life, gypsy society has its own aspirations and systems of values yet its members are subject to the allocations of a political system which is dominated by different outlooks, while the gypsies fall foul of a system of labelling and segregation. Sibley writes that

> there is a common local authority conception of 'the gypsy problem', the definition of a problem, in itself, implying that gypsies are marginal to mainstream society. There are a number of related strands of theory which help in understanding this conception, particularly, argument concerned with consensus, deviance, and the cateogorization of social groups . . . In relation to so-called marginal groups, such as the occupants of squatter settlements, indigenous minorities like Eskimos and gypsies, both deviance and deprivation can be seen as convenient myths which are instrumental in the extension of social control. The categories 'deprived' and 'deviant' assist in legitimating official policy.[15]

Differing in many cultural and economic respects from the remainder of the community, the gypsies can be seen by officialdom as a form of pollution which periodically threatens areas of urban space and the spatial response involving a rigid classification of space and a maintenance of the boundaries around those areas which are to remain 'unpolluted'. 'If a function of planning is to support the social system through boundary maintenance, then non-conforming groups must be changed so that they fit accepted classifications. Otherwise, they must be segregated so that they do not constitute pollution.'[16] The authority, performing a role as the agent of consensus views, finds itself in conflict with the weak and supposedly deviant community of travellers. As a result of such conflicts there is a greater dependency by the minority which, because of the authority's powers to impose classifications on space and maintain exclusive boundaries around space, must depend upon whatever crumbs in the way of designated sites may fall from the planners' table.

Within societies which may be labelled loosely 'pluralistic', great variation may be found between the abilities of different groups to launch forceful programmes of demands which command the attention of allocating authorities while the resources necessary to sustain demand-making are unevenly distributed and the receptivity of the political system varies according to the origins and nature of demands. While one would expect to find some relationship between the system inputs of demand and support and the allocations of the system, much more work on the input-output relationship is needed. One can easily find examples to show how demand-making organized in relation to a specific allocation objective can produce the desired response from the political system. There are also studies which show that a variety of factors govern the outcome of such situations. In a study of policy-making in the London Borough of Kensington and Chelsea, Dearlove found that the councillors evaluated pressure groups in relation to whether their demands were in harmony with the policy preferences of their representatives and according to their images and modes of operation.[17] The groups which obtained the most effective access to the system were those whose demands passed the test of acceptability and whose styles of action did not affront the councillors through vocal or disruptive attempts to apply pressure. What remains to be established is whether there is a clear input–output relationship operating as a long-term process and at a more generalized level. Such would operate for example if voting behaviour and the outcomes of elections as inputs could be shown to affect outputs in the form of resource allocation policies. Linkage might exist to affect the choice of policy areas in terms of favouritism for those sectors – roads, hospitals, schools, etc – which the electorate was deemed to have considered as having a high priority. Secondly, the linkage could exist in the form of payoffs to those voting areas which had rewarded the victors with their votes, or to areas which could be expected to play a crucial role in subsequent elections.

The possible connections between urban policy output and voting behaviour were explored by Glassberg.[18] The two study areas were carefully chosen; both London and New York had recently experienced a change in political control terminating periods of stable party domination. In New York the period came to an end with the election of John Lindsay in 1965 as a Republican–Liberal mayor while in London, the Conservative Party won control of the Greater London Council in 1967 to end a long period of Labour control. 'For both New York and London, the last administration prior to the shift in control is taken as a "base line". Spending patterns in the *ancien régime* are compared with patterns of voting behaviour in the elections which produced a political shift.'[19] The research set out to test a hypothesis of continuous feedback:

> voters make electoral choices and through these electoral choices give elected office-holders power and legitimacy. Elected office-holders make allocational decisions which may be different from those which would have been made had an alternative set of representatives been elected. Voters, observing the allocational decisions of elected representatives, act in the next election at least partially on the basis of their satisfaction or dissatisfaction with the decisions made.[20]

(In both cities the new regimes were returned to power with reduced majorities in the ensuing elections.)

In the event it was found that populist democracy was not operating in the arena of linkage between voting behaviour and capital budgeting; purely electoral considerations did not determine budgeting decisions while the capital allocations of the local authority were not a dominating factor in relation to subsequent voting behaviour. In New York there was a general pattern of weak relationships between allocations and voting behaviour while in London the relationship was generally absent. The study concluded with a warning concerning the nature of interview data and comparative studies: in New York, whatever the true nature of the relationship, there was a widely-spoken assumption that a payoff relationship existed and that interviews conducted without reference to actual capital allocations would misrepresent the real situation and exaggerate the contrasts between linkages in New York and London.

Social scientists have engaged in a pursuit of general rules and concepts, and it is easy to undervalue the uniqueness of different situations and locations. Much of the best work on allocational behaviour has been done by investigators who accept the perspectives of the radical left; Marxists however are prone to blanket assumptions concerning capitalist societies while a widespread reluctance to consider the operation of political systems in the socialist world is apparent. Generalization can undervalue the specific characteristics of particular systems and, as Glassberg points out,

> These surface similarities in political situation between London and New York should not obscure the large differences in structure between the two cities. New York has a relatively centralized administration (a fact currently causing considerable political dispute), while the subdivisions of Greater London, the thirty-two London Boroughs and the City of London, are regarded by some observers as holding more power than the overall Greater London government.[21]

The problems concerning generalization, model-building and comparative study are underlined by Elkin:

> Lima, Peru, has no city government, the central city being divided into several municipalities including a portion governed by Lima Province. Similarly, Valencia, Venezuela is largely governed by a variety of central governmental agencies over which the local authority exercises limited influence. In contrast, Zagreb, Yugoslavia has a metropolitan area government which can vote its own budgets, pass laws and establish agencies without central control. In Calcutta, India, the chief executive is

appointed by the state government, but locally elected councillors have considerable voice in a variety of administrative matters and personnel appointments, decisions in Calcutta reflecting these two apparently evenly balanced actors. In Lodz, Poland, however, local decisions are largely made in central departments and in conflict between the council and ministerial orders, the latter tend to dominate.[22]

While the difficulties of comparative study continue to pose problems, more work is also needed on the processes concerning the distribution of goods and services to the different elements in the community and in particular, the causes which underlie various patterns of allocation. Neither populations nor public goods are distributed evenly, and as Jones and Kaufman point out,

> Some neighbourhoods may receive more of a particular service than others, or the service delivered may be of a higher quality. This may be accomplished either by direct delivery, or by locating better facilities nearer these neighbourhoods, since consumption of such services depends heavily on access. Since urban neighbourhoods are distinctive in their composition, by distributing services unequally to neighbourhoods governments are distributing those services unequally to categories of citizens.[23]

The authors go on to describe four examples or models of service delivery systems. In the 'equality of service distribution' example, each neighbourhood shares equally in service outputs, irrespective of the varying levels of demand and need; in the 'humanitarian' example, the system is responsive to the needs rather than to the demands of the different sections in the community and the allocations are made in such a way as to achieve an equality of distribution; thus the system is redistributive. Different forms of allocation would obviously result from the operation of these contrasting systems. Under the former, goods and services like libraries, skilled teachers and so on would be located with a view to equalizing the quality of service throughout the governmental area, while in the latter, the best facilities would become concentrated in the formerly deprived areas with the objective of equalizing the quality and opportunity of school leavers and educational standards throughout the area by giving most to those who started with least.

The third example is based on 'pressure and response' and here, the service delivery system is demand-dominated and the decision-makers are more sensitive to well-supported demands than they are to the needs of deprived areas. In this case, the allocations are concentrated in those areas which contain the most vocal and influential populations. The final example is that of a 'linear service function' and here the service delivery system responds in a nondiscriminatory fashion both to increases in demand and in need, rewarding rises in intensity of either. Clearly, each real world delivery system has its own inherent acquired and imposed characteristics and they will vary in the degree to which general policies, constraints and ideological perspectives colour the pattern of allocation, as they will vary in their relative sensitivity to demand and need. Even so, these four models provide useful yard-sticks against which the character of particular systems may be measured.

Environment, Politics and Allocation: American state and local government experience

One of the more consistent observations in studies of how governments provide goods and services is the marked variation apparent between jurisdictions in the supply of the same function. That is, governments of the same type – state or local – vary in their allocative behaviour. The differences can often be substantial: for example, per capita unemployment compensation benefits in the most generous states in the USA can be twice those of states providing the lowest levels. More generally differences in welfare payments between states closely parallel variations in income between the jurisdictions. Such disparities raise questions of welfare and equity, although equally they pose questions as to their possible explanation. Comparative studies of the factors 'explaining' such differences in output have been extensively developed in relation to the behaviour of state and local governments in the United States.

The systems model has provided the general framework within which most studies have been discussed. According to it governments will seek to transform demands generated by the environment into public policies, so that differences in the environment between jurisdictions can be used to help explain variations in policy outputs. This is tantamount to saying, as Dye has put it, that policy outputs are 'the result of *forces* brought to bear upon a *system* and causing it to make particular responses'.[24]

Fig. 7.2 is an expanded version of the systems model introduced in Chapter 1. The outputs of the process, normally measured by the patterns of spending within different fields (housing, welfare and specific programmes within such fields) reflect the differing socio-economic character of the territorially bound governments and those factors relating more to the working of the political apparatus.

These would include the effect of the party system, the electoral system including apportionment, the constitutional framework and interest group behaviour (some of which we have discussed in previous sections). The model oversimplifies the pattern of interrelationships which link the environmental and political system variables. Hence, as a number of studies of local (city) politics have shown, different types of government are associated with cities of a particular size, and these differently styled governments exhibit characteristic patterns of allocative behaviour. For example, in small towns (less than 5,000) and very large cities the mayor–council form of government predominates in contrast to the manager–council form in medium-sized communities (25,000 to

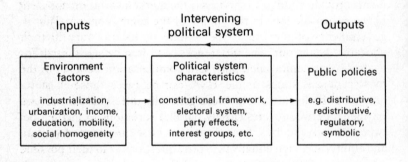

Fig. 7.2. Systems model of public policy-making.

250,000). At least in the very large cities the mayor–council form is the more usual because it is better able to conciliate among the numerous competing interests and values typical to a large, socially heterogeneous urban environment. In the small town the predominance of the mayor–council form of government is presumed to be due to the system being able to accommodate itself to the more tightly-drawn and widely-accepted community values and norms; to appoint a manager, most likely not a member of the community, could set in train its own conflicts. What is important, though, is that these two factors, population size and form of government, together with other ecological and political variables have been linked to specific policy-making patterns among local governments. Fluoridation of the water supply (to cite one case) is more likely in smaller cities in which the manager–council form of government is found – its size implies a degree of social homogeneity while the manager form is the stronger of the two modes of government.[25]

The question of which factors of the social environment might correlate with and act as the determinants of the policy outputs of state governments was first systematically analysed by Fabricant in *The Trend of Government Activity in the United States since 1900*.[26] Fabricant demonstrated that 72 per cent of the variation in expenditures could be explained by differences in levels of urbanization, population density and per capita income. Of these per capita income was the most powerful factor, a finding which subsequent analyses have confirmed, although as a determinant of spending differences its importance varies according to policy field. In some (but not all) of the state welfare programmes and in the provision of education income differences are the dominant explanatory variable, while these are of far less importance in explaining differences in per capita highway expenditures between states. Variables such as income and urbanization assess the need and in some cases the possible resources available to meet the delivery of services.

Besides the need for action and the availability of resources to meet demand the fashioning of public policies depends on the 'disposition' of the political and administrative institutions responsible. Such dispositions reflect a wide range of factors; they may include attitudes of politicians and bureaucrats towards needy groups, the power of various groups and the effects of the party system. Of the latter it was Key's classic study of Southern politics which argued convincingly that states with one-party as opposed to two-party systems differed in their treatment of the less privileged.[27] In the one-party state it would be easier for a few power interests to dominate the state government whereas in the the two-party state, common in North-Eastern, North Central and Western states, 'anxiety over the next election pushes political leaders into serving the interests of the unprivileged element of society, thereby using countervailing power against the party in control'.[28] Such differences could be used to explain variations in welfare policies between Southern and non-Southern states. Furthermore, as Lockard argued,[29] these differences in party system could in part be attributed to differences in the socio-economic make-up of the states – the two-party systems of Northern states such as Ohio, New York or Pennsylvania reflected the diversity of their economic structure.

Table 7.1 and Fig. 7.3 illustrate the major findings of Sharkansky and Hofferbert's study[30] of the social and political differences

Table 7.1. **The Association between Socioeconomic, Political and Policy Factors in the United States – 48 States.**

	Welfare– Education	Highways– National Resources
	Simple and partial correlation	
Professionalism– Local Reliance	·39 (·26)	−·54 (−·24)
Competition–Turnout	·68 (·47)	·25 (−·02)
Industrialization	·37 (·17)	−·69 (−·55)
Affluence	·69 (·43)	·43 (·53)
	Multiple correlation and determination	
Socioeconomic factors	·77 (·59)	·82 (·68)
Political factors	·78 (·61)	·60 (·36)
Socioeconomic and political factors	·83 (·69)	·84 (·70)

Notes: Measured by coefficient of correlation. In the upper table the figure in brackets refers to the partial coefficient of correlation, *viz.* where other factors are 'held' constant. In the lower table the figure in brackets refers to the multiple coefficient of determination, in which unity (1·0) is the measure of 'total explanation'.

Source: Adapted from R. I. Hofferbert, *The Study of Public Policy*, Bobbs-Merrill, New York, 1974, p. 219.

characterizing states and their relationship with policy allocations. Their method relied substantially on the ability of the factor analytic techniques used to isolate major social, political and policy dimensions. In terms of socioeconomic differences two dimensions accounted for 58 per cent of the variance, measuring industrialization and affluence, the latter distinguishing Northern from Southern states. These two factors were labelled professionalism–local reliance and competition–turnout. States scoring high on the former were more likely to be industrial, while those in the second factor, specifically where suffrage laws are liberal and turnouts in gubernatorial elections relatively high include the less industrial, non-Southern states.

These socioeconomic and political factors correlate varyingly with the two policy factors, welfare/education and highways/natural resources. The affluence of the state and its electoral competitiveness both have positive relationships with their spending in the welfare/education field. Spending in the highways/natural resources field was negatively associated with industrialization. Evidently Sharkansky and Hofferbert are able to provide evidence countering the argument which suggested that differences in political structure and process (e.g. the competitiveness of elections) were insignificant compared to the impact of economic differences, although they concluded that there is no single answer to the question 'Is it economics or politics that has the greatest impact on public policy-making?'.

Allocations and Externalities

One important sphere of governmental allocation policy has concerned the location of those controversial public facilities which impose significant negative externalities upon sections of the community, with the burden of externalities tending to be borne by those neighbourhoods which already existed in deprived circumstances. Again, the policy options open to allocating authorities are varied, and the situation can be clarified by reference to a set of models concerning approaches to the location of controversial facilities which have been developed by Mumphrey, Seley and Wolpert.[31] The 'minimum physical cost' model operates purely on economic considerations where the location of externality-imposing facilities is regarded purely on the grounds of comparative physical costs. Such a model makes no allowance for the consequent political activity and socio-political costs which may accrue and cause delays and possible cancellations when opposition places obstacles in the path of the locators, and such opposition will render the model unviable in a majority of cases. As a consequence, two further models were developed.

The 'political placation' model provides a short-run approach to locational problems and the outcomes reflect the varying abilities of different groups in the community to exact concessions or payoffs from the locators. These are made to those groups with significant resources of power, and the model can be used either as a descriptive tool or as a normative approach to location. There is no guarantee that side payments will be proportional to the disamenity costs borne by affected groups and they are more likely to reflect the power, influence and degree of organization of the opposed groups. The 'welfare distribution' model provides a long-run approach and prescribes a more equitable distribution of controversial facilities and associated side-payments. Bargaining power is regarded as being proportional to the adverse effects of the facilities concerned; thus those groups which are the most disadvantaged are granted the greatest redress. The vital difference between the two approaches concerns the methods of discounting the political consequences of the initial locational decision. The long-run approach involves side-payments to groups who need not be placated on purely political grounds in the short run, but it avoids the accumulation over time of a concentration of disamenities which might politicize the otherwise uncompensated weaker groups. Here, concessions are divided between short-run opponents who have the immediate power resources to oppose the project concerned and long-run opponents who would acquire this power to resist future projects as a result of their experience of disamenities accruing from the project in question.

The authors conclude that

> Traditional least-cost solutions to the problem of locating public facilities with significant spatial externalities tend to be quite costly in the long run when they fail to anticipate opposition ... Obviously, the short run approach is easier to operationalize and can be used to describe many existing cases of public facility decision-making. For planners concerned with future stability, however, the more difficult long term model suggests a way to convince politicians to look beyond immediate power struggles to the predictable results of their present action.[32]

The paper amounts to a not unconvincing argument that spatial justice can make economic sense, although this lesson may be lost on a wide range of authorities.

Cox has described how the problem of externalities can be viewed as one of locational conflict since the magnitude of externalities experienced in any location is to a large degree related to the spatial juxtaposition of resource allocators.[33] The resolution of conflicts, he points out, may be achieved either through private co-ordination in which some of the parties involved move out of the neighbourhood concerned – a relocation strategy – or in which bargaining between the actors leads to successful compromise. An outcome of the relocation strategy – for example when middle-class families move out of decaying inner city neighbourhoods to exclusive suburbs – is the creation of discrete territories in which positive externalities are shared and which are homogeneous with regard to social class and race. This outcome may resolve the problem of externality-creating allocations for those who move, but it does not solve but intensifies the problems faced in the abandoned neighbourhoods.

Public co-ordination through government activity may seek to influence private locational decisions, for example by seeking to check private relocations by offering tax incentives to those who remain in inner city locations. Governments may also engage in bargaining through which an inner city authority may negotiate subsidies for suburban municipalities in order to improve the quality of city centre amenities. In the USA in particular, however, the advantages of public co-ordination may be offset by the fragmentation of the urban unit by the boundaries of separate jurisdictions. As a result conflicts both between and within jurisdictions are anticipated. A jurisdiction may produce externalities experienced by the populations of neighbouring jurisdictions, as when the high quality of public goods available as a result of high income from taxes in a 'desirable middle-class jurisdiction' attracts further middle-class families from nearby municipalities which can scarce afford to lose elements of its high-income population and where revenue and the standards of resource provision are low. Conflicts within jurisdictions may arise as a result of unevenness in the allocation of public goods or in the imposition of externalities.

Within the city, a range of locational conflicts may be resolved through the creation of a superordinate authority which can take an overall view and produce city-wide policies with individual jurisdictions releasing some of their sovereignty over the property rights of their constituent, decision-making units to the larger authority. However, 'The collectivization of property rights and the vesting of them in a superordinate authority, therefore, creates new decision-making units on a new and larger geographical scale'.[34] In turn, the enlarged jurisdiction may be expected to create externalities for other units of similar or smaller scales and new cycles of conflict and conflict resolution are initiated.

In a broad sense, the locational conflicts which Cox has described operating at the scale of the city are a part of a conflict continuum which extends upwards to include the population of sovereign states. 'The division of accessible space into political units has produced an unequal allocation with some states much weaker than others and unable, under present conditions, to function very effectively as providers of goods and services.[35]

The magnitude, range and pattern of the allocation of public goods produces spatial outcomes which are the products of intertwined variables. From unit to unit and from decision to decision, the degree to which the political ideologies of the allocators of goods or their masters intrude upon decisions will vary. The paramountcy of ideology in the socialist states is well publicized, but it may also be evidenced from time to time in the western democracies, for example in the blanket hostility of the Thatcher government in the UK towards 'quangos', irrespective of the usefulness of the role of the institution concerned. The receptivity of the political system to demands in general and to sectors of demand is variable while the levels of demand-making are uneven both within and between units of government. In some countries demand-making is constricted within avenues of acceptability and where freedom exists, different elements in the community issue demands at different intensities, and these levels are seldom proportional to need.

In the search for generalized concepts and models the researcher must not be blind to the differences in allocative behaviour which result from differences in the powers, functions and financing of different political structures.

> In the United States a greater proportion of the money spent is raised locally, mainly from taxes levied on property (the state fixes the limits on debt held by the local units however, and this is one of the reasons for the creation of so many special districts . . .) In the United Kingdom, on the other hand, more than 60 per cent of the money spent by local authorities comes from the central government by way of rate-support grants. The central government is in a strong position, therefore, to intervene in order to even out what it considers to be gross inequality in patterns of expenditure by local authorities, and can put pressure on the local spenders to make changes in the priority they give to different services.[36]

A behavioural approach to the problems of the allocation of public goods is buttressed by the fact that the decisional bodies are not efficient machines capable of producing optimal outputs and distributions constructed from the objective assessment of all relevant and perfectly weighted inputs, but consist of human actors, vessels for all the frailties which humanity entails. Such actors are responsive to pressure and coercion, personal and collective biases and conduct imperfect appraisals of information and the consequences of their choices. A spatial approach is favoured because 'the "where" enters the situation because the political system can only operate in space, and it therefore needs to create a geographical organization of space. It is within this structure of government and administration that competition, conflict, and co-operation take place'.[37]

Discussion Points and Further Reading

In recent years geographers of various political persuasions have recognized the importance of the allocation of goods and resources as vital geographical processes. Although the economic, social and urban geographers have been in the forefront, the political significance of their work is obvious and allocational studies form an important strand in the new political geography. Most problems revolve around the relationship between a national or local political system and its geographical, political and social environments. Studies of demand-making show that in both public and private sectors the allocative systems often prove more responsive to organized demand rather than objective needs. Political perceptions and interests strongly influence the allocation of public goods.

The most influential text is Harvey (1973). Several interesting concepts were further developed by Cox (1973). The articles by Runciman (1966) and Bertsch (1973) provide interesting introductions to the concept of relative deprivation. An important case study of public participation in urban planning was provided by Ferris (1972), while Lowe (1976) offers a useful review of British environmental pressure group activity. The nature of demand making in a socialist country is explored in the articles by Oliver (1968), and Friedgut (1978).

G. K. Bertsch, 'The Revival of Nationalism', *Problems of Communism* (1973), **22**, 1–15.

K. R. Cox, *Conflict, Power and Politics in the City*, McGraw-Hill, New York, 1973.

J. Ferris, *Participation in Urban Planning: The Barnsbury Case*, Bell, London, 1972.

T. H. Friedgut, 'Citizens and Soviets: Can Ivan Ivanovich Fight City Hall?', *Comparative Politics*, July 1978.

D. Harvey, *Social Justice and the City*, Edward Arnold, London, 1973.

P. D. Lowe, 'Amenity and Equity: a Review of Local Environmental Pressure Groups in Britain'. *Environment and Planning* (1976), **9**.

J. H. Oliver, 'Citizen Demands and the Soviet Political System', *American Political Science Review* (1968), **63**, 465–75.

W. G. Runciman, *Relative Deprivation and Social Justice*, University of California Press, Berkeley, 1966.

Notes

1. Professor Kirk elaborates on the difficulties involved in the notes to the address (see note 2 below).
2. W. Kirk, 'The Road to Mandalay: Towards a Geographical Philosophy', *Transactions of the Institute of British Geographers* (1978), **3**, 4, 391–2.
3. W. Taubman, *Governing Soviet Cities*, Praeger, New York, 1973, p. 109.
4. T. H. Friedgut, 'Citizens and Soviets: Can Ivan Ivanovich Fight City Hall?', *Comparative Politics*, July 1978.
5. J. H. Oliver, 'Citizen Demands and the Soviet Political System', *Amer. Pol. Sci Rev.* (1968) **63**, 465–75.
6. Friedgut, 'Citizens and Politics', p. 475.
7. Oliver, 'Citizen Demands', p. 475.
8. *Ibid.* p. 473.
9. W. G. Runciman, *Relative Deprivation and Social Justice*, University of California Press, Berkeley, 1966.
10. G. K. Bertsch, 'The Revival of Nationalism', *Problems of Communism* (1973), **22**, 1–15.

11. J. Ferris, *Participation in Urban Planning: The Barnsbury Case*, Bell, London, 1972.
12. R. Gregory, 'The Voluntary Amenity Movement', in M. MacEwan (ed.), *Future Landscapes*, Chatto and Windus, London, 1976, pp. 199–217.
13. P. D. Lowe, 'Amenity and Equity: a Review of Local Environmental Pressure Groups in Britain', *Environment and Planning* (1976), **9**, 55.
14. D. Sibley, 'Classification and Control in Local Government: a Case Study of Gypsies in Hull', *Transactions of the Institute of British Geographers* (1978), **3**(3), 319–27.
15. *Ibid.* pp. 319–20.
16. *Ibid.* p. 321.
17. J. Dearlove, 'Councillors and Interest Groups in Kensington and Chelsea', *British Journal of Political Science* (1971), **1**, 129–53.
18. A. Glassberg, 'Linkage between Urban Policy Output and Voting Behaviour', *British Journal of Political Science* (1973) **3**, 341–61.
19. *Ibid.* p. 343.
20. *Ibid.* p.342.
21. *Ibid.*
22. S. L. Elkin, 'Comparative Urban Politics and Inter-Organisational Behaviour', *Policy and Politics* (1975), **2**, 3, 289.
23. B. D. Jones and C. Kaufman, 'The Distribution of Urban Public Services', *Administration and Society* (1974), **6**, 3, 338.
24. T. R. Dye, *Politics, Economics and the Public: Policy Outcomes in the American States*, Rand McNally, Chicago, 1966, p. 3.
25. See the general discussion contained in P. Conter, 'American Community Politics: The Policy Perspective', in J. A. Riedel, (ed.), *New Perspectives in State and Local Politics*, Xerox, Mass., 1971, pp. 43–76.
26. S. Fabricant, *Trend of Government Activity in the United States since 1900*, National Bureau of Economic Research, New York, 1952.
27. V. D. Key, *Southern Politics*, Alfred Knopf, New York, 1949.
28. A. S. Harbert, *Federal Grants-in-Aid*, Praeger, New York, 1976, p. 69.
29. D. Lockard, *New England State Politics,* Princeton University Press, Princeton, 1959.
30. I. Sharkansky and R. I. Hofferbert 'Dimensions of State Politics, Economics and Public Policy', *American Political Science Review* (1969), **63**, 867–79.
31. A. J. Mumphrey, J. E. Seley and J. Wolpert, 'A Decision Model for Locating Controversial Facilities', *Journal of the American Institute of Planners* (November 1971), 397–402.
32. *Ibid.* p. 402.
33. K. R. Cox, *Conflict, Power and Politics in the City: A Geographic View*, McGraw-Hill, New York, 1973.
34. B. E. Coates, R. J. Johnston and P. L. Knox, *Geography and Inequality*, Oxford University Press, London, 1900, p. 193.
35. Cox, *Conflict, Power and Politics*, p. 15.
36. Coates, Johnston and Knox, *Geography and Inequality*, p. 194.
37. *Ibid.* p. 203.

8 International Behaviour

The study of the international behaviour of states – or more accurately, of statesmen and other political actors – is the concern of students of international relations.[1] Not all international relationships are greatly influenced by considerations arising directly from the geographical environment and not all the outcomes of these relationships exert a great impact upon this environment. Relevant political geographical inquiry will concern those relationships which have been largely or partly conditioned by spatial factors such as distance and relative proximity and variations in the distribution of geographical resources. It will also concern those relationships whose outcomes or whose spillover effect bring about changes in the geographical environment. A sizeable proportion of the literature of political geography has been pitched at the international level, but until recently such work tended to be presented without any deep exploration of the political character of the states concerned or the behavioural motivations of their decision-makers. The result of this was the production of studies which tended to be incomplete and descriptive, using approaches which were analogous to the study of agricultural land-use while neglecting the whys and wherefores of the farmer's choice.

Influencies and Goals

The study of international behaviour is largely a study of decisions and decision-making, and since most of the relevant decisions at the international level are made by politicians, it is a study of how politicians handle and are influenced by information, values, pressures and existing relationships. The ability to generalize about international political behaviour depends upon our being able to devise a model or stereotype of the political decision-maker, and since such actors are no more predictable than other members of the human race and operate in an environment which is infinitely varied and ever-changing, only a coarse caricature of their goals and behaviour can be attempted. Some leading actors are dictators, but normally the important political decision-makers are servants of the state and consequently their most fundamental motivation can be identified as the pursuit of the 'national interest'. In theoretical terms it can be argued that absolute state or national interests exist and as a consequence at any point in time there are a series of best decisions which should be taken for the most perfect furtherance of the national interest. However, for all practical purposes we are not concerned with the unrecognizable absolute national interest but with those characterizations of national interest which form in the minds of political actors. Were the national interest readily identifiable and not amenable to varying interpretations, there would be little need for the elaborate diplomatic machines which most states support, and arguably, for political parties either. The national interest which concerns us here is a subjective phenomenon and so we can say that the fundamental motivation which helps to determine political behaviour at the international level is the pursuit of a perception of the national interest.

Having introduced the word 'perception' the flood gates are opened for all manner of complications and qualifications. The national interest which we have confidently identified as being the basic goal of political action now becomes an intangible, a matter of opinion. It is not likely to be the product of only one mind, for a foreign secretary for example who is faced with a particular problem or opportunity will form a perception of the best course of action which is likely to embody the various perceptions of national interest as generated by his advisors and which is coloured by perceptions of relevant aspects of party policy. Even where the ethic of national interest is held to be paramount, the boundary between national interest and party interest is unlikely to be clearcut and circuitous debate is difficult to avoid. The politician can argue that it is in the national interest that his party should dominate the political life of his state and consequently decisions which concern the national interest should be aligned with the party interest. Perceived national interest does not carry clearcut guidance concerning the time scale over which national interest should be considered, and this may lead to contradictions. For example, a policy of armament may appear to be favoured in a consideration of the short-term interests of a state but be in conflict with a long-term interest in disarmament. Perceptions of the national interest will frequently be clouded by the emotional intrusion of certain political values which strongly influence members of the dominant political group. For example, members of the British Conservative party have been unable to formulate a foreign policy which accords with the realities of black Africa largely because of the emotional but irrational attachment to considerations of 'kith and kin' relating to the precarious white settler regimes which have existed in Rhodesia and South Africa.

The elusive nature of the national interest can be examined briefly by reference to the case of a French coastal atomic waste-disposal plant. The fishing community of nearby Guernsey is concerned that this plant may lead to the contamination of the fish stocks upon which their livelihood depends. If there is such a thing as an absolute national interest then it must be a composite of sectional and regional interests and, other things being equal, the state government should seek to promote regional interests as elements of the overall national interest. However, if the UK government were to bring diplomatic pressures to bear upon the French government in the single-minded support of the Guernsey fishing community, a number of complications might arise which could be seen to be at variance with broader perceptions of the UK national interest. Any questioning of the safety margins of nuclear waste disposal plants might have the embarrassing effect of focusing attention upon the expanding British plant at Windscale. National interest can be interpreted in many different ways; it may be in the financial interest of states like Britain and France to establish lucrative international waste-disposal systems, but then these states have the greatest proximity to the areas of potential disaster and the probabilities of disaster cannot be calculated with accuracy. It is apparently in the short-term interest of all states that plants should exist for the disposal of rising output of nuclear waste, but long-term environmental implications may or may not reveal a common interest in abandoning this dangerous mode of power generation. National interest has some parallels with organized religions; it is the major factor motivating behaviour, but it can also be invoked to legitimize decisions reached and influenced by a variety of peripheral considerations.

At least we can be sure that national interest is a selfish doctrine and its pursuit is a barrier to the proper exploration of the collective interests of mankind. Humanity is geographically and politically fragmented within a series of sovereign states and national perspectives have become entrenched while internationalism is a poorly explored or developed concept.[2] The world is a closed system and its geographical resources are finite. The pursuit of national interest involves to a considerable degree the attempt to control resources such as territory, minerals and zones of marine, agricultural and industrial production, and the finite nature of these resources ensures that international conflict and competition predominate over global co-operation.

Problems of conflict and competition at the national level may ultimately require resolution by a supreme arbiter in the form of the sovereign government of the state concerned with vested powers to make and enforce decisions which are binding upon the national community as a whole. There is, however, no supreme arbiter for international disputes, and while agencies such as the United Nations and the International Court might seek to fill this vacuum, they are not sovereign institutions and their decisions are not binding upon the sovereign governments whose actions they might wish to control.[3] International conflicts of interest therefore tend not to be solved by the intervention of higher authorities but by complex processes involving power, coercion and bargaining, if in fact they are resolved at all.

Power, like national interest, is a fundamental but intangible factor in determining the nature and outcome of international relationships and it is of significance to the geographer in a number of ways. First, state power is derived in part from the control of geographical resources such as territory, industrial minerals and fuels; secondly, power in one form or another is likely to be an important consideration in the formation of decisions which bear upon the geographical landscape; thirdly, power is geographically interesting because it is unevenly distributed throughout the international system of states.

There can be no doubt that power is of central importance in political geography and were we able to measure power we would, for example, be able to assess the degree of its impact upon international decision-making and analyse its international distribution, perhaps constructing isoline maps to contour the global distribution of power. Unfortunately, there is no accurate means of measuring power, and while each student will have a somewhat vague perception of its distribution, with the greatest concentrations in the superpowers, the USA and the USSR, with power troughs in areas such as Andean America or Polynesia, the precise calculation of state power is, and will probably remain, unknown. While power is in part derived from a number of tangible resources such as territory, location, population, minerals and production, it is in total a resource which can not be appreciated in any but subjective terms.[4]

Certain geographical components of power such as the possession of energy sources or of skills within a population clearly contribute to the power ranking of the state while obviously the impact of mobilized power will depend to a considerable extent upon the adroitness with which diplomats, the military and industrialists apply these resources to the support of policies, strategies and production plans. However, in addition to being the sum of a vast complexity of mobilized resources, power is relative to the contexts in which it is applied. State A may be more powerful than State B but less powerful than State C; however if State A and State C confront each other in situation x, State C will not automatically emerge the victor. An obvious example concerns the Vietnam war when the vast resources of US military power were not equal to the task of defeating the army of North Vietnam and the Viet Cong in the context of guerilla jungle warfare and when harnessed to a policy of limited commitment against a background of considerable US domestic dissent. Had the contexts of the war been different, for example involving a US policy of total commitment within a desert environment, a swift and different outcome would clearly have resulted.

Situations involving the full mobilization of the power resources of opposed states behind certain goals, as occurred in the 1914–18 and 1939–45 wars, are fortunately rare, and power is normally influential in international decision-making in terms of perceptions of its potential. Not surprisingly, the perceptions held by political actors in respect of the power resources, intentions and capabilities of their allies and adversaries vary greatly in their accuracy. On occasions certain perceptions may be so deeply entrenched as to prevent the acceptance of crucial information which would rationally be assimilated into the decision-making process. Early in the 1939–45 war, the belief of the French commanders that the capability to direct tanks through the difficult terrain of the Ardennes did not exist was so firmly rooted that even air photographs depicting such a German advance were discounted – with disastrous consequences. There are many examples of the distortion of power factors by the perception process; at the time of the Munich crisis in 1938, the British negotiators apparently did not believe that they possessed the power resources necessary to deflect the Nazi armies from the occupation of Czechoslovakia. Conversely, Marshal Keitel in his testimony at the 1946 Nuremberg war trial stated that had the western powers stood firmly by Prague, the German strategists did not believe that their military resources would be adequate in an armed confrontation. The political geographical implications of this interplay of poorly developed perceptions included the absorption of Bohemia, the creation of a Slovak puppet state and ultimately the full devastation of the world war.

Those who contribute to the formation of decisions which have international implications must attempt an assessment of their own power resources, those of their supporters and those of their opponents and they must try to determine the degree to which each of the parties involved will be prepared to mobilize resources in order to modify the outcome. Such decisions are based upon perceptions whose accuracy can only be assessed retrospectively. For example, the Chinese strategists and politicians who planned the invasion of Vietnam in 1979 were correct in their assumptions that the USSR would not commit Soviet forces to the defence of their Vietnamese ally, and they were correct in thinking that China had the power to inflict defeat upon Vietnam. On the other hand, they were wrong in assuming that the regular Vietnamese forces engaged in the occupation of neighbouring Cambodia would be cripplingly depleted and diverted on a grand scale to the defence of the homeland and they underestimated the military capabilities of the militia and reservists which their armies encountered.

By degrees, a picture of the behavioural processes conditioning political action at the international level begins to emerge. It is clear that these relations take place within an anarchical political system in which no actor exercises universal sovereignty and is able to impose lawful authority. The political representatives of the various states are motivated primarily by the pursuit of perceptions of the respective national interests, and this leads them into competition for the control of scarce resources. The uneven nature of the distribution of power constrains the goal-seeking behaviour of the actors, each of whom must adjust his chosen role in accordance with a perception of relative capabilities, and consequently the objectives pursued by the lesser powers will be of a different order and nature from those pursued by greater powers.

One highly geographical influence upon international decision-making is that of distance. Perhaps the most obvious demonstration of the effect of distance and relative location concerns the large number of conflicting territorial claims which involve states which share a common boundary; but distance also exerts its influence in more subtle ways. It is very easy for the political geographer to state the obvious and very difficult to elucidate the less prominent but significant factors. Particular obstacles in the development of impressive and intensely geographical theories and models concerning the relationship between distance and policy include the uniqueness of the individual state in its history, geography and diplomatic priorities and the nature of each geographical state's location, with the complex assemblages of neighbours, resources, problems and opportunities which that location provides. It is easy to suggest that the more powerful a state the wider will be its international commitments and the greater its concern and ability to influence events in the more distant parts of the globe. Clearly, a comparative study of the foreign policies, involvements and objectives of superpowers such as the USA and USSR and those of lesser powers such as Bolivia or Botswana would support this assumption. There are other obvious examples which show that the distance from its borders over which a state may exert a significant influence is not directly proportional to its power. In the post-war era, West Germany has become a leading economic superpower while keeping a very low diplomatic profile beyond the contexts of the EEC and NATO theatres of action. Cuba in contrast is a dwarf according to most standards of power analysis but has pursued a militant and aggressive African policy and is a major influence on the political affairs of Latin America.

Numerous examples can be quoted to demonstrate the effects of distance and relative location on policy in which the geographical factor is so obvious as to be hardly worth quoting. Such examples include the frequent tendency of pairs of states to form alliances against a mutually adjacent neighbour, e.g. France and Scotland versus England or Germany and Russia versus Poland. There is the tendency of states with far-reaching trading commitments to attempt to preserve peace and protect commercial stability, a role played by the UK in the previous century and the USA in the post-war period. Equally obvious is the tendency of the expansionist state to probe areas of weakness along adjacent frontiers, exemplified by Russian policy towards the Turkish Empire in the nineteenth century. The development of more profound insights into the political geographical implications of distance will require much patient research and the unique will always intrude to a considerable degree.

We cannot begin to understand the effect of distance upon

politics if the concept of distance is narrowly considered in terms of linear distance. Until Columbus, sailing westward hopefully to Japan, struck land on the offshore islands of the American continent, we can assume that European political influences in the Americas were to all intents and purposes nil. Within a relatively short period of time, European values and conflicts came to dominate the political life of the continent. Obviously the Americas had not come any closer to Europe in these intervening years and the importance of distance in politics is in part related to the ability or inability to extend influences across distance, and to the time it takes to transmit these influences. Distance will exert part of its effect as linear distance, but in many contexts it is best expressed not in terms of a linear scale, but in terms of travel time. While linear distance is constant, travel time will change with each technological improvement in transport. The statesman reacts to distance in relation to a wide variety of considerations, such as proximity of one area to another of prime strategical importance, the range of military aircraft and missiles of various kinds, relative capabilities of power transmission, distance in relation to respected spheres of influence, and so on.

Some basic refinements to the concept of distance have been briefly suggested by Tiwari using the context of colonial Africa, where he thought that three different forms of distance affected the relationship between the politicians of the imperial heartland, their colonial administrators and the indigenous populations of the colonies.[5] These were linear distance, a constant; time distance, which was progressively reduced with each improvement in communications which shortened the distance between the respective parties; and social distance which was effective through the value and class systems and prejudices of the different groups. Both the temporal and linear forms of distance located the natives and colonial administrators closely together but distant from the imperial government, while social distance put the members of the government and their administrators in proximity but far removed from the native populations.

The effect of the various forms of distance upon decision-making could only be appreciated following a study of the goals and behaviour patterns of the participants, and the nature of information transfer was crucial, with the colonial decision implementors seeking to insulate the European decision-makers from the colonial areas affected by their decisions and attempting to ensure that only such information as reflected favourably on the colonial administrations was able to filter back to Europe.

Proximity is not only a function of linear distance, and proximity of outlook may be unaffected by distance, or even enhanced by it. Although they are widely dispersed, the states which constitute the Third World display a considerable proximity of outlook. Significantly they tend to show a linear proximity to the equator, and a temporal proximity to a colonial past.

Just as the effects of distance are transformed by technological revolutions in the field of communications, so relative location, while fixed in the spatial sense, will change in the functional sense. Two useful examples of the implications of such functional locational changes have been provided by Bradshaw.[6] 'Until the 1950s Nepal could be considered as occupying a location which was secure and something of a political backwater by virtue of the extremely difficult nature of the surrounding mountainous terrain, while the large adjacent states of India and China lacked both the endeavour or the capability to disturb Nepalese isolation. However, during the 1950s and early 1960s both these states began to take an interest in the territories of their frontier zone as both developed transport facilities which improved their accessibility in relation to the Himalayas. The Nepalese political response to these changes in relative location which had been made evident was to convert the natural neutrality which had been endowed by the environment into the active pursuit of a specific policy of neutrality which was buttressed in the quest to preserve independence by attempts to co-operate with the neighbouring great powers.

Changes in the functional nature of relative location will also obviously be transformed by changes in capabilities of power transmission. Until the early 1950s the Soviet Union in all probability possessed the land power capability to overrun the states of Western Europe, but this capability was largely nullified by the US airborne capability to penetrate Soviet air defences and inflict untold damage in the interior of the Soviet Union while the Soviet state lacked the ability to cause reciprocal damage in the USA. This American immunity endowed by relative location affected the behaviour of the component members of the Atlantic alliance, with the USA being more ready to explore policies of brinkmanship than were the exposed European allies. Subsequently the relative location of the USA deteriorated with the development of a Soviet capacity for long-range air and missile attacks.

The relative power status of the state and its relative location are two factors which help to determine the nature of its international policy, and a third factor is that of size. There is no direct relationship between the size of a state and the scope of its impact upon international affairs, and at different periods of history modestly sized states such as England, Portugal and Spain have exerted global roles which were quite disproportionate to their size. By virtue of a location which coincides with vast oil reserves, Kuwait is an example of a modern state which is capable of playing a substantial role in international affairs. One remarkable feature of the political partitioning of the modern world concerns the enormous diversity in both the size and the international influence of states, with a considerable number of small states being in existence whose GNP figures are less than the annual turnover of many western industrial corporations. It has been pointed out that six large states cover 49·7 per cent of the total land area of the world, while twenty very small states together occupy only 1·2 per cent of the land surface.

In the past it could be said that excessive size in itself could constitute a problem for the state with over-large states possessing territory which exceeded the organizational capacity of their governmental structures, the Russian decision of 1867 to sell Alaska to the USA being offered as an example. During the course of this century a variety of technological refinements in the means of communication have eroded the problem of administrative distance and since the start of the second quarter of this century the Soviet Union, which is by far the largest state in the world, has been subjected to a highly centralized form of government which has been quite capable of imposing its will upon the most peripheral portions of its territory.

The problem of smallness, however, is severely encountered in the majority of smaller states. Characteristically it emerges in a variety of forms and concerns the absence of a broad and varied industrial base, the lack of a domestic market which will support the economies of scale of mass production and dependence upon a limited range of export commodities which are subject to severe price fluctuations and enjoy restricted access to potential markets as a result of the operation of tariff or quota restrictions. The political life of such states is typically dominated by a pervasive government apparatus which often exists to articulate the interests of a small educated elite which may be composed of members of the dominant economic interest groups. The claustrophobic political arena of the small states often produces an intensely factional and personalized form of political life in which the broader and more objective political issues become submerged in a morass of sectional antagon-isms.[7]

Each state will tailor its international diplomacy to the size of its political cloth and while examples have been given to show that the scope of a state's international involvement is not directly related to either its power or its territorial characteristics, we may expect to find a correlation between the international roles and objectives of states and their inherent geographical characteristics. Rather than having a comprehensive international policy, the small state of the developing world will commonly be active in international affairs only in respect of a limited range of issues which generally involve attempts (often in association with groups of states with similar problems) to obtain improved access to developed markets, efforts to attract foreign aid and investment and bilateral negotiations with the foreign corporations which may dominate the limited range of production in the small state concerned. International policy tends to be overshadowed by domestic policy which is preoccupied by problems of raising standards of living, initiating programmes of industrial development or, as is frequently the case, maintaining the political status quo within a heterogeneous and divided society.

The historical background of the state will obviously exert a considerable influence upon the political perspectives of its policy-makers and in extreme cases the leading element in the *raison d'être* of the state may involve a determination to avoid control by a traditional adversary. The basic norms which govern diplomacy were developed in the context of eighteenth- and nineteenth-century Europe and subsequently superimposed or adopted in the remaining parts of the world where they are often found to be at variance with more deeply established political outlooks and entities. The fundamental unit of international rela-tions is the sovereign state which is essentially the product of evolu-tion in Europe where pre-existing kingdoms and empires provided the geographical basis for compartmentalization while the accep-tance of the sovereign rights of rulers which developed during the period following the Treaty of Westphalia in 1648 established a basis for the development of certain norms of diplomacy. The subsequent growth in Europe of a political philosophy of national-ism culminated in the arrangement of political organization around the norm of the sovereign nation state described by Soja as

the most prevalent organizational structure in human history. Its 'suc-cess' story in political evolution rests on the establishment of a territori-ally defined focus of mass-identity and political action which was sufficiently large in scale to permit the societal differentiation, specialization and participation that was necessary for the massive changes engendered by industrialization.[8]

This form of state was successfully adopted with a federal variation by the USA, and the American republican state in turn provided a model widely used in the establishment of independent states in the southern part of the continent. Paralleling the rise of the sovereign nation state in Europe was the development of European imperialism which achieved the (generally arbitrary) partitioning of Africa and Asia into a patchwork pattern of colonial territories whose political geographical characteristics often bore little resemblance to indigenous patterns of race, culture or economy.

With the retreat of European imperialism the communities inhabiting each of the former colonies had little choice but to adopt the European sovereign state as the vehicle for their future political existence. Each colony had incubated its own particular movement for 'national' independence and the few subsequent attempts at the amalgamation of former colonial territories to form more viable economic and political units such as the Central African Federation, the Mali union, the Caribbean Federation and the proposed East African Federation were notably unsuccessful. In each case the heterogeneous and divided populations of the amalgamations lacked any decisive feeling of identity with the new or proposed unions. Diversity of identity was almost as great within most of the former colonies, driving the new regimes into feverish attempts to create a sense of national unity sufficient to override the deeply entrenched tribal, ethnic and economic identities of their heterogeneous populations.

The newly independent states emerged into a world in which the norms of statehood and the procedures of diplomacy were standardized and there was no alternative but to subscribe to and adopt the sovereign nation state either in a parliamentary, republican or federal form. Accepted along with the state were the institutions and protocols of international diplomacy, no matter how poorly adapted were the European state and its political accessories to the conditions which prevailed in the developing world. Since statehood was the goal of every colonial political leader, the question of alternatives to the sovereign nation state will seldom have been considered other than through nebulous speculation concerning the long-term prospects of Pan-Africanism.

While the newly established rulers in the developing world were unanimous in their adoption of the sovereign nation state as a vehicle for the organization of internal and external affairs, the attempts by the European powers to recreate the political institutions which they operated and admired within their departing colonies were singularly unsuccessful. As Colebatch and Scott remark,

> In 1960, all but three of the recently independent states of tropical Africa possessed a system of competitive political parties operating within a European-style parliamentary framework. A decade later, it was difficult to find a single example of a state where the constitution still functioned along the lines intended by the departing colonial power. The normal pattern of post-independence politics was the transition of the ruling party in a competitive situation into an authoritarian structure which absorbed or suppressed its opponents.[9]

The international politics of the states of the developing world reflect their economic condition and their history. The priority given to attempts mounted on either individual or collective bases to achieve a more equitable trading relationship with the developed world is entirely justified in terms of the generally unstable and unequal character of trade between the developed and developing spheres. The experiences of the colonial past have often seemed to encourage the formation of emotional and undiscriminating attitudes towards supposed instances of imperialism, while the precarious nature of the political structures in many of the countries of the developing world have encouraged tendencies both to attempt to divert attention away from internal problems towards alleged external threats and, in Africa at least, to develop powerful taboos against interference in the domestic affairs of other black states. Both these tendencies were clearly exhibited in the events which culminated in the Tanzanian overthrow of the Amin regime in Uganda in 1979. The action began with a Ugandan invasion of Tanzania in support of a stage-managed territorial claim which was almost certainly designed to divert the attention of Ugandan civilians and soldiers away from the worsening economic and political situation within Uganda. While the subsequent Tanzanian invasion and eviction of the Amin regime was joyfully received within Uganda, removing from the global arena a ludicrous dictator who symbolized all that was worst in black African politics, the support of other African leaders for the Tanzanian initiative was never more than lukewarm and clearly the precedent of external intervention against an insecure regime struck a number of chords of insecurity.

The political ideology and preferences of government are obviously an important factor in determining the international relations of a state. Political values and perceived national interest are often uneasy bedfellows with the latter consideration generally, but not always, emerging supreme. The western democracies have seldom had great difficulty in deciding to ignore democratic values when important national interests have encouraged economic or strategical association with authoritarian and reactionary regimes. Equally, while the foreign policy of the Soviet Union could be characterized as that of a militantly Communistic regime, the Soviet concern to protect the state against western powers by exerting a strong political influence over the territories of its western approaches and the search for warm-water naval bases could easily be interpreted as an extension of Tsarist policies. The desertion of its Somali ally and the switch of Soviet support to the Ethiopian invasion of Somalia in 1977 had little to do with ideology and much to do with pragmatism.

Where ideology and values conflict with perceived national interest, the makers of international policy must assess the extent to which the one is threatened by the other and assign respective priorities; beyond this it is difficult to generalize. Such a conflict confronts several African leaders, say Colebatch and Scott:

> South Africa possesses capital, skills and natural resources which could rapidly accelerate economic development in the rest of Africa as well as provide short-term employment opportunities for the inhabitants of poorer states. But here, as with Rhodesia, most of the African states accept that Pan-African ideals must be weighed against national self-interest. The African majorities in South Africa and Rhodesia are not being abandoned by an acceptance of continuing European minority rule. Dr. Banda's Malawi, and the client states of Lesotho, Botswana and Swaziland, are exceptional in stifling criticism because of the economic advantages accruing from friendly relations with the white-controlled areas.[10]

The formation of international policy involves the permanent and political staff of the foreign departments of government, the head of state or government and other senior members of the dominant political party whose vested departmental interests may conflict with those of the department charged with the formation of diplomatic policy. The combination of political actors involved in decision-making will of course vary from issue to issue and from state to state. In any event, the decisions made are aligned with the fundamental objective of furthering the national interest as this is perceived by the political actors involved. To a greater or lesser extent, these decisions will also be influenced by attitudes derived from historical experience and by political values relating to the issues concerned. The nature and scope of these decisions are made to conform with assessments of the capabilities for successful action derived from an appraisal of the relative power of the state concerned within the political geographical arena under consideration. In all cases, the decisions and policies which are espoused are formed in relation to a perspective of the world which is centred on the relative locational characteristics of the state concerned.

The political perceptions of the world as developed by leading statesmen on the basis of experience, preference, information and interpretation are of vital importance in the formation of international policy, although it is not always easy to infer the characteristics of mental maps pertaining to political statesmen. Occasionally statements made by these figures provide insights into their political geographical perspectives, as with General De Gaulle's declaration of 1955 that 'when all is said and done, Great Britain is an island; France, the cape of a continent; America, another world'. Collectively or individually and consciously or subconsciously the makers of international policy form decisions in relation to political geographical mental maps. These maps include the distribution of friendly and antagonistic powers, areas of opportunity, the spheres of influence of respective powers and critical zones over which the *status quo* must be upheld or changes attempted or resisted. There was never any question of US intervention during the Hungarian uprising of 1956 owing largely to the tacit recognition that East Europe lay within the Soviet sphere of influence; however, a few years later the US was prepared for a full-scale military intervention when the Soviet Union attempted to introduce missiles in Cuba which lay well within the US sphere of influence. Boulding has introduced the concept of 'critical boundaries', lines which are firmly marked on the mental maps of the makers of foreign policy as vital political or ideological watersheds which must be enforced at almost any cost.[11] Assuming that the Soviet Union has an objective of westward expansion, the security of Western Europe could be said to depend upon Soviet belief in the US intention to resort to nuclear warfare in order to maintain the critical boundary between East and West Germany. Cohen has suggested that when a great power suffers a loss of influence in one portion of the globe it will attempt to redress this loss through the more active pursuit of advantages in another.[12] This being the case one might anticipate increased US involvement in Israel and Egypt following the collapse of US influence with the overthrow of the Shah's regime in Iran.

Forms of Relationship

Each state has international relationships with every other state and there is great variation in the intensity and amity of these relationships, varying from armed conflict at one extreme to joint membership of purposeful regional organizations at the other. Forms of international association are varied; there are trading relations, imperial relations between the metropolitan country and its colonies and those which develop between members of international economic, political and defensive organizations.

The attitudes which are generated in the course of political relationships do not tend to remain confined to the sphere of politics and there are various studies which show that the climate of a political relationship is exported and reflected in economic, social and perceptual arenas. Not only are political attitudes influenced by economic and cultural considerations, the reverse relationship is also encountered. Any serious inquiry into the pattern of world trading will reveal the inadequacy of analysis based solely on the consideration of purely economic factors concerning the relative distribution of areas of supply and demand and the forces of economic competition. Patterns of political preference are clearly an important factor influencing – and in some cases governing – the trading behaviour of states. Relevant policies include the establishment of a trading bias with politically acceptable partners and the use of selective restrictions upon trade in the form of embargoes, or more commonly, tariff and quota systems which are applied at the boundaries of the state. The use of tariffs and quotas to constrain and inhibit the commercial relationships of the state – and consequently those of its potential economic partners – may be motivated by a variety of considerations. It may reflect the intent to provide an artificially favourable economic environment for selected newly established industries during a difficult incubation period, or the preservation of employment in ageing and outmoded industries, the protection of politically strategical forms of production, the redress of an unfavourable balance of trade, a more sweeping policy of autarchy or simply the use of tariffs as a crude but easy way of raising state revenue.

Investigation of the political factors involved in trading bias is made difficult by what is known as the 'problem of existence'. This is to say that one can describe the trading behaviour of a selected state, but one cannot say with any measure of certainty what the trading pattern would be if selected influences and constraints such as political preference were removed. An elegant yet rough and ready attempt to sidestep the problem of existence involves the use of the interactance hypothesis whereby one looks for significant real world deviations from a null model which assumes that the level of trade between any pair of states will be proportional to the degree of involvement of each state in global trade. One weakness of this technique concerns its blindness regarding the maldistribution of specific scarce economic resources and distance friction. The quantitative techniques involved are complicated and space does not permit their description; however, a competent and informative study of patterns of economic partnership in the North Atlantic area by Alker and Puchala provides a useful application.[13]

It can be argued that, despite all its obvious shortcomings, the interactance hypothesis is the most valuable and versatile of the techniques available to the geographical study of international political behaviour, particularly because negative deviations from the predictions of the null model can be interpreted as an exaggeration of the distance factor involved in the relationship between two locations. Its use is not confined to the study of economic patterns of association and the most widely acclaimed applications have concerned the investigation of the ways in which political and cultural perceptions have constrained the development of international and intranational social relationships. Of such studies, two based upon significant deviations between real and predicted levels of telephonic communication are amongst the most frequently cited studies in the whole literature of political geography. Mackay's influential study of levels of communication between French and non-French Canadians and French Canada and the USA and Soja's study of the deterioration in the levels of communication in East Africa following the erosion of hopes for the establishment of a union between the component states of the region are classics in the field.[14]

International organizations of states are, along with the development of a bipolar power system and the withdrawal of European colonialism, a key characteristic of patterns of political change and adjustment in the post-war world. However, the emergence of a multiplicity of organizations need not be regarded as marking a stage in the abandonment of the sovereign nation state and it can more credibly be interpreted as a vital component in the attempt to perpetuate this mode of political organization through the manipulation of international conditions in such a way as to create a modified environment within which the previously maladjusted state can regain its viability. Viewed in this light, the organizations emerge as nationally motivated responses to a new set of conditions in which all by the greatest powers – confronted by the emergence of overwhelmingly formidable military superpowers and economic giants, notably the USA, armed with the economic advantage derived from mass production for a voracious domestic market – sought to preserve their independent existences. Their political survival demanded such limited sacrifices of sovereign independence as were demanded by a pooling of military resources or a merging of domestic markets. Consequently, the organizations so formed can be regarded as vehicles for the preservation rather than the further erosion of state sovereignty. This interpretation would be more completely applicable were it not for the existence of one organization, the EEC, with avowedly sovereign aspirations and the legitimate capability to impose organizational decisions – albeit of a largely trivial nature – upon its component sovereign members. However, a study of many aspects of organizational policy formation encourages the belief that the organization is manipulated to serve collective needs only in so far as these needs do not conflict with nationally perceived interests (persistent British attempts to modify and resist important aspects of the common agricultural and fisheries policy provide a clearcut example). Nevertheless this organization may possess the potential ability to generate an independent life of its own and European rather than nationally motivated politicians and academics have developed and attempted to act upon the concept of a 'Europe of regions', partly expressing an enthusiasm for the regional devolution of power, but partly because any dilution of power at the national governmental level must assist the reconcentration of power at the international organizational level.[15]

Forms of international association based on political colonialism are, at least in the institutionalized form of the imperial system, a thing of the past and contemporary interest focuses upon the problems encountered in the aftermath of political imperialism. A systems-based analysis of the processes involved in the disintegration of imperial systems was developed by Merritt; it identifies the exploitation by the metropolitan country of the unequal trading relationship derived from a policy of mercantilism as the *raison d'être* of imperialism, while the disintegration of the imperial system is seen to occur as the dependent subsystems or colonies succeed in exchanging political, economic and psychological relationships which focus on the metropolitan country for relationships with each other and with political entities located outside the imperial system.[16] Of the limited range of political geographical studies of imperialism, this, along with Tiwari's distance-based hypothesis, is probably the most useful of those of a generalized nature.

Equally rare are political geographical studies of the consequences of that most intense of international relationships, warfare. A recent volume of the *Transactions of the Institute of British Geographers* was exclusively devoted to the theme of settlement and conflict in the Mediterranean world and goes some of the way to redressing this obvious imbalance in the literature of political geography.[17] Thompson demonstrates how, in the case of Corsica,

> The form of domination has evolved from being one of political control imposed by warfare, through a phase of more passive domination when the island lost control of its own economic destiny, to the present phase of less overt domination by investment by organizations and increasingly by settlers from outside the island. The settlement pattern has responded to each of these phases in terms both of distribution and form.[18]

Wagstaff investigated the extent to which the eighteenth- and early nineteenth-century desertion of villages in Morea was the consequence of warfare or of social and economic changes;[19] Harris described the demographic consequences of the Arab-Israeli War of 1967 upon the Golan Heights and Jordan Rift,[20] while amongst other valuable contributions Sutton and Lawless analysed the consequences of warfare and stress upon the rural settlement pattern of Algeria.[21]

Techniques, Concepts and the Macroscale

A number of studies undertaken by political scientists concerned with the wider and more generalized aspects of international relationships are of distinct interest to the geographer. Prominent amongst these is the elaborate and heavily computerized investigation undertaken by Russett in his study in political ecology of the existence of international relationships within the international system of states.[22] A series of factor analyses were applied in the quest to discover regional subsystems of the world which, while lacking an institutionalized existence, nevertheless displayed traces of unity by virtue of shared characteristics, function and behaviour. The most elaborate and arguably the most valuable of these exercises involved a factor analysis of 54 variables for 82 countries in an attempt to identify underlying regions of social and cultural homogeneity.

The gross environmental determinism of Mackinder's Heartland concept,[23] its development by Spykman[24] and the greater flexibility of Meinig's reinterpretation[25] will be known to most geographers. For a more generalized but perhaps more relevant consideration of the behavioural implications of different patterns of global power distribution, the reader may refer to Kaplan's speculation upon the ways in which different distributions of power will giver rise to different power systems, each system being characterized by its own specific rules for international behaviour.[26] In consequence, any major change in the distribution of power between the unipolar and multipolar extremes will automatically produce changes in the processes which govern international behaviour. While one of the theoretical models which Kaplan devises involves a 'unit veto' system in which each independent unit possesses the capability to annihilate any other unit, the impact of nuclear capabilities upon power relationships is uncertain. Speculation on the behaviour resulting from the conversion of one power system into another is nevertheless particularly relevant in the contemporary world where the long-awaited arrival of a third superpower in the shape of China must now be imminent.

Many of the baffling complexities involved in the study of international relationships may be clarified if not resolved through the adoption of a systems-based approach, which should at least lead to the identification of relevant actors or behaviour units and of the various relationships which link the actors in forms of association. The value of a systems approach as a teaching aid is beyond dispute, but its usefulness as a means for actual discovery as well as providing a convenient analytical framework or device for the initial ordering of complex information will depend upon its performance and adaptability in respect of specific research problems. One variant of the systems approach which is applicable to problems of international politics is that of linkage politics, although it has been scarcely explored by geographers.[27]

Linkage politics has its own language and concepts and analyses linkages which have their origins in one system and their outputs or terminal stages in another. Various forms of linkage exist; in the case of an 'emulative linkage', one unit will attempt to emulate the achievements of another, for example the Soviet drive to emulate the US development of nuclear weapons; in the case of a 'penetrative linkage', one unit is partially able to determine the nature of developments within a second, penetrated unit, as in an imperial system, while in the case of a 'reactive linkage', an unpenetrated unit reacts to developments in another unit, as when a state arms itself in response to hostile policies developed within a potential aggressor.

Linkage politics could provide an organizational framework for a variety of geographical studies, and the case of Malta could well be a subject for a study organized in this perspective. The archaeologist MacKie writes:

> The twin islands of Malta and Gozo possess between them an area of only about 308 square kilometres yet during their long history they have experienced three periods during which the island culture has flowered remarkably. At these times impressive monuments and constructions have been built there of a kind which, in the two most recent cases at least, were well beyond the resources of the native islanders themselves. The last two episodes were, first, from the sixteenth to the late eighteenth centuries when the islands were the headquarters of the Knights of St. John and, secondly, from 1783 onwards when they came under the protection of Britain and provided a base and dockyard for the British navy. During both these periods energetic foreigners came to Malta and built great military installations. But in the first great cultural flowering, far back in prehistoric times, the building had been apparently religious-based – a series of temples.[28]

Blouet, who completed a geographical study of war and rural settlement in Malta, writes:

> In the years 1547–66 a large proportion of the island's settlements were placed under stress by successive invasions, and many might well have been abandoned had not the victory of 1565 ensured that the Knights would refinance the local economy. During the remainder of the Order's rule, although the arrival of the Turks was constantly predicted, the rural settlement pattern showed little response to this threat. Under the protection of the Order the large, compact, socially cohesive villages, which are characteristic of the twentieth century landscape, developed not as a response to conflict but as a product of population growth, economic expansion, and increasing social interaction.[29]

Although neither of these writers employs a linkage approach, the relevance of such to the geography of Malta and course to a host of other associated spatial units seems obvious.

While this book is mainly concerned with spatial behaviour at the national and intranational levels, a behavioural approach is equally applicable to the study of such behaviour at the international level. Unfortunately, it is at this level that the diplomatic and security-oriented restrictions upon information are the most severe; the student may, therefore, be severely inhibited and obliged to work at more generalized levels, rely upon speculative interpretations or undertake historical investigations on subjects amenable to detailed investigation following the removal of restrictions concerning key documents after the lapse of a specified period of security classification.

Discussion Points and Further Reading

This chapter introduces the behavioural background to international decision-making. International political behaviour is seen to be conditioned by a range of variables, including the still-vital phenomenon of state sovereignty which defines the parameters for international relations, state power and a variety of spatial factors, of which distance is of immense importance. Although state power and the impact of distance upon international behaviour present several insurmountable obstacles to the investigator, they remain crucial variables which cannot be overlooked.

A general introduction to political geographical approaches to the international system is provided in R. Muir, *Modern Political Geography* (1977). Of particular value are the articles on transaction flow analysis by Mackay (1958), Alker and Puchala (1968) and Soja (1968). Other valuable contributions include Merritt's application of a systems approach to the study of imperial distintegration (1964), Tiwari's introduction to the problem of distance (1972) and Russett's computerized search for international regions of various types (1967).

H. Alker and D. Puchala, 'Trends in Economic Partnership in the North Atlantic Area, 1928–63', in J. D. Singer (ed.), *Quantitative International Politics*, Free Press, New York, 1968.

J. R. Mackay, 'Interactance Hypothesis and Boundaries in Canada: a Preliminary Study', *Canadian Geographer* (1958), **2**, 1–8.

R. L. Merritt, 'Systems and the Disintegration of Empires', *General Systems* (1964), **8**.

R. E. Muir, *Modern Political Geography*, Macmillan, London, 1977.

B. H. Russett, *International Regions and the International System*, 1967; repr. Greenwood Press, Conn., 1975.

E. J. Soja, 'Communications and Territorial Integration in East Africa: an Introduction to Transaction Flow Analysis', *East Lakes Geographer* (1968), **4**, 39–57.

R. C. Tiwari, 'Distance in Decisions: Some Aspects of Colonial Administration in Tropical Africa', *Scottish Geographical Magazine* (1972), **88**, 208–10.

Notes

1. For discussion on the relationship between geography and international relations see J. Gottman, 'Geography and International Relations', *World Politics* (1951), **3**, 153–73, and R. Muir, 'Political Geography and the Political Scientist', *Discussion Paper*, Cambridge College of Arts and Technology.

2. For a well-organized statement of the internationalist case see W. O. Douglas, *Towards a Global Federalism*, New York University Press, New York, 1968.

3. For a discussion on problems of interpreting the doctrine of

sovereignty see W. Stankiewicz, 'Sovereignty as Political Theory', *Political Studies*, **14**, 2, 141–157.

4. For studies on the quantification of power see F. C. German, 'A Tentative Evaluation of World Power', *Journal of Conflict Resolution* (1960), **4**, 138–44, and R. Muir, *Modern Political Geography*, Macmillan, London, 1975, pp. 147–52.

5. R. C. Tiwari, 'Distance in Decisions: Some Aspects of Colonial Administration in Tropical Africa', *Scottish Geographical Magazine* (1972), **88**, 208–10.

6. P. G. Bradshaw, 'Geography and International Relations: An Attempt at Synthesis', Ph.D thesis, University of Southampton, 1971.

7. B. E. Coates, in B. E. Coates, R. J. Johnston and P. L. Knox, *Geography and Inequality*, Oxford University Press, Oxford, 1975, pp. 189–91.

8. E. J. Soja, *The Political Organization of Space*, Resource Paper No. 8, Commission of College Geography, Association of American Geographers, Washington, 1971.

9. H. K. Colebatch and R. Scott, 'New Guinea and the Relevance of the African Experience', in R. Scott (ed.) *The Politics of New States*, Allen & Unwin, London, 1970, p. 150.

10. *Ibid.* p. 164.

11. K. E. Boulding, *Conflict and Defense: A General Theory*, Harper and Row, New York, 1962.

12. S. B. Cohen, *Geography and Politics in a Divided World*, Methuen London, 1964.

13. H. Alker and D. Puchala, 'Trends in Economic Partnership in the North Atlantic Area, 1928–63', in J. D. Singier (ed.), *Quantitative International Politics*, Free Press, New York, 1968.

14. J. R. Mackay, 'Interactance Hypothesis and Boundaries in Canada: a Preliminary Study', *Canadian Geographer* (1958), **2**, 1–8, and E. J. Soja, 'Communication and Territorial Integration in East Africa: an Introduction to Transaction Flow Analysis', *East Lakes Geographer* (1968), **4**, 39–57.

15. R. A. Rhodes, 'Regional Policy and a "Europe of Regions": a Critical Assessment', *Regional Studies* (1974), **8**, 105–24.

16. R. L. Merritt, 'Systems and the Disintegration of Empires', *General Systems* (1964), **8**.

17. *Transactions of the Institute of British Geographers* (1978), **3** (3).

18. I. B. Thompson, 'Settlement and Conflict in Corsica', *ibid.* p. 272.

19. J. M. Wagstaff, 'War and Settlement in the Morea, 1685–1830', *ibid.* pp. 295–308.

20. W. W. Harris, 'War and Settlement Change: the Golan Heights and the Jordan Rift, 1967–77', *ibid.* pp. 309–30.

21. K. Sutton and R. I. Lawless, 'Population Regrouping in Algeria: Traumatic Change in the Rural Settlement Pattern', *ibid.* pp. 331–50.

22. B. M. Russett, *International Regions and the International System*, 1967; repr. Greenwood Press, Conn., 1975.

23. H. J. Mackinder, *Democratic Ideals and Reality*, 1919; repr. Norton, New York, 1962.

24. N. J. Spykman, *The Geography of the Peace,* 1944; repr. Archon Books, Hamden, Conn., 1969.
25. D. W. Meinig, 'Heartland and Rimaland in Eurasian History', *Western Political Quarterly* (1956), **9**, 553–69.
26. M. A. Kaplan, *System and Process in International Politics*, Wiley, New York, 1957.
27. J. N. Rosenau (ed.), *Linkage Politics*, Free Press, New York, 1969.
28. E. MacKie, *The Megalith Builders,* Oxford University Press, Oxford, 1977, p. 25.
29. B. L. Blouet, 'The Impact of Armed Conflict on the Rural Settlement Pattern of Malta (AD 1400–1800)', *Transactions of the Institute of British Geographers* (1978), **3**, (3) 379.

Select Bibliography

Alford, R. R., *Party and Society*, Rand McNally, Chicago, 1963.
Alker, H. and Puchala, D., 'Trends in Economic Partnership in the North Atlantic Area, 1928–63', in J. D. Singer (ed.), *Quantitative International Politics*, Free Press, New York, 1968.
Allison, L., *Environmental Planning. A Political and Philosophical Analysis*, Allen & Unwin, London, 1975.
Allison, L., 'Politics, Welfare and Conservation, A Study of Meta-Planning', *British Journal of Political Science* (1971), **1**, 438–9.
Almond, G. A. and Powell, G. B., *Comparative Politics: A Developmental Approach*, Little Brown, Boston, 1966.
Berelson, B. R. *et al.*, *Voting*, University of Chicago Press, Chicago, 1954.
Berger, B. M., *Working-class Suburb: A Study of Auto Workers in Suburbia*, University of California Press, Berkeley, 1960.
Bergman, E., *Modern Political Geography*, Brown, Dubarque, 1975.
Bersch, G. K., Clark, R. P., and Ward, D. M., *Comparing Political Systems: Power and Policy in Three Worlds*, Wiley, New York, 1978.
Bersch, G. K., 'The Revival of Nationalism', *Problems of Communism* (1973), **22**, 1–15.
Binder, *et al.*, *Crises and Sequences in Political Development*, Princeton University Press, Princeton, 1971.
Blewett, N., 'Redistribution Procedures', in H. Mayer and H. Nelson (eds.), *Australian Politics: A Third Reader*, Cheshire, Melbourne, 1972, pp. 295–300.
Blondel, J., *Voters, Parties and Leaders*, Penguin, Harmondsworth, 1965.
Blouet, B. L., 'The Impact of Armed Conflict on the Rural Settlement Pattern of Malta (AD 1400–1800)', *Transactions of the Institute of British Geographers* (1978), **3**(3), 367–80.
Boulding, K. E., *Conflict and Defense: A General Theory*, Harper and Row, New York, 1962.
Bourne, L. S., 'Through the Looking Glass: Comments on Behavioural Approaches in Geography', in J. Rees and P. Newby (eds.) *Behavioural Perspectives in Geography*, Middlesex Polytechnic Monographs in Geography No. 1, 1973, pp. 94–106.
Bradshaw, P. G., 'Geography and International Relations: an Attempt at Synthesis', Ph.d. thesis, University of Southampton, 1971.
Brecher, M., *The Foreign Policy System of Israel: Setting, Image and Process*, Yale University Press, New Haven, 1972.

Brunn, S. D., *Geography and Politics in America*, Harper and Row, New York, 1974.

Buchanan, W., Cantril, H. *et al., How Nations See Each Other: A Study in Public Opinion*, University of Illinois Press, Urbana, 1953.

Budge, I. and Urwin, D. W., *Scottish Political Behaviour*, Longman, London, 1966.

Bush, K., 'Environmental Problems in the USSR', *Problems of Communism* (1972), **21**, Jul.–Aug., 27–9.

Butler, D. E. and Stokes, D. E., *Political Change in Britain: Forces Shaping Electoral Choice*, Macmillan, London, 1974.

Buttimer, Sr. A., *Values in Geography*, Commission on College Geography, Resource Paper No. 24, Association of American Geographers, Washington, 1974.

Campbell, A. *et al., The American Voter*, Wiley, New York, 1960.

Capecchi, V. and Galli, G., 'Determinants of Voting Behaviour in Italy: a Linear Causal Model of Analysis', in M. Dogan and S. Rokkan (eds.), *Quantitative Ecological Analysis in the Social Sciences*, M.I.T. Press, Cambridge, Mass., 1969, pp. 235–84.

Castles, F. G., *Pressure Groups and Political Culture*, Routledge & Kegan Paul, London, 1971.

Castles, F. G., Murray, D. J., Potter, D. C. and Pollitt, C. J., *Decisions, Organisations and Society*, Penguin, Harmondsworth, 2nd edn., 1976.

Christenson, R. M. *et al., Ideologies and Modern Politics*, Nelson, London, 1971.

Civic Trust, The, *The Local Amenity Movement*, London, 1976.

Coates, B. E., Johnston, R. J. and Knox, P. L., *Geography and Inequality*, Oxford University Press, Oxford, 1975.

Cobban, A., *National Self-Determination*, Oxford University Press, London, 1944.

Cohen, S. B., *Geography and Politics in a Divided World*, Methuen, London, 1964.

Cohen, S. B., and Rosenthal, L. D., 'A Geographical Model for Political Systems Analysis', *Geographical Review* (1971), **61**, 5–31.

Cole, J. P., and Whysall, S., 'Places in the News: A Study of Geographical Information', *Bulletin of Quantitative Data for Geographers* (1968),7, University of Nottingham.

Colebatch, H. K. and Scott R., 'New Guinea and the Relevance of the African Experience', in R. Scott (ed.), *The Politics of New States*, Allen & Unwin, London, 1970.

Connor, W. (1967), 'Self-determination: The New Phase', *World Politics,* **20**.

Conway, M. and Feigert, F. B., *Political Analysis*, Allyn and Bacon, Boston, 2nd edn., 1976.

Cox, K. R., 'The Spatial Structuring of Information Flows and Partisan Attitudes', in M. Dogan and S. Rokkan (eds.), *Quantitative Ecological Analysis in the Social Sciences*, M.I.T. Press, Cambridge, Mass., 1969, pp. 157–85.

Cox, K. R., *Conflict, Power and Politics in the City: A Geographic View*, McGraw-Hill, New York, 1973.

Cox, K. R., *Location and Public Problems*, Blackwell, Oxford, 1979.

Crewe, I. and Payne, C., 'Another Game with Nature: an Ecological Regression Model of the British Two-Party Vote Ratio in 1970', *British Journal of Political Science* (1976), **6**, 43–81.

Crossman, R. H. S., *Diaries of a Cabinet Minister*, vol. III, Hamilton and Cape, London, 1977.

Dahl, R. A., *Who Governs?*, Yale University Press, New Haven, 1961.

Dahl, R. A., 'Power', in *International Encyclopedia of the Social Sciences*, vol. XII, Macmillan, New York, 1968.

Dahl, R. A. and Tufte, E. R., *Size and Democracy*, Stanford University Press, Stanford, 1973.

Dale, E. H., 'The State-Idea: Missing Prop of the West Indies Federation', *Scottish Geographical Magazine* (1962) **78**, 166–76.

Davis, E. E. and Sinnot, R., *Attitudes in the Republic of Ireland Relevant to the Northern Ireland Problem*, Vol. 1. *Descriptive Analysis And some Comparisons with Attitudes in Northern Ireland and Great Britain*, Economic and Social Research Institute, Dublin, 1979.

Dearlove, J., 'Councillors and Interest Groups in Kensington and Chelsea', *British Journal of Political Science* (1971), **1**, 129–53.

Despres, L. A., *Cultural Pluralism and Nationalist Politics in British Guiana*, Rand McNally, Chicago, 1967.

Deutsch, K., *Politics and Government. How People Decide their Fate*, Wiley, New York, 1975.

Dikshit, R. D., 'The Retreat from Political Geography', *Area* (1977), **9**(4), 234–9.

Dogan, M., 'Political Cleavage and Social Stratification in France and Italy,' in S. M. Lipset and S. Rokkan (eds.), *Party Systems and Voter Alignments*, Free Press, New York, 1967, pp. 129–95.

Douglas, W. O., *Towards a Global Federalism*, New York University Press, New York, 1968.

Downs, R. M., 'Geographic Space Perception: Past Approaches and Future Prospects', *Progress in Geography* (1970), **2**, 65–108.

Duchacek, I. D., *Comparative Federalism*, Holt, Rinehart and Winston, New York, 1970.

Eckstein, H., *Pressure Group Politics: The Case of the British Medical Association*, Allen & Unwin, London, 1960.

Elazar, D. J., *American Federalism: A View from the States*, Crowell, New York, 1972.

Elkin, S. L. 'Comparative Urban Politics and Inter-Organisational Behaviour', *Policy and Politics* (1974), **2**(3).

Enloe, C. H., 'Central Governments' Strategies for Coping with Separatist Movements', in W. H. Morris-Jones (ed.), *The Politics of Separatism*, Institute of Commonwealth Studies, Seminar Papers, London, 1974.

Ferris, J., *Participation in Urban Planning: The Barnsbury Case*, Bell, London, 1972.

Fitton, M., 'Neighbourhood and Voting: a Sociometric Explanation', *British Journal of Political Science* (1973), **3**, 445–72.

Fletcher, P., 'The Results Analysed', in L. J. Sharpe (ed.), *Voting in Cities*, Macmillan, London, 1967, pp. 290–321.

Friedgut, T. H., 'Citizens and Soviets: can Ivan Ivanovich Fight City Hall?', *Comparative Politics* (July 1978).

Furnivall, J. S., *Netherlands India*, Cambridge University Press, Cambridge, 1939.

Garson, G. D., *Handbook of Political Science Methods*, Holbrook Press, Boston, 2nd edn, 1976.

Geertz, C., 'The Integrative Revolution: Primordial Sentiments and Civil Politics in the New States', in C. Geertz (ed.), *Old Societies and New States: The Quest for Modernity in Asia and Africa*, Free Press, New York, 1963.

German, F. C., 'A Tentative Evaluation of World Power', *Journal of Conflict Resolution* (1960), **4**, 138–44.

Ginsburg, N., 'On the Chinese Perception of a World Order', in Tang Tson (ed.), *China's Policies in Asia and America's Alternatives*, University of Chicago Press, Chicago 1968, vol. 2, pp. 73–91.

Glassberg, A., 'Linkage between Urban Policy Output and Voting Behaviour', *British Journal of Political Science* (1973), **3**, 341–61.

Goldthorpe, J. H. *et al.*, *The Affluent Worker: Political Attitudes and Behaviour*, Cambridge University Press, Cambridge, 1968.

Golledge, R. G., Brown, L. A. and Williamson, F., 'Behavioural Approaches in Geography: An Overview, *The Australian Geographer* (1972), **12**(1), 59–79.

Gottman, J., 'Geography and International Relations', *World Politics* (1951), **3**, 153–73.

Gottman, J., *Le Politique des Etats et leur géographie*, Colin, Paris, 1952.

Gregory, R., *The Price of Amenity*, Macmillan, London, 1971.

Gregory, R. in P. J. Smith (ed.), *The Politics of Physical Resources*, Penguin, Harmondsworth, 1975.

Gregory, R., 'The Voluntary Amenity Movement', in M. MacEwan (ed.), *Future Landscapes*, Chatto and Windus, London, 1976, pp. 199–217.

Gurr, T. R., *Why Men Rebel*, Princeton University Press, Princeton, 1970.

Hall, G. H., 'The Myth and Reality of Multiple-Use', *Natural Resources Journal* (1963), **3**, 287.

Harris, W. W., 'War and Settlement Change: the Golan Heights and the Jordan Rift, 1967–77', *Transactions of the Institute of British Geographers* **3**(3), 309–30.

Hartshorne, R., 'The Functional Approach in Political Geography', *Annals of the Association of American Geographers* (1950), **40**, 95–130.

Henning, D. H., 'The Politics of National Resources Administration', *Annals of Regional Science* (1968), **2**.

Inglehart, R., 'The Nature of Value Change in Postindustrial Society', in L. N. Lindberg (ed.), *Politics and the Future of Industrial Society*, McKay, New York, 1976, pp. 57–99.

Jacob, P. E. and Jeune, H., 'The Integrative Process: Guidelines for Analysis of the Bases of Political Community', in P. E. Jacob and J. R. Toscano, *The Integration of Political Communities*, Lippincott, Philadephia, 1964.

Jackson, W. A. D. and Samuels, M. S. (eds.), *Politics and Geographic Relationships*, Prentice-Hall, Englewood Cliffs, 2nd edn., 1971.

Johnson, S. P., *The Politics of Environment*, Stacey, London, 1973.

Johnston, R. J., *Political, Electoral and Spatial Systems*, Clarendon Press, Oxford, 1979.

Jones, B. D. and C. Kaufman, 'The Distribution of Urban Public Services', *Administration and Society* (1974), **6**.

Kaplan, M. A., *System and Process in International Politics*, Wiley, New York, 1957.

Kasperson, R. E., 'Environmental Stress and the Municipal Political System', in R. E. Kasperson and J. V. Minghi (eds.), *The Structure of Political Geography*, University of London Press, 1969.

Kasperson, R. E., 'Political Behaviour and the Decision-Making Process in the Allocation of Water Resources Between Recreational and Municipal Use', *Natural Resources Journal* (1969), **9**, 176–211.

Kasperson, R. E. and Minghi, J. V., *The Structure of Political Geography*, University of London Press, 1969.

Kaufman, H., *The Forest Ranger: A Study in Administrative Behaviour*, Johns Hopkins Press, Baltimore, 1960.

Kendall, M. G. and Stuart, A., 'The Law of Cubic Proportions in Election Results', *British Journal of Sociology* (1950), **1**, 183–97.

Kennet, W., 'The Politics of Conservation', in A. Warren and F. B. Goldsmith (eds.), *Conservation in Practice*, Wiley, London, 1974.

Kirk, W., 'Historical Geography and the Concept of the Behavioural Environment', *Indian Geographical Society, Silver Jubilee Edition* (1951), pp. 152–60.

Kirk, W., 'Problems of Geography', *Geography* (1963), **48**, 357–71.

Kirk, W. 'The Road from Mandalay: Towards a Geographical Philosophy', *Transactions of the Institute of British Geographers* (1978), **3**(4), 391–2.

Kristof, L. K. D., 'The Russian Image of Russia: An Applied Study in Geographical Methodology', in C. A. Fisher (ed.), *Essays in Political Geography*, Methuen, London, 1968, pp. 345–87.

Lambert, W. E. and Klineberg, O., *Children's Views of Foreign Peoples*, Appleton, New York, 1967.

Lazarsfield, P. *et al.*, *The People's Choice: How the Voter Makes up his Mind in a Presidential Campaign*, Dwell, Sloan & Pearce, New York, 1944.

Levin, P. H., 'On Decisions and Decision Making', *Public Administration* (1972).

Levin, P. H., *Government and the Planning Process*, Allen & Unwin, London, 1976.

MacDougall, J. A., 'Birth of a National: National Identification in Singapore', *Asian Studies* (1976), **16**, 510–24.

Mackay, J. R., 'Interactance Hypothesis and Boundaries in Canada: a Preliminary Study', *Canadian Geographer* (1958), **2**, 1–8.

MacKie, E., *The Megalith Builders*, Oxford University Press, Oxford, 1977.

Mackinder, H. J., *Democratic Ideals and Reality*, 1919; repr. Norton, New York, 1962.

Manis, J. C. and Stine, L. C. 'Suburban Residence and Political Behaviour', *Public Opinion Quarterly* (1958), pp. 485–9.

Martin, P., 'Conflict Resolution Through the Multiple-Use Concept in

Forest Service Decision-Making', *Natural Resources Journal* (1969), **9**, 228–36.

Maslow, A. H., 'A Theory of Human Motivation', *Psychological Review* (1963), **50**, 370–96.

Meinig, D. W., 'Heartland and Rimland in Eurasian History', *Western Political Quarterly* (1956), **9**, 553–69.

Merritt, R. L., 'Systems and the Disintegration of Empires', *General Systems* (1964), **8**.

Merritt, R. L., 'Noncontiguity and Political Integration', in J. N. Rosenan (ed.), *Linkage Politics*, Free Press, New York, 1969, pp. 237–72.

Milbrath, L. W., *Political Participation*, Rand McNally, Chicago, 1965.

Minghi, J. V. 'Recent Developments and Future Trends in Political Geography Research in North America', paper presented at I.B.G. Conference, Lancaster, 1980. Forthcoming in A. Burnett and P. J. Taylor (eds.), *Politics and Geography: Anglo-American Perspectives*, Wiley, London, 1980.

Moodie, G. C. and Studdert-Kennedy, G., *Opinions, Publics and Pressure Groups*, Allen & Unwin, London, 1970.

Morris-Jones, W. H., 'In Defence of Apathy', *Political Studies* (1954), **2**(1).

Muir, R. E., *Modern Political Geography*, Macmillan, London, 1977.

Muir, R. E., 'Political Geography: Dead Duck or Phoenix?', *Area* (1976), **8**(3), 195–200.

Mumphrey, A. J., Seley, J. E. and Wolpert, J., 'A Decision Model for Locating Controversial Facilities', *Journal of the American Institute of Planners* (1971), pp. 397–402.

Oliver, J. H., 'Citizen Demands and the Soviet Political System', *American Political Science Review* (1968), **63**, 645–55.

Okpu, U., *Ethnic Minority Problems in Nigerian Politics, 1960–65*, Almquist, Uppsala, 1977.

Open University, *Decision Making in Britain*, pts 1–3, Open University Press, Milton Keynes, 1972.

Orbell, J. M., 'An Information-Flow Theory of Community Influence', *Journal of Politics* (1970), **32**, 322–38.

O'Riordan, T., *Perspectives on Resource Management*, Pion, London, 1971.

Owens, P. L., 'A Managerial Issue: Conflict Between Norfolk Broads Coarse Anglers and Boat Users', in M. J. Moseley (ed.), *Social Issues in Rural Norfolk*, CEAS, Norwich, 1978.

Paddison, R., 'Factors Underlying Variations in Local Electoral Turnouts', unpublished paper, Department of Geography, University of Glasgow, 1976.

Paddison, R., 'Spatial Bias and Redistricting in Proportional Representation Systems: a Case Study of the Republic of Ireland', *Tijdschrift voor Economische en Social Geografie* (1976), **67**, 230–40.

Parsons, T., *The Structure of Social Action*, McGraw-Hill, New York, 1937.

Parsons, T., *The Social System,* Free Press, New York, 1950.

Patrick, R. A., *Political Geography and the Cyprus Conflict 1963–1971*, University of Waterloo, Department of Geography Publication Series no. 4, Waterloo, 1976.

Piaget, T. and Weil, A., 'The Development in Children of the Idea of

Homeland and of Relations with Other Countries', *International Social Science Bulletin* (1951), **3**, 561–78.

Pocock, D. C. and Hudson, R., *Images of the Urban Environment*, Macmillan, London, 1978.

Prescott, J. R. V., 'The Functions and Methods of Electoral Geography', *Annals of the Association of American Geographers* (1959), **49**, 296–304.

Pulzer, P. G., *Political Representation and Elections in Britian*, Allen & Unwin, London, 1972.

Putnam, R. D., *The Beliefs of Politicians: Ideology, Conflict and Democracy in Britain and Italy*, Yale University Press, New Haven, 1973.

Rabushka, A. and Shepsle, K. A., *Politics in Plural Societies*, Merrill, Columbus, 1972.

Rae, D. W., *The Political Consequences of Electoral Laws*, Yale University Press, New Haven, 1971.

Ratzel, F., 'The Laws of the Spatial Growth of States', in R. E. Kasperson and J. V. Minghi (eds.), *The Structure of Political Geography*, University of London Press, 1970.

Rees, J. and Newby, P. (eds.), *Behavioural Perspectives in Geography*, Middlesex Polytechnic Monographs in Geography No. 1, 1973.

Reich, C. A. C., *Bureaucracy and the Forests*, Center for the Study of Democratic Institutions, Santa Barbara, Calif. 1962.

Rhodes, R. A., 'Regional Policy and a "Europe of Regions": a Critical Assessment', *Regional Studies* (1974), **8**, 105–24.

Roberts, G. K., 'The Federal Republic of Germany', in S. E. Finer (ed.), *Adversary Politics and Electoral Reform*, Wigram, London, 1975.

Rogin, M., 'Politics, Emotion and the Wallace Vote', *British Journal of Sociology* (1969), **20**, 27–49.

Rokkan, S. and Campbell, A., 'Citizen Participation in Political Life: Norway and the United States of America', *International Social Science Journal* (1960), **12**, 69–99.

Rokkan, S. and Valen, H., 'Regional Contrasts in Norwegian Politics', in E. Allardt and S. Rokkan (eds.), *Mass Politics*, Free Press, New York, 1970, pp. 190–250.

Rose, R. and Urwin, D., 'Social Cohesion, Political Parties and Strains in Regimes', in M. Dogan and R. Rose (eds.), *European Politics: A Reader*, Macmillan, London, 1971.

Rosenau, J. N. (ed.), *Linkage Politics*, Free Press, New York, 1969.

Royal Commission on Local Government in England, vol. II, *Memorandum of Dissent*, H.M.S.O., London, 1969, Cmnd 4040–1.

Runciman, W. G., *Relative Deprivation and Social Justice*, University of California Press, Berkeley, 1966.

Rush, M., and Althoff, P., *An Introduction to Political Sociology*, Nelson, London, 1971.

Russett, B. M., *International Regions and the International System*, 1967; repr. Greenwood Press, Conn. 1975.

Saarinen, T. F., 'Student Views of the World', in R. M. Downs and D. Stea (eds.), *Image and Environment*, Aldine, Chicago, 1973, pp. 148–61.

Sacks, P., 'Bailiwicks, Locality and Religion: Three Elements in an Irish Dail Constituency Election', *Economic and Social Review* (1970), **1**, 531–54.

Savage, R. L., 'Patterns of Multilinear Evolution in the American States', *Publius* (1973), **3**(1), 75–108.

Sibley, D., 'Classification and Control in Local Government: a Case Study of Gypsies in Hull', *Transactions of the Institute of British Geographers* (1978), **3**(3), 319–27.

Simon, H. A., 'Theories of Decision-Making in Economics and Behavioural Science', *American Economic Review* (1959), **49**(3).

Smith, A. D., *Nationalism in the Twentieth Century*, Martin Robertson, Oxford, 1979.

Smock, A. C., 'Education and National Integration in Ghana', in D. R. Smock and K. Bentsi-Erchill (eds.), *The Search for National Integration in Africa*, Free Press, New York, 1975.

Snyder, R. C. 'A Decision-Making Approach to the Study of Political Phenomena', in R. Young (ed.), *Approaches to the Study of Politics*, Northwestern University Press, Evanston, Ill., 1958.

Soja, E. J., 'Communication and Territorial Integration in East Africa: an Introduction to Transaction Flow Analysis', *East Lakes Geographer* (1968), **4**, 39–57.

Solesbury, W., 'The Environmental Agenda', *Public Administration* (1976), **54**, 379–97.

Sprout, H. and Sprout, M., *The Ecological Perspective on Human Affairs, with Special Reference to International Politics*, Princeton University Press, Princeton, 1965.

Spykman, N. J., *The Geography of the Peace*, 1944; repr. Archon Books, Hamden, Conn., 1969.

Stacey, B., *Political Socialization in Western Society*, Edward Arnold, London, 1978.

Stankiewicz, W., 'Sovereignty as Political Theory', *Political Studies*, **14**(2), 141–57.

Sutton, K. and Lawless, R. I., 'Population Regrouping in Algeria', *Transactions of the Institute of British Geographers* (1978), **3**(3), 331–350.

Taubman, W., *Governing Soviet Cities*, Praeger, New York, 1973.

Taylor, A. H., 'Journey Time, Perceived Distance and Electoral Turnout–Victoria Ward, Swansea', *Area* (1973), **5**, 59–63.

Taylor, P. J. and Gudgin, G., 'The Myth of Non-Partisan Cartography: a Study of Electoral Biases in the English Boundary Commissions Redistribution for 1955–70', *Urban Studies* (1976), **13**, 13–25.

Taylor, P. J. and Johnston, R. J., *Geography of Elections*, Penguin, Harmondsworth, 1979.

Thompson, I. B., 'Settlement and Conflict in Corsica', *Transactions of the Institute of British Geographers*, (1978), **3**(3), 259–73.

Tiwari, R. C., 'Distance in Decisions: Some aspects of Colonial Administration in Tropical Africa, *Scottish Geographical Magazine* (1972), **88**, 208–10.

Trent, J., 'The Politics of Nationalist Movements – a Reconsideration', *Canadian Review of Studies in Nationalism* (1974), **3**, 157.

Verba, S., 'Sequences and Development', in L. Binder *et al.*, *Crises and Sequences in Political Development*, Princeton University Press, Princeton, 1971.

Verba, S., Nie, N. H. and Jim, J., *Participation and Political Equality*,

Cambridge University Press, Cambridge, 1978.

Verba, S. and Nie, N. H., *Participation in America: Social Equality and Political Democracy*, Harper and Row, New York, 1972.

Wagstaff, J. M., 'War and Settlement in the Morea, 1685–1830', *Transactions of the Institute of British Geographers* (1978), **3**(3), 295–308.

Weiner, M., 'Political Participation: Crisis of the Political Process', in L. Binder *et al.*, *Crises and Sequences in Political Development*, Princeton University Press, Princeton, 1971.

White, G. F., 'The Choice of Use in Resource Management', *Natural Resources Journal* (1961), **1**, 23–40.

Whittlesey, D., 'The Impress of Effective Central Authority upon the Landscape', *Annals of the Association of American Geographers* (1935), **25**, 85–97.

Whittlesey, D., *The Earth and the State: A Study of Political Geography*, Holt, New York, 1939.

Wicker, A. W., 'Attitude versus Actions: The Relationship of Verbal and Overt Behavioural Responses to Attitude Objects', *Journal of Social Issues* (1969), **25**.

Wilson, T., 'The Economic Costs of the Adversary System', in S. E. Finer (ed.), *Adversary Politics and Electoral Reform*, Wigram, London, 1975, pp. 99–116.

Wilson, J. Q. and Banfield, E. C., 'Public-Regardingness as a Value Premise in Voting Behaviour', *American Political Science Review* (1964), **58**, 876–87.

Wirt, F. M. *et al.*, *On the City's Rim: Politics and Policy in Suburbia*, Heath, Lexington, 1972.

Wise, M., 'Policy-making Studies in Political Geography', paper presented at the Institute of British Geographers 1978 conference.

Young, O. R., *Systems of Political Science,* Prentice-Hall, Englewood Cliffs, 1968.

Ziegler, H. and Peak, W., 'The Political Functions of the Educational System', *Sociology of Education* (1970), **43**, 115–43.

Index